Psychological Care for Families:
Before, During and After Birth

Psychological Care for Families: Before, During and After Birth

A research-based guide for midwives, health visitors, nurses and other health care professionals

Catherine A. Niven RGN, BSc (Psychology), PhD
Lecturer in Psychology, Glasgow Polytechnic

Foreword by Mary Cronk RGN, RM, NCDN, ADM
Elected Member of the English National Board for Nursing, Midwifery and Health Visiting; Independent Midwife

Butterworth-Heinemann Ltd
Linacre House, Jordan Hill, Oxford OX2 8DP

PART OF REED INTERNATIONAL BOOKS

OXFORD   LONDON   BOSTON
MUNICH   NEW DELHI   SINGAPORE   SYDNEY
TOKYO   TORONTO   WELLINGTON

First published 1992

© Catherine A. Niven 1992

British Library Cataloguing in Publication Data
Niven, Catherine A.
  Psychological care for families: Before, during
  and after birth.
  I. Title
  618.2001

ISBN 0 7506 0060 8

Library of Congress Cataloguing in Publication Data
Niven, Catherine A.
  Psychological care for families – before, during, and after birth/
  Catherine A. Niven.
  p. cm.
  Includes bibliographical references and index.
  ISBN 0 7506 0060 8
  1. Pregnancy – Psychological aspects. 2. Childbirth – Psychological aspects. 3.
  Parenthood – Psychological aspects. 4. Obstetrical nursing. I. Title.
  RG560.N58   1992
  618.2′001′9–dc20   91–36065
                                                          CIP

Printed and bound in Great Britain by Biddles Ltd, Guildford and King's Lynn

To my family

Contents

Foreword

The childbearing years are, for most families, a time when there is a great deal of input by professionals into ensuring that the woman's physical health is carefully monitored, and that she is helped to approach childbirth healthy and fit. While physical needs are met, and British women at the end of the twentieth century are, in general, well nourished and healthy, their psychological needs are not always perfectly understood and sometimes downright neglected. Our wish to improve outcomes and statistics, and reach minimum figures for perinatal mortality, can lead us to neglect the emotional and social aspects of maternity care. This book clearly spells out the importance of psychological care and the positive effect on outcomes when it is done well.

Our goal of minimal perinatal mortality has been responsible for births taking place in hospitals in almost 100 per cent of cases, and while hospital is now being questioned as the safest place to be born, women will very likely continue to be 'confined' in hospitals for some time to come. Women are territorial mammals, and when they are removed from their homes many are vulnerable and insecure. Good psychological care based on research will benefit not only the immediate family, but the community and society. Anxious, depressed, insecure people are unlikely to be competent, confident parents. We who care for women and their families have a responsibility to ensure that our care does not harm, and hopefully helps, those we care for. This book will help us achieve that aim.

I feel that everyone who reads this book will gain in their understanding of the emotional needs of families, and be able to improve the care they provide. Chapter 1 should be required reading for all responsible for setting staffing levels, as it demonstrates the improvements in outcomes that result from increased input by midwives and health visitors.

Kate Niven is not a midwife. I have to admit that my first knee-jerk reaction to this information was of the 'what does she think she knows about maternity care' variety. As I read through the book it became eminently clear just what she does know. The range and depth of her knowledge of, and feeling for, the psychological needs of childbearing women and their families is matched by academic rigour of the highest category. Kate writes as a psychologist, a nurse and as a mother, and most importantly as a researcher who as a non-midwife takes a fresh look at midwifery and obstetric care.

I commend this book to all who are involved in providing care to childbearing women and their families, and to those studying to become providers of that care. We are special, and are specially privileged. It is our responsibility to assess the outcomes of the care we give in psychological, as much as physical, terms. Thank you Kate for helping us to do that.

Mary Cronk

Preface

The aim of this book is to improve the quality of psychological care provided for families during pregnancy, birth and the first few months of the postnatal period. It is written for all health professionals who are involved in their care but it focuses on student and qualified midwives, health visitors and nurses involved in obstetrics and paediatrics. They are the people best placed to give good psychological care to babies and their siblings, to their mothers and to the husbands/partners/lovers/ friends or relatives who care for them and support them. However, physiotherapists in obstetrics and gynaecology should be interested in the sections on preparation for childbirth and on labour pain; community psychiatric nurses in the material on postnatal depression and other psychiatric disorders associated with childbearing; hospital doctors in the sections relating to hospital based care; and general practitioners in those related to community based care (though publishers tell me that 'general practitioners never buy books'!).

The book deals with the many psychological aspects of pregnancy, birth and early parenthood and with their applications in community and hospital based settings. More than 95 per cent of its material is based on research findings. Therefore the book is not restricted to my opinions or experiences (however wonderful they might be) but is solidly grounded in the results of hundreds of research studies. I have concentrated on recent British research wherever possible, to facilitate the application of research findings. However, a smattering of American, European and Commonwealth studies are thrown in for good measure. I constantly relate the results of the studies I discuss to the realities of midwifery, health visiting and nursing practice and I only discuss in depth, studies which can be applied in this way.

Psychological Care for Families is organized into six chapters which follow a rough chronological order beginning with (surprise, surprise) pregnancy and ending in the postnatal period. Midwives might feel that they can concentrate on the first four chapters and leave out those related to the postnatal period (beyond puerperium) and its associated problems. Health visitors might correspondingly be tempted to skip the sections on pregnancy and birth. However, 'pre to postpartum' is a continuous process for the mother, baby and family. They cannot miss out bits of it. In order to understand any segment of that process, you really need to understand what went before it and what is likely to come afterwards. So the book will be of more use if you at least skim every chapter, even if you only study some more thoroughly.

My name is Catherine Niven, usually known as Kate. I'm a nurse who went on to take a first and second degree in Psychology. I work as a lecturer in Psychology, specializing in Developmental and Health Psychology. Amongst my students are midwives, health visitors, community psychiatric nurses and degree student nurses doing placements in paediatrics and obstetrics, all of whom teach me as much about their specialities and about the current day-to-day realities of working in these jobs, as I teach them about psychology. I have been involved in research into labour pain, prematurity, attachment, postnatal depression and I am currently investigating stress in health care professionals.

This book was, therefore, written from the viewpoint of a nurse, a psychologist and a researcher who is fascinated by every aspect of childbearing. It was also influenced by my experiences as a mother and as a health care consumer. I have two children, now grown up. Almost as soon as I got the contract for this book I was amazed and delighted to discover that I was expecting a baby, so I have had recent experience of being the recipient of modern 'high tech' health care in pregnancy. Tragically I lost the baby a few months later. This is bound to have influenced the way this book was written.

As I say at the beginning of the introduction, I have written this book with the aim of improving the psychological care given by midwives, health visitors, nurses and other health care professionals. This does not imply that I think that the care you give just now is bad. On the contrary, I have the greatest admiration for most of the psychological care that is given. But much of it is given instinctively, rather than being the result of proper training, and lots of it is based on the professional's own experience rather than on the distilled experience of others which is provided by research. There could also be more of it, and it could be awarded a higher status.

I've tried to give practical advice on how to implement the results of research in order to improve psychological understanding and care but these are just guidelines, not prescriptions for how you should behave and what you should or shouldn't do. Giving professionals rules and regulations of that sort is, in my opinion, insulting. You are the experts in midwifery, health visiting etc., not me. It's up to you to use your expertise in selecting the material from the book which you find helpful;

to try out some of the suggestions to see if they work for you and the families in your care; and to fight to implement them if they are worthwhile but to reject them, but not the research upon which they are based, if they turn out to be unhelpful or impractical.

Kate Niven

Acknowledgements

I would firstly like to thank Susan Devlin and the staff at Butterworth-Heinemann for their support and encouragement. Mary Cronk, their midwifery adviser, gave me confidence by her enthusiastic appraisal of the book, and her humorous, down-to-earth and informative comments were greatly welcomed.

Many people in Glasgow Polytechnic were helpful, most notably David Bell, Christina Knussen, Anne McLean, Ron McQueen, Alison Smith and Cathie Wright. My students in the Health and Nursing Department have taught me much about modern-day nursing and midwifery practice and have kept me in touch with the realities of their world. I hope I have been able to teach them something useful in return. The now defunct Faculty of Life and Social Sciences funded my sabbatical leave during which this book was written, and my home department of Psychology provided the word processor on which it was inscribed.

While I was writing this book, I was secretary of the Society for Reproductive and Infant Psychology, a society which is particularly concerned with the psychological aspects of pregnancy, birth, parenthood and infancy. Much of the material in this book has been published in its journal, and many of its members are involved in research which is reported here. I would like to take this opportunity to record my thanks to those SRIP members and to all the other researchers whose work I have utilized in this book.

Finally I want to thank my family. Seonaid and Campbell, my children, gave me the encouragement and understanding that all mothers deserve. Eric epitomized everything I have said in this book about providing practical and emotional support. The practical support included rescuing me from various word-processing disasters. His emotional support was equally essential, especially his firmly held belief, which I didn't always share, that I would actually finish this book. Authors often say 'this book wouldn't have been written without the support of my partner'. It's certainly true in this case. If this book seems to reflect an unduly optimistic view of men, one which I certainly would not always have espoused, then Eric is to blame.

Kate Niven

Introduction: In the beginning is the family

During pregnancy, birth, the puerperium and the postnatal period, the professionals involved in midwifery, health visiting, obstetrics and paediatrics are used to considering the joint needs of mothers and babies. I contend that this consideration should be extended to all the members of the family unit. The fetus and the mother are an indivisible unit, but it takes two to make a fetus so the father is an automatic member of that unit whether he maintains contact with the mother or not. During pregnancy, birth and the postnatal period the mother deserves constant practical and emotional support to enable her to optimally care for herself and for her baby at the same time. The person who gives her that support is vital to her well-being and thus to the well-being of the baby. That person is therefore a member of the family unit, whether he or she is related or not. The adults who care for a baby, who may or may not be its biological parents, develop an interdependent reciprocal relationship with the baby and with one another. They therefore also constitute a family unit. Other family members need looking after as well as the baby and the care they need may detract from the care that can be given to their newest member.

Every chapter in this book demonstrates the individual and inter-related needs of the fetus/baby, the mother/primary caretaker, and the father/primary supporter. So the provision of health care during pregnancy, birth and the postnatal period involves the giving of psychological care to all the members of these family units.

The family

Before describing what I mean by psychological care, I want to expand on the nature of family units. In the UK today the person most likely to provide long-term, regular, practical and emotional support for mothers and babies is the father. A baby's primary caretaker is most likely to be her or his biological mother but the most likely regular secondary caretaker is the father. This is a recent development, a product of the nuclear rather than the extended family and of the changing role of women. (Female relatives are more likely to be employed outside the home and to be geographically distant from parturients in the 1990s than in the 1900s. They are therefore less able to be involved in the day-to-day practical and emotional support of mothers and babies than they were in the past.)

However, a few parturients will sadly be supported by no one, while a substantial proportion will be supported by mothers, sisters and best friends rather than by husbands/partners/fathers of the baby (usually but not necessarily synonymous). The reasons for this may be practical – an absent partner; emotional – where the mother chooses to have no further contact with the father; cultural/social – where the norm for the mother's cultural, social or familial group is that female rather than male relatives are involved in childbirth and child-rearing; or personal – where the mother has a particularly close, mutually supportive relationship with her sister or best friend or where her chosen partner is female.

The provision of maternal support by females is traditional in many societies and may have many benefits, since the supporter and the supported can share the same experiences. However, it is no longer the norm within our society and many women in the UK today would quail at the thought of having their mother or mother-in-law attendant during pregnancy, birth and the puerperium rather than their husband.

The provision of support by husbands/partners/fathers of the child is potentially problematic – especially for the husbands. In this age of so-called equality of the sexes there is still one central inequality – men can't have babies! They can't get pregnant and they can't give birth. No matter how well intentioned, empathic or sympathetic they may be, it is impossible for them fully to understand these aspects of female experience. Furthermore, they have to come to terms with prospective fatherhood (an experience that women can't fully understand) at the same time as supporting the prospective mother through her mysterious maternal adjustments. (Chapter 1 details these separate adjustments.) This makes pregnancy, birth and the postnatal period tough for men as well as for women and can interfere with the quality of support available to the parturient and consequentially to her baby. There is therefore a very special need to understand and support the father so that he can adequately support his partner and child.

This principle of caring for the carer and supporting the supporter encompasses the mother – who cares for the baby; the husband, partner, relative or friend – who cares for the mother, and the midwife, health visitor or nurse – who cares for all of them. All of these people need good psychological care if they are to be able to give proper care in their turn.

Psychological care

The giving of good psychological care to families by midwives, health visitors and nurses does not involve family therapy or marriage guidance. These are the jobs of experts. Good basic psychological care involves respect, compassion, reassurance, the giving of information, the provision of choice, the acknowledgement of concerns, the sharing of joys and sorrows. These are components of good midwifery, health visiting and nursing care too which have been variously embodied in concepts such as holistic care or empowering the parturient. The task of the health care professional is to extend that good care to all the members of the family unit, each of whom thus becomes part of her/his professional responsibility. In order to carry out this extended remit s/he needs to understand the family's experiences from the family's point of view. That understanding cannot come from personal experience alone. It can come from studying the results of research into psychological aspects of pregnancy, birth, parenthood and infancy, many of which are described in the remainder of this book. It can also come from listening to the families in your care who will tell you their worries, their needs, their joys and sorrows, what information they want, what choices they want to make and what reassurance they seek.

Health care professionals are generally bad at listening. We haven't been trained for it; talking is much more our line. And – 'there isn't time!' – the eternal cry. But listening can be done at the same time as carrying out physical care or practical tasks. It could replace all that superficial chitchat about visitors, flowers and the weather – appropriate enough at times but not when a mother or father is worried sick about something, or is deeply upset.

Listening can also be more efficient than talking. Giving information to a mother-to-be who is too upset to take it in or who doesn't want to hear it is a waste of time (see Chapter 2), whereas listening to her concerns and anxieties will calm her and allow the midwife, health visitor or nurse to give more appropriate information at a more appropriate time (Chapters 1–3). Professing false understanding: 'Oh, I know exactly how you feel', or offering superficial platitudes, 'There are others worse off than you', 'Never mind, you can always have another baby', can be not only a waste of time but can cause deep distress (Chapter 4). Listening quietly to a person in distress, putting an arm round them, giving them an actual or metaphorical shoulder to cry on can be much more helpful than anything you can say (Chapters 4 and 6).

Psychological care for the carers

Listening can be harder than talking, because sometimes you hear things you would rather not. Listening to families in your care may upset you, anger you or lead you to identify more closely with their experiences – 'If it can happen to them, it can happen to me!' In fact, giving good psychological care can generally be hard on the health professional. S/he can spend all her/his working time caring for 'patients', i.e. mothers, fathers and babies, then go home and start again caring for family and friends.

But who cares for the carer? Senior staff can seem unappreciative; 'patients' occasionally ungrateful; and everybody else takes the carer for granted. Eventually, the caring midwife, health visitor or nurse, just like the caring mother or father, can run out of 'caringness' if someone doesn't care for her or him. The exhaustion of the caring response is often glorified by the trendy term 'burn-out', but it's something much more simple and ubiquitous. What carers need is respect, support and appreciation (and the ability to say 'enough is enough'). These are what midwives, health visitors and nurses need if they are to be able to give good psychological care.

Where is this respect, support and appreciation to come from? From senior staff, and here midwives are fortunate in that their supervisor of midwives is designated to provide just such support. However, although the old authoritarian, perfection-seeking, nit-picking, task-oriented style of health care management is changing, many health care professionals still do not receive adequate respect, support and appreciation from their managers. Professional carers have no right to demand or expect appreciation from those in their care, far less support, but research has shown that they sometimes do (Butterworth and Faugier, in press). Neither should their families have to compensate for the short-comings of management, but they undoubtedly do. If midwives, health visitors and nurses are to preserve their ability to care for others, they must learn to care for themselves and for one another so that psychological care isn't just something that's given to those individuals for whom the professional has responsibility but is also given to colleagues and taken by oneself.

So throughout this book runs a constant theme of psychological care – health professionals caring for one another; health professionals caring for families; families caring for one another; and at the end-point of this chain of caring, the baby, who cares for no one and demands care of exceptional quantity and quality.

Reference

Butterworth A., Faugier J. *Clinical Supervision and Mentorship in Nursing.* London: Chapman and Hall (in press).

1 Pregnancy

- The mother's adjustment to pregnancy
- The father's adjustment to pregnancy
- Relationship changes during pregnancy
- The fetus
- The effects of psychological distress during pregnancy
- Social support during pregnancy
- Alleviation of psychological distress during pregnancy
- Overview and summary
- Further reading
- References

The mother's adjustment to pregnancy

A variety of theoretical views have been advanced concerning the psychological and emotional aspects of pregnancy. Deutsch (1947), for instance, describes pregnancy as a calm dream-like period, the attainment of which fulfils a woman's deepest yearnings. Bibring (1959) on the other hand sees pregnancy as inherently a period of emotional, psychological and social stress. Both these views are still evident in our society with the 'rosy glow' view being perpetrated widely in the media, especially in relation to the numerous royal pregnancies which have occurred in the last few years. In contrast, the 'grim reality' view is more prevalent in the tales of old wives and the intimate discussions of younger ones.

The results of empirical research indicate that for most women pregnancy is not entirely pleasurable. Physical discomforts are common; for example, in a study of 105 married pregnant London women, 43% reported indigestion, 68% a lack of energy, 46% breathlessness, 68% leg cramps, 48% backache and 66% urgency of micturition (Wolkind and Zajicek, 1981). The same study, which utilized a longitudinal methodology with the same subjects being interviewed repeatedly over the course of their pregnancy, showed that crying (53%), misery (50%), nervousness (34%) and worrying (29%) were quite common in the second and early third trimester. A recent English study carried out in nine hospitals in four NHS regions found that 74% of subjects reported that they felt happy in early pregnancy and 46% felt anxious. Major worries reported at this stage of pregnancy included the possibility of miscarriage (31%); that something was wrong with the baby (28%); and money (26%). Even in early pregnancy, 14% of women reported that they were worried about going into hospital, with 18% being worried about internal examinations (Green, 1990). Another London-based study found that anxiety was more common in pregnant women than amongst the non-pregnant general public and that certain kinds of negative feelings, particularly concerning the birth, peak in the third trimester (Elliot et al., 1983). A more recent Australian study found that over 60% of female subjects reported an increase in anxiety, depression and irritability during their pregnancy, compared with their non-pregnant state (Condon, 1987). Some studies of postnatal depression, which is discussed in detail in Chapter 6, have found that a proportion of postnatally depressed women were also depressed during the antenatal period. For instance, a community-based study of depression carried out in London (Sharp, 1989) found that out of 32 women who were rated as being depressed at 3 months after birth, 22 had been depressed at either 14 or 36 weeks of pregnancy or on both occasions.

Some pregnant women may never experience these negative emotions, reporting increased rather than decreased psychological well-being in pregnancy (Elliot et al., 1983; Condon, 1987). Others may suffer reactions severe enough to be categorized as psychiatric disorder. Overall, occasional feelings of depression and anxiety are probably best regarded as a normal part of pregnancy, that is, a typical feature of pregnancy which does not imply abnormal adjustment or poor psychological functioning. Those caring for women during pregnancy should therefore expect them to be anxious, to worry, to be easily upset – these psychological reactions are as common as morning sickness (Fairweather, 1968) – and should treat them accordingly. Of course most mothers-to-be are happy and optimistic for much of the time but the less positive aspects of pregnancy should be acknowledged. This would release the pregnant woman from the necessity of pretending to be blissfully happy all of the time. It would allow the professionals who care for her to be more understanding and constantly to seek to reduce her anxiety and distress.

Worrying in pregnancy may be helpful to some degree. Janis (1958) has shown the efficacy of anticipatory 'worry work' in reducing the harmful impact of traumatic events such as major surgery, and Doering et al. (1980) found that women who had worried about childbirth during pregnancy had a more positive birth experience. In a study of labour pain carried out in Scotland, I found that women who had realistic as opposed to idealistic expectations of childbirth had lower levels of labour pain, their realism reflecting a certain amount of anticipatory anxiety (Niven and Gijsbers, 1984).

However, while some degree of psychological negativity is probably unavoidable in pregnancy, this may be unnecessarily exacerbated by the way mothers-to-be are cared for within the current health care system. Thus anxiety and depression associated with poor-quality care or restricted choices of care should not be regarded as normal; that is, normal in the sense that they are acceptable or inevitable. Instead they should be taken as evidence that the system is failing its clients in some way and that changes should be made accordingly. For instance, it seems unfortunate that 14% of women in the early weeks of their pregnancy are preoccupied by worries about going into hospital (Green, 1990; see above). While no one likes the idea of going into hospital, it may be that much of the parturient's concern could be ameliorated by improving the psychological care she receives there, for example by empowering the mother, or of course by increasing the provision of community-based maternity care so that the need for hospitalization is reduced or removed.

Furthermore, it has been shown that excessive anxiety in pregnancy is associated with depression in the postnatal period (Watson et al., 1984) and is likely to reflect high levels of stress and distress in the mother-to-be. These high levels of stress and distress can adversely affect the fetus (see below) and the mother's relationship with her partner, friends and family. For the woman herself, excessive anxiety can make pregnancy 9 months of total misery – it could perhaps be compared to the way you feel the day before a huge exam which you think you might fail, but lasting for months on end. Thus high levels of anxiety in pregnancy are a major cause for concern.

A number of factors have been related to high levels of anxiety, stress and distress in pregnancy. Some are obvious and are exactly the same factors that would stress any of us at any time: factors such as homelessness, severe financial worry or the breakdown or loss of a long-term relationship.

Some factors are more clearly related to the pregnancy itself. Wolkind and Zajicek's London study, discussed above, found that a small group of women who had psychiatric problems in pregnancy (i.e. had psychological problems such as anxiety and depression severe enough to be characterized as psychiatric disorder when rated by a psychiatrist using standardized interview techniques; see Wolkind and Zajicek, 1981) had negative feelings about being pregnant. This finding was echoed by Condon (1987) and by Sharp (1989) who reported that women who had seriously considered terminating the pregnancy were more likely to show high levels of psychological symptomatology. However, it would be wrong to think that every woman who has second thoughts about being pregnant or who initially rejects an unplanned pregnancy will be distressed and disturbed throughout her pregnancy because of this. Wolkind and Zajicek (1981) demonstrated conclusively that the desirability of a pregnancy is not an unchanging attribute. Many of their subjects, whether married, cohabiting or single, who were initially upset to find that they were pregnant, were positive about the pregnancy when interviewed at 7 months. In contrast, some subjects who had planned and welcomed their pregnancy became negative about it later on. It was therefore clear that attitudes towards being pregnant often changed markedly over the three trimesters. The subjects who became more negative about their pregnancy as it developed were the ones who were more likely to become psychiatrically disturbed.

Wolkind and Zajicek did not find that unmarried or non-cohabiting subjects suffered from significantly higher levels of psychiatric morbidity than married or cohabiting subjects. There was a tendency for their teenage subjects, both married and single, to have slightly higher levels of disturbance. All of their subjects were in their first pregnancy. Studies which have utilized multiparous subjects as well have shown, somewhat surprisingly, that they report more psychological distress than primiparous women during pregnancy. This is generally attributed to the additional stresses these women suffer in caring for their already existing child or children at the same time as adjusting to the current pregnancy (Condon, 1987). It supports the view that the woman's experience of pregnancy must be considered in the light of her family framework.

A pregnancy which is threatened with miscarriage or stillbirth or with the possibility that 'something is wrong with the baby' is associated with anxiety, depression and irritability (Condon, 1987). Raised serum alpha-fetoprotein levels are a source of intense anxiety (Fearn et al., 1982) as are the results of other tests which indicate rightly or wrongly that the fetus is abnormal or at risk. Awaiting the results of such tests can be immensely stressful, with some women reporting that they smoked more and took tranquillizers during this time (Farrant, 1980): a far-from-positive consequence of prenatal screening, though one which has not always been found (Green, 1990). Negative findings on ultrasound scans can therefore be very reassuring and are associated with significant reductions in maternal anxiety (Tsoi and Hunter, 1987) but of course confirmatory results will increase anxiety and may set in motion the grieving process (see Tsoi and Hunter, 1987 and Chapter 4). Long-term follow-up of mothers who have had false-positive results from, for example, phenylketonuria or hypothyroidism screening programmes show that some continue to be anxious about their babies for months or even years despite medical reassurance (Bodegard et al., 1983) so it is not safe to conclude that the anxiety raised by such results will necessarily be dissipated by subsequent negative findings.

A pregnancy which appears to the professionals to be completely healthy and to be proceeding totally normally may be the source of intense anxiety because of previous reproductive problems. Miscarriage (Gannon, in submission), stillbirth and neonatal death (MacCarthy, 1969), previous cot death (Mandell and Wolfe, 1975) and handicap in the baby (Helper et al., 1968) are all associated with intense anxiety in the subsequent pregnancy. Women who have had a previous preterm baby are also more likely to be anxious in a subsequent pregnancy (Van den Akker et al., 1990). Infertility, infertility investigation and infertility treatment are all highly stressful so that a long-awaited pregnancy, as well as being very precious and therefore a source of some anxiety, may also reflect the continuation of the stress the woman has been undergoing in participating in treatment programmes such as in vitro fertilization (Reading et al., 1989; Niven et al., in press).

Some of these past problems may be obvious to all the professionals caring for the woman during her subsequent pregnancy. Others may be hidden. For instance, a history of secondary infertility, cot death or handicap is not reflected in 'para 1 + 0' and so staff who do not have ready access to such information will be unaware of the impact this reproductive history is having on women in their care. Of course some pregnant women will share their anxieties with maternity staff but others will find recalling the previous events too painful even to mention. A research study carried out in a gynaecological ward has shown that nurses are typically inaccurate in their understanding of the worries of those in their care, worries which fellow patients found all too easy to empathize with (Johnston, 1982). This kind of insensitivity can afflict maternity staff as well, especially if the women they care for do not display their anxiety in an obvious manner. The pregnant woman who, like me, trembles and goes faint when faced with some potentially traumatic investigation like chorionic villus sampling, conveys her anxiety clearly and will (usually) receive a lot of support and sympathy. The woman who covers her anxiety with loud-mouthed bravado may not be treated so sensitively if the staff do not appreciate why this particular test is so upsetting.

Women who have suffered a previous reproductive loss or handicap may cope with the subsequent pregnancy by trying to avoid attachment to the fetus (Niven et al., in press), so they act as if they were totally detached from the events of the current pregnancy. This detachment has gone beyond the stage of the previous miscarriage or until the fetus is viable, or it may last for longer, interfering with the woman's attachment to her new baby. Uncompleted grieving following miscarriage, stillbirth, neonatal or infant death is relatively common (see Chapter 4 and Oglethorpe, 1989) and may interfere with the mother's reaction to the current pregnancy. Occasionally she may be unable to separate her feelings about the baby she has lost from the baby that she is expecting or may think of them as one and the same baby. More commonly the course of the current pregnancy (and birth) brings back all the traumatic events of the past (Tylden, 1990), so that certain stages in pregnancy which, for example, correspond to when the previous pregnancy had started to go wrong, or when the lost baby had been born prematurely, or the estimated date of its delivery, have tremendous significance and engender both renewed grief for the baby that has died and tremendous anxiety for the baby that is to be born.

A history of intense psychological disturbance or psychiatric morbidity has been shown to be associated with marked depression and anxiety in pregnancy in some studies (Sharp, 1989; Wolkind and Zajicek, 1981). This may indicate that the pregnancy has exacerbated an underlying predisposition to affective disorder or may simply reflect some continuing psychological disturbance.

In our culture pregnancy is regarded as a special time; a period of great personal and medical significance when the woman is preoccupied by thoughts and feelings about her pregnancy, birth and baby, and when health care is directed towards bringing about the best possible outcomes for mother and baby. Women who come from other cultures do not always appear to share these views. For instance, Currer (1986) has studied a group of Pathan women who had migrated within the previous 10 years from Pakistan to Bradford and who followed traditional religious (Muslim) and cultural practices, especially those involving purdah – the social system whereby women are secluded from unrelated men and from public life. For these women, pregnancy is seen as an inevitable stage of the female lifespan and not as something special. It is also regarded as embarrassing and not something which should be mentioned in front of children or elders (as it was in British ethnic majority society until fairly recently) or even close female relatives. Because of these factors, pregnancy is not announced, preparations for the baby are rarely made before the birth and antenatal clinic attendance, especially early in pregnancy, is regarded as strange and unnecessary. Ritual fasting is also usually observed, despite the advice of health educators that this should be avoided during pregnancy.

Health care workers might therefore conclude that these women do not care about the well-being of the fetus. However, most of Currer's subjects attended antenatal clinics, despite the problems this caused them in having to discuss their pregnancy and be attended by male doctors. They put up with these problems (the breaking of purdah is seen as a very serious matter) and go against their own inclinations and beliefs about appropriate pregnancy behaviour in order to improve the chances of having a healthy baby. Currer comments: 'It was [this] outcome which was most important for the women, and the NHS was seen by all to offer a high chance of a healthy baby and healthy mother. It was greatly appreciated for this reason' (Currer, 1986, p. 26).

Their participation in ritual fasting during the holy month of Razam, if it fell during their pregnancy, was regarded by the women as especially important to their spiritual well-being as servants of their God. Normally they would be precluded from fasting when menstruating as they are regarded at that time as unclean and thus unable to pray. Pregnancy thus provided an opportunity to fast for the whole of the holy month and this was generally regarded as more important than any (to them) unproven link with the well-being of the baby. Thus the advice to avoid fasting was usually ignored. As one woman commented: 'They think we don't understand. We do, but our ways are different' (Currer, 1986, p. 20).

The women Currer studied are probably atypical of ethnic minority women in this country, many of whom do not follow their traditional practices rigorously but have to some extent adopted the majority culture's norms (see Chapter 2). They may not even be typical of all Pathan women or of all practising Muslim women. Therefore health care workers should not assume that all or most ethnic minority women in their care will share the feelings and beliefs expressed above. However, the results of Currer's research give an insight into a belief system which is different from that which prevails in the UK. This should encourage midwives, health visitors and nurses working with women who come from different cultures to be sensitive to the possibility that their ideas about what is right and wrong for pregnant women may not be shared.

The father's adjustment to pregnancy

The father's personal adjustment to the development of his offspring during pregnancy is likely to be different from the mother's. After all, he gets no physical feedback to prove to him that this baby exists. Once the fetus's presence is obvious and he can see it and feel its movement, he gets that evidence, but only second-hand. In the early months, however, he has no physical evidence at all whereas the mother will be feeling sick or running to the toilet or craving chocolate or buying a larger bra. So it's not surprising that fathers seem to lag behind mothers in adjusting to pregnancy itself and to the prospect of fatherhood.

However, perhaps as a compensation for the lack of physical changes they experience in pregnancy, some fathers experience or report experiencing higher than normal levels of physical symptomatology during their partner's pregnancy. When these symptoms resemble those of women during pregnancy they are often labelled as the couvade syndrome, 'couvade' being the term used by anthropologists to describe the ritual practices carried out in some so-called 'primitive' tribes of a husband taking to bed and screaming and groaning while his wife gives birth. For instance, a study by Shereshevsky and Yarrow (1974) compared a group of fathers-to-be with a matched control group of men whose partners were not currently pregnant. Twenty per cent of the fathers-to-be reported nausea, vomiting and loss of appetite during the course of the study, compared with only 9% of the control group. Similarly, Wolkind and Zajicek (1981) in their study of pregnancy (see above) found that approximately 50% of their subjects' husbands complained to them of pregnancy-like symptoms.

A number of studies have shown that fathers-to-be, like mothers-to-be, find pregnancy stressful. Clinical studies have noted that men who are receiving psychotherapy often relate the onset of their problems to their partner's pregnancy, e.g. Wainwright (1966). A study of 100 Nottingham fathers (Lewis, 1986) found that 20 of them spontaneously reported that they had consistent fears for their partner or for the baby during pregnancy; six had psychiatric symptoms and one had experienced a nervous breakdown necessitating hospitalization for six months during a previous pregnancy. Lewis concludes: 'Worries about the risk of pregnancy and birth begin to prey on them and their wives. Men firstly feel helpless about and partly responsible for, the possible dangers which face both mother and child' (Lewis, 1986, p. 53).

An Australian study found that 32% of male subjects reported an increase in anxiety during their partner's pregnancy, 26% an increase in irritability and 16% an increase in depression. This compares with increases of 61%, 62% and 61% for each of these symptoms respectively for their female partners (Condon, 1987). For the male subjects the increase in psychological distress was strongly related to feelings of marital insecurity, defined as a fear that parenthood would result in a decrease in closeness within the marriage or that the spouse would be closer to the child. Scott-Heyes (1984; see below) found that fathers-to-be who were depressed and anxious during pregnancy felt that they gave less affection to their partners, and that male depression in pregnancy was also related to low levels of nurturance received from the mothers-to-be. Thus the quality of the marital relationship seems to affect, and be affected by, the father-to-be's adjustment to his partner's pregnancy.

Relationship changes during pregnancy

The mother's adjustment to pregnancy might be considered to be dominated by her developing relationship to her baby; her relationship to its father takes second place. The father's adjustment is more concerned with his changing relationship to the mother, the relationship with the baby being mediated through her. Certainly pregnancy causes major changes within the marital or cohabiting relationship (long-term, committed cohabitation being here considered as the equivalent of a marital relationship) which of course presage those which will be caused by the birth and rearing of the child. A number of these changes appear to be to the disadvantage of the male partner and may therefore colour his experience of pregnancy.

Scott-Heyes (1983, 1984), working in Northern Ireland, conducted a study into love, marriage and childbearing. She found that the major change in the relationship between husband and wife during pregnancy concerned the degree of nurturance (looking after and caring for) and dependence (being looked after and cared for) shown by each partner to the other. During pregnancy 85% of the wives became more dependent on their husbands than they had been before; 73% of the husbands provided more nurturance to their wives than before and, if she was multiparous, received less in return. However their wives still felt that they were not being nurtured sufficiently.

Consequently, in 50% of cases the women's needs were unsatisfied, as were some of the men's (35%), and the men's increased provision of nurturance was to an extent unappreciated. A discussion of fatherhood in Sweden by Hwang (1988) pointed to a similar pattern of findings. Hwang suggests that in Sweden, as elsewhere in the world, wives are the principal source of emotional support for husbands. The wife is the provider of comfort and reassurance, a shoulder on which to cry and a sympathetic ear to listen to his troubles. She thus plays a central role in his emotional life. During pregnancy this changes. Emotional support is sought by the wife, not given. As in Scott-Heyes' study, the picture is of a husband deprived of a customary source of support. This support is rarely available from male friends or colleagues, even in advanced liberated Sweden. So the husband has to do without. And at the same time he is being called upon to provide a kind of support which he has had little opportunity to practise giving.

What Hwang describes as emotional support and Scott-Heyes labels as nurturance is what this book calls psychological care (see Introduction). It is a skill which needs to be practised and refined. In our still unequal society women practise it more than men. So when men are suddenly called upon to provide psychological care for their partners, they are likely to be relatively unskilled. Women need psychological care in pregnancy to help them to cope with the fears and anxieties typical of pregnancy (see Alleviation of psychological distress during pregnancy, this chapter). So without it they suffer. For instance, Scott-Heyes (1984) found that women who received less affection and nurturance from their partners during pregnancy were more likely to be depressed. Men need it too. Being sick during their partner's pregnancy may reflect male anxieties or it may be a way of saying 'I need looking after too'. But if there are already children in the family, then *they* get the 'looking after', not their fathers, so the fathers suffer as well (Scott-Heyes, 1984; see above).

Men 'don't get it' during pregnancy in another sense. A number of studies have found a marked drop in sexual activity during pregnancy (Kumar et al, 1981; Wolkind and Zajicek, 1981; Scott-Heyes, 1983, 1984). Scott-Heyes' findings demonstrated that this was in part attributable to a decrease in sexual desire on the part of the mother, as well as to the couple's caution about the effects of intercourse on the pregnancy. The fathers-to-be reported no decrease in sexual desire, so again they were experiencing a negative change in their marital relationship.

These male deprivations during pregnancy can be related to the findings of Condon (1987) that a number of men feel a sense of 'marital insecurity' during pregnancy (see The father's adjustment to pregnancy, this chapter). They need however to be set against findings which emphasize the positive aspects of prospective fatherhood. For example, 70 of 91 male subjects in Wolkind and Zajicek's study were 'delighted', 'over the moon', when they learned that their wives were pregnant. Lewis found that 43% of expectant fathers expressed a sense of increased responsibility – 'It made me grow up more' (Lewis, 1986, p. 48) – and that many of the couples seemed to grow closer as they engaged in joint 'nest-building'.

Sympathy for the 'pregnant' male's plight needs to be balanced by the acknowledgement that women also have a difficult time of it during pregnancy, and it is they who give birth to the baby after all! But in understanding a little more of what pregnancy is like for fathers as well as for mothers, we can see again how the needs of both have to be considered.

The fetus

So far in this chapter we've looked at the father's and mother's experience of pregnancy and at how their adaptation to it is influenced by their interactions with one another. The third member of this embryonic family, the fetus, is affected by these experiences and interactions too.

The idea that the fetus exists in a warm, wet world, safe from all external influences is a consoling one. But it's not accurate. The fetal autonomic system is very sensitive to environmental changes as perceived by the mother, which affect her catecholamine levels. Also affected is the uterine splanchnic bed, the placental circulation and the contractility of uterine muscle (see Newton, 1988). This means that it is possible for the mother's emotional and psychological state to affect the well-being of her fetus directly (see below).

The fetus can also be adversely affected by various drugs the mother ingests, inhales or injects, such as tobacco or alcohol, heroin or cocaine. Most mothers (even the so-called addicts) attempt to stop using these drugs during pregnancy. Unfortunately all these drugs act as potent, if temporary, stress relievers. They make you feel better and help you to forget your troubles for a time. Consequently, the highly stressed mother is more likely to continue using them, especially if she has little support from other quarters. It's very easy to condemn these mothers but just imagine if you were told that for the next 9 months, no matter how hard things were at work or outside it, you were never to have a cup of tea or coffee – substances we are nearly all addicted to. And imagine you had nobody sympathetic to talk to. Wouldn't you break the rules occasionally?

Stress in the mother can therefore affect the well-being of the fetus indirectly through the action of harmful drugs. Other factors which are sometimes associated with stress, such as poor nutritional status, late antenatal booking and poor clinic attendance, can also have adverse effects on the health of a pregnancy (Hall et al., 1980; Luke et al., 1981). Animal studies have demonstrated that gestational stress has adverse effects on fetal well-being (Istvan, 1986). Human studies have established significant correlations between maternal stress and anxiety levels, maternal catecholamine levels and fetal condition (Lederman et al., 1978), and between the occurrence of stressful life events in pregnancy (such as serious illness in a close family member or unemployment in the husband) which will give rise to high levels of stress and anxiety in the mother, and both low birthweight and premature delivery (Newton and Hunt, 1984). Newton and Hunt's study, carried out in Manchester, also found an association between cigarette smoking and low birthweight which in some cases interacted with the effect of stressful life events. Women who had experienced the largest number of stressful life events in pregnancy were also the most likely to be late bookers or to default on clinic attendance.

Newton and Hunt's study therefore demonstrates how the effects of maternal stress may operate directly on the fetus and the fetal environment, with raised maternal catecholamine levels leading to placental insufficiency and low birthweight or to increased uterine contractility and premature delivery. Indirect effects of stress mediated through tobacco inhalation and poor clinic attendance could also have affected maternal and fetal well-being. (This study was carried out prospectively, which means that life stress was measured during pregnancy *before* any measure of low birthweight or prematurity could be taken. Retrospective studies, e.g. where mothers of premature babies are asked about any stressful life events which had occurred during pregnancy, may be inaccurate because the mother searches to find some reason why she went into labour prematurely and so reports events as being stressful which she would not have done if asked during the course of an apparently normal pregnancy. Prospective studies are usually considered to be methodologically superior to retrospective studies, since memory effects and a search for meaning can render recall inaccurate. However a retrospective study carried out by Newton and others in 1979 into the effects of stressful life events in pregnancy produced the same results as their subsequent prospective study – that they are associated with premature delivery (see Newton and Hunt, 1984). Therefore the dangers of the retrospective technique may sometimes be exaggerated.)

Other studies have shown that mothers who have previously experienced spontaneous abortion after 12 weeks' gestation, perinatal death or infant death have an increased risk of having a low birthweight baby (Chamberlain et al., 1975). It is most likely that this relationship is primarily due to biological factors (Newton, 1988). However since these mothers are likely to suffer considerable anxiety and distress during their pregnancy, the effects of this may further compromise the well-being of the fetus.

The effects of psychological distress during pregnancy

Psychological distress in pregnancy can therefore affect the mother and father-to-be independently; it can affect their relationship with one another, and it can affect their baby before and after birth, since low birthweight and premature delivery can have prolonged consequences for infant health (Illsley and Mitchell, 1984).

When one member of a married or cohabiting couple experiences high levels of psychological distress, this will affect the other members of his or her family. If the male partner is distressed, rejects the pregnancy or disrupts the marital relationship, this is likely to make it more difficult for his wife to adjust easily to her pregnancy (e.g. Helper et al., 1968; Scott-Heyes, 1984). On the other hand, a supportive marital relationship can alleviate maternal distress during pregnancy. A study by Nuckolls et al. (1972) showed that women who experienced a stressful pregnancy were less likely to have pregnancy complications if they had supportive social assets, prominent amongst which was a supportive marital relationship. And in a clinical study (Blake-Cohen, 1966) of women who had suffered severe childhood trauma, the author noted the crucial role played by the husbands in affecting their partners' well-being during pregnancy. These women were considered by their clinicians to be at risk of psychological disturbance during pregnancy because of the damaging effects of their childhood experiences. Instead, with the support of their male partners, they adapted to pregnancy well and did not show any marked psychological symptomatology.

A number of studies of postnatal depression have shown that women who are highly distressed, anxious or depressed during pregnancy are more likely to experience depression postnatally (Watson et al., 1984; Elliot et al., 1988; Sharp, 1989). These findings may reflect a state of continuing depression, starting prenatally (or even before pregnancy) and continuing on into the postnatal period. Alternatively, it may be that women who are highly distressed prenatally are predisposed to a subsequent but separate depression occurring some time after the birth. Women who have poor marital relationships during pregnancy are more likely to be depressed (Scott-Heyes, 1984) and are more susceptible to postnatal depression (Elliot et al., 1988) so again the link between the quality of the marital relationship during pregnancy and the psychological well-being of the mother is evident.

Studies of postnatal depression have also focused attention on the relationship between the new mother and her own mother (Kumar and Robson, 1984; Cox, 1989) and the importance of this relationship is obvious to many health professionals caring for a woman in pregnancy. Although research has not yet focused on the manner in which the dynamics of this relationship alter over pregnancy, a sensitive midwife may be able to guide the mother-to-be towards resolving any difficulties she may have with her mother, so that these will not continue to have a disruptive effect during birth and the postnatal period.

Social support during pregnancy

In the Introduction, I noted that the concept of the family should be applied to the mother, her offspring and the person or persons who give her continued long-term support. Although this supporting person is often her partner and the father of her child, other relatives and friends, male or female, can occupy this role, for instance, the woman's parents (her mother perhaps being especially important here; see above) her sister, her best friend.

In addition, most of us are fortunate enough to have a network of friends, relatives, neighbours and colleagues who support us to some extent both emotionally and practically. No one member of this social network provides continued, long-term support, so they don't qualify as 'family' according to the terms of this book. However, collectively, they act as a vital source of support for pregnant women, just as for all of us. They are the colleagues who cover for the mother-to-be with morning sickness, and who help her to celebrate her new status. They are the neighbours who will give her a lift home with the heavy shopping. They are the friends who will lend her maternity clothes and who will listen when she has a moan about her sore back, her irritable and irritating kids, her inconsiderate husband. They are the relatives who will lend her money, or take the kids off her hands for a while and the babysitters who will let her and her husband out for the evening so she can discover that he's not so inconsiderate after all. These people may also act to sustain other members of the family apart from the mother-to-be. So the father's support network or the sister's or the best friend's may support the pregnant woman indirectly by supporting her primary supporter. Together with the primary support figure, these people provide what the literature calls 'social support', 'psychosocial assets', 'emotionally sustaining behaviour', 'available coping resources' (see Oakley, 1988).

A number of studies show that having social support is helpful for pregnant women, especially when they are experiencing a stressful pregnancy. For instance, Yamomoto and Kinney (1976) found a negative correlation between anxiety in pregnancy and the coping resources women on low income had available to them at that time – the more resources they had available, the less their anxiety. Robinson et al. (1984) showed that social support ameliorates anxiety associated with amniocentesis to some extent. Nuckolls et al. (1972) showed that women who experienced a number of stressful life events in pregnancy but who had considerable psychosocial assets had a pregnancy complication rate of 33% compared to women with similarly stressful pregnancies but few psychosocial assets, who had a complication rate of 91%. A more recent prospective study confirmed the buffering effect of social support in protecting women who were experiencing high levels of stress and distress in pregnancy from pregnancy complications (Norbeck and Tilden, 1983). However, the effect was not as dramatic as that found in Nuckolls' study.

While good friends and neighbours may counteract the effects of poverty to some extent, as Yamamoto and Kinney's study shows, there is no doubt that having money helps an expectant couple to cope with the demands of imminent parenthood. As discussed above (see The mother's adjustment to pregnancy, and The fetus), stressful life events often involve financial worries, homelessness or unemployment for the husband. These events are obviously associated with lack of money.

Social class is clearly related to health in general and reproductive health in particular, with women from lower social classes being at increased risk of miscarriage, stillbirth, infant death, low birthweight and handicap (Oakley et al., 1982; Office of Population Censuses and Surveys, 1987). Some of the relationship between social class and poor reproductive outcome could be accounted for by the effects of poverty in exacerbating or failing to alleviate stress during pregnancy: Kehrer and Wohin (1979), for example, found that direct income supplementation was effective in enhancing pregnancy outcome, though only in women who had high-risk pregnancies. However, mothers of lower social class also experience a larger number of stressful life events during pregnancy (Newton and Hunt, 1984) and after birth, and are less likely to have a confiding relationship with their husbands (Brown and Harris, 1978), so a variety of psychosocial factors are associated with lower social class. These may account for its relationship with comparatively poor reproductive outcome, together with physical and medical factors such as inadequate nutrition and poor general health.

Alleviation of psychological distress during pregnancy

The material presented in this chapter so far makes it clear that the occurrence of some psychological stress in pregnancy is inevitable. It's a time of change and adjustment, and that always causes stress, even when the change is positive and highly desired, such as when moving house or changing job. So no matter how hard you try, you can't totally abolish stress in pregnancy.

You can give information and reassurance, but that won't stop a 40-year-old woman worrying about the result of a chorionic villus sampling, an alpha-fetoprotein test or an amniocentesis. Those caring for a couple in pregnancy who have suffered a previous miscarriage or stillbirth can give them access to frequent medical checks, scans and monitoring. But they can't convince them that 'it will be all right this time'. You can't replace a missing husband, a lost job or inadequate housing. It's important for all who care for the pregnant woman and her family to recognize that there are things you cannot do. That leaves more energy to do the things that can be done and stops you feeling a failure because you can't work miracles. What you can do is acknowledge the worries and anxieties that families have during pregnancy. Ignoring them, pretending they don't exist, doesn't make them go away. It just makes *you* feel more comfortable. Once you recognize their worries it becomes clearer what information and reassurance is needed. Table 1.1 lists factors which are likely to increase anxiety in mothers and fathers-to-be. But remember that you will only find out what is worrying this particular mother or father-to-be at this particular time if you ask, and then take time to listen to the answer.

Table 1.1   Factors associated with increased anxiety during pregnancy

---

Stressful life events – e.g. bereavement, unemployment for the husband, family illness

Marital problems

Lack of social support

Risk of miscarriage

Risk of stillbirth

Risk of low birthweight or prematurity or other condition which will threaten the life or well-being of the baby

Risk of handicap – therefore screening tests in at-risk mothers

Raised serum alpha-fetoprotein levels or other positive results on screening tests, even if false positives

Previous history of miscarriage, stillbirth or neonatal death

Previous history of infant illness or death

Previous history of infertility, infertility investigation and treatment

Negative attitude to pregnancy in third trimester

Previous psychiatric illness

In Chapter 2, I deal with the provision of information in detail when discussing preparation for childbirth. Giving information in pregnancy – about fetal or maternal risks, about the possibility that the baby might be handicapped or that the pregnancy may not be sustained – is somewhat different. The midwife who is preparing a patient for childbirth has considerable freedom to choose what, when and how to tell her about the many different aspects of parturition. Conveying information about pregnancy is not like that. There are strong moral and ethical reasons why mothers and fathers-to-be should be told about the risk of handicap in their baby, or about maternal risks, or about their baby's condition in utero. Staff do not have the right to withhold information of that kind.

Therefore staff will often be placed in the position of having to tell families in their care potentially upsetting news, or having to explain risk factors and test results which have been conveyed by medical staff. (This can be problematic. Preliminary results from a recent study (Marteau, 1990) showed that different doctors working within the same hospital quoted the risk of miscarriage following amniocentesis as anything from 1 in 100 to 1 in 300/400 and tended to convey information about prenatal testing in a way which accentuated the risks of handicap and downplayed the risks of miscarriage following testing.)

Ley, in his work on communication from doctors to 'patients', has shown that the recipients' satisfaction with such communication is dependent on their understanding of what they have been told, and their memory of it. Their memory of what the doctor said is also crucially affected by their understanding, so that people who do not understand what the doctor said won't remember it accurately (Ley, 1982). Therefore explaining test results and risk factors clearly, in language the recipient understands, is the most important aspect of such communication. Many people faced with unclear communications from health care practitioners listen quietly, say 'thank you very much', go home and realize they didn't understand a word that was said to them. This may be partly because they didn't comprehend what was said but didn't want to admit it, or because they didn't want 'to be a bother to you when you're busy', but also because they were so anxious that they couldn't attend to what was said. Perhaps they heard 'at risk', or 'Down's syndrome' or 'negative result' and panicked so much that they heard nothing else, just like latching on to one word in an exam and ignoring the rest of the question. They don't understand what's being said because they haven't heard it.

Ley recommends that information should be given simply, clearly, in small amounts, in a setting as free of distractions as possible. Vital information should ideally be mentioned first and repeated again at the end of the communication. This is in order to utilize what are known as primacy (beginning) and recency (end) effects, which enhance recall (are more likely to be remembered). All important material should be repeated, given in writing in a personalized form as well as orally, and provision should be made for those receiving the information to contact staff again if they have any further questions or confusions (Ley, 1982). The midwife or health visitor conveying important information to families during pregnancy should follow this advice. This will make it more likely that those in their care understand and remember the information they have been given so that they do not misinterpret positive or negative information. It will also allow them to make any necessary decisions on the basis of full and accurate knowledge.

Although research has indicated that the recipients of health care generally want to know as much as possible, even when the news is bad (Ley, 1982), this does not lessen their anxiety while awaiting test results, nor their distress if the results confirm miscarriage or handicap. Everything possible should be done to reduce the waiting time for test results, since the high anxiety, increased cigarette smoking and tranquillizer use which the wait may induce (see The mother's adjustment to pregnancy, this chapter) could be harmful to the fetus, whether it is healthy or 'at risk'.

Breaking bad news (see Chapter 4) is better done in person rather than by phone or letter. That is, it is usually better for the recipient of the news, who can ask questions and for clarification and can be comforted by the person who brings it. It is not generally better for the bearer of the news. There are few things more upsetting than telling someone that their beloved baby-to-be is dead, at risk, or will be handicapped. Midwives and health visitors perform a great service for families in such situations by telling them in person and by waiting with them to comfort them as far as possible (see Chapter 4 for details of how best to comfort families following a bereavement). However they must acknowledge the cost to themselves. They too should be able to receive comfort and support in these circumstances (see Introduction).

Reassurance can be equated with the giving of positive information, good news or optimistic findings. It doesn't entail lying to people or pretending that their anxieties are groundless. Doing that may reassure them briefly, but once you have been proved wrong they will never trust you again. In a study of information given during labour, Kirkham (1989) found that midwives sometimes used reassurance to deny a parturient's apprehensions, e.g. Woman in second-stage labour: 'I'm scared'; midwife: 'You mustn't be scared' (Kirkham, 1989, p. 129), or, according to the author, a midwifery sister and researcher, to reassure themselves rather than the parturient – the 'this-won't-hurt' phenomenon! However, genuinely reassuring information about, for instance, progress in labour was not always given, whereas potentially negative information sometimes was. These findings may be generalizable to pregnancy where midwifery and other health care staff are often engaged in transmitting potentially negative information. Their laudable efforts to transmit information accurately and their knowledge of what can go wrong may lead them to be very punctilious about conveying information about possible risks, complications and dangers to the baby while forgetting to be equally accurate in their transmission of positive information. Reassurance also entails boosting a person's confidence whenever appropriate and involves assuring the mother or father-to-be of your continuing ability to care for them properly. Thus, even when things go wrong, when it's bad news, or it does hurt, reassurance can still be employed – 'With help you will be able to cope', 'All of us here will give you every possible assistance', etc.

Parents whose pregnancies are very precious because of previous infertility or reproductive loss, or whose current pregnancy is at risk of miscarriage, stillbirth or possible handicap, can be reassured to some extent by seeing the fetus on the ultrasound scanner (see The mother's adjustment to pregnancy). But studies show that many mothers feel that they need more explanation of the scan from the person performing it and from doctors, and the opportunity to ask questions and have the image on the monitor screen explained clearly (Tsoi and Hunter, 1987). Careful provision of reassuring information is again shown to be vitally important. Similarly, negative results after amniocentesis are associated with the greatest stress reduction when the results are communicated directly to the mother rather than when she is left to assume that all is well if she has not heard by a specific date (Robinson et al., 1984). Yet often it is regarded as more important to convey a positive result (the bad news) directly than to convey the good news. Telling mothers-to-be good news is good for them, as Robinson's study shows, and it is good for the teller, so we should do more of it!

Oglethorpe (1989), in his review of parenting after perinatal bereavement, concludes that vigilance and support rather than psychotherapy are the best forms of psychological treatment for the family in pregnancy who have previously lost a child. This vigilance and support may be provided by psychologists or psychiatrists in some circumstances. The midwife caring for the family throughout the pregnancy is however best placed to provide regular comfort, understanding and reassurance. This is especially important around the times which are of most significance to the family, for example around the anniversaries of the previous loss and previous estimated date of delivery.

Psychotherapy, which involves probing painful feelings, may be hazardous in pregnancy, though extremely useful after the birth in helping the parents to come to terms with their original loss (see Oglethorpe, 1989 and Chapter 4). Midwives or other health care professionals caring for such families during pregnancy should not therefore discuss the family's loss unless prompted by the parents. A subject of mine who had lost a baby previously said she dreaded the inevitable repetition of her reproductive history: 'I just wished they would skip over that part. I tried not to think about it because it upset me so much! But the doctors went over it every time they saw me' (Niven et al., in press). So, as always, it is best to be guided by the mother or father. If they want to talk about it, fine. If they don't, then leave it alone.

The vigilance that Oglethorpe (1989) refers to concerns the psychological state of the family. These couples are at risk of severe psychological disturbance, especially if the current pregnancy is close in time to the previous loss. Those caring for them should be looking for signs of intense anxiety and/or depression, for signs of unusual detachment from the current pregnancy and/or for signs of severe marital strain. If these are observed then specialist help should be offered to the couple.

This raises the vexed question of where to go for such help. The psychologically aware midwife or health visitor caring for the family during pregnancy, birth and the postnatal period needs to know of psychiatrists and psychologists who are experienced in treating psychological disturbance associated with childbirth or with bereavement, to whom the family can be referred. These specializations are not as common as they should be, so it should not be assumed that every psychiatrist or psychologist will have the necessary skills. Midwives working within a hospital setting may have better access to a range of specialists through the auspices of their (hopefully) sympathetic and knowledgeable consultant. Midwives and health visitors working in the community may be able to call on the resources of the community psychiatric nursing service or, in some areas, on a psychologist working in primary care, as well as on other members of the community health team. The voluntary societies may also be a useful source of expertise and are sometimes more acceptable to the family than psychologists or psychiatrists (see Appendix for a list of such agencies).

Another area which may necessitate specialist expertise involves the care of a mother who is using drugs during pregnancy. Pregnant women who are addicted to opiates need highly skilled management since both opiate addiction and maternal opiate withdrawal during pregnancy can have serious obstetric consequences (see Green and Gossop, 1988). Such women tend to avoid normal antenatal clinics and to present late in pregnancy or in labour. This exacerbates the difficulties associated with their management. Current attempts to reach and support these women have involved community-based health care clinics for drug users which may be more acceptable to the mothers-to-be than hospital or statutory drug agency-based provision (Gerda and Dawe, 1990), and flexible educational and supportive programmes where continuity of care is ensured in order to build up trust between the mother and the health care professionals involved in her care.

One such programme has recently been evaluated. In this programme all the staff involved in the care of the women co-ordinated their efforts so that the mother-to-be received consistent, supportive, non-judgemental treatment. Her drug prescriptions were issued at the antenatal clinic and were gradually and carefully reduced, with all mothers achieving some reduction in drug usage over the course of pregnancy and some mothers coming off drugs completely. Evaluation showed that women who had participated in the programme did not differ significantly in the outcome of their pregnancy from a control group of non-drug-using women who were matched for age, parity, social class and racial origin (Riley, in press), whereas drug-using women who had not participated in the programme had a much higher rate of fetal loss.

Mothers-to-be who are using alcohol or nicotine are also placing their pregnancy and their baby at some risk (and postnatal development of the baby may be affected by passive smoking too). Health education can be effective in reducing the use of these substances (see, for example, Stevens et al., 1988) but good psychological care is also important in alleviating some of the stress and anxiety which drives mothers-to-be (like the rest of us) to seek relief in drink or tobacco.

Antenatal classes seek amongst other things to provide health education and to alleviate anxiety about pregnancy, birth and baby-care. The effectiveness of antenatal training is dealt with in more detail in Chapter 2. It should be noted here, however, that attendance at classes is associated with some reduction in anxiety during pregnancy, although this does not appear to be due to the increase in knowledge which the classes aim to impart (Hiller and Slade, 1989). Attending classes allows women to meet other mothers-to-be and the subjects of Hiller and Slade's study, carried out in the north of England, gave this as one of the important reasons for their participation. The development of lasting friendships between participants was particularly strong in the community-based classes rather than in the hospital classes where the women had come from a wider catchment area. These friendships will have provided a social support network for the women and this may have acted to reduce their general anxiety at that time. Grouping pregnant women together may not always reduce their anxiety however. Lilford and colleagues in Leeds have used group counselling to provide mothers-to-be with information about the various screening tests available during pregnancy. Preliminary findings indicate that this is an efficient method of communication but that it increases anxiety in the short term (Lilford, 1989).

It should be obvious from reading the previous sections of this chapter that social support is central to ameliorating stress in pregnancy. The best social supporters are likely to be the primary supporters – the partners, sisters, mothers, best friends of the mother-to-be and of the father-to-be – acting in conjunction with the wider network of colleagues, neighbours, friends and family (see Social support during pregnancy). They are the people you can confide in, the people you can tell your innermost thoughts to, and they won't laugh or think you're silly. They are the comforters, the providers of cuddles, cheering up and chat. The professionals can provide some social support but it's the amateurs who do it best. For instance, a recent study of social support in women at risk of having low birthweight babies (see Oakley et al., 1990, and below) found that 65% of the subjects rated their partner as being the most helpful person in pregnancy, compared to 5% who rated the research midwife who provided professional contact and support as the most helpful (Garcia, 1990). So we come back to the husband and wife supporting each other, with him taking a more prominent role than he did before her pregnancy, and to their friends and family who may play the part of principal supporters or who may act as second-order supporters, supporting the primary supporters.

The professionals – you – are second-order supporters with regard to the father/husband/partner. If you can support him adequately, you will help him to support his wife and, in turn, help the baby. So giving

him information, reassuring him, listening to his worries and addressing his concerns can be the most effective way of caring for her. Of
course sometimes you never see him. And sometimes he's there in body
but not in spirit. In these cases there is nothing you can do to support
him directly. (You might consider talking about his needs to his wife, or
you might feel that would be adding too much to her burden of care.)
But when he is there, don't treat him like part of the furniture, ignoring
him unless he gets difficult, or faints. The material presented in this
chapter shows that his concerns during pregnancy are not identical to
those of his partner. The couple need to be regarded as separate
individuals, not as some kind of amalgam where you can talk to one
and assume that what you are saying addresses the needs of the other
as well.

I would hate to think that anyone reading this book would imagine
that I was advocating psychological care for men at the expense of
psychological care for women. The pregnant woman is and always
must be your first concern. But the pregnant man needs caring for also.

Pregnant women are sometimes unsupported, not necessarily
because they are unmarried – so-called single mothers often have a
primary supporter who may or may not be the father of their child.
Unsupported pregnant women may be married or cohabiting but their
partner is unavailable, either in the practical or psychological sense.
Garcia, Oakley and colleagues carried out a study with English women
at risk of having a low birthweight baby. They found that around 10%
of their sample received very little help in pregnancy, having no friends
and uninterested, unhelpful husbands (Garcia, 1990). Without the
benefit of such studies it is difficult to predict which mothers-to-be are
likely to be adequately supported and which are not. It has been found
for instance that teenage mothers who are often regarded as a deprived
group are commonly well supported, especially by their mothers
(Phoenix, 1991) but that midwives often overestimate the number of
people available to support more advantaged women (Goodenough,
1990). These findings would suggest that careful but tactful enquiry is
necessary to establish whether or not a pregnant woman has adequate
support and that the mere existence of a potential supporter, such as a
husband, should not automatically be taken to mean that the required
support will be available.

Women who receive little support from family and friends, along
with women who are experiencing a highly stressful pregnancy or
whose pregnancy is at risk, need to be provided with extensive support
from professional carers. A number of programmes have been devel-

and emotional support for pregnant women. In this chapter, I will outline three programmes designed to help women at risk of having a low birthweight baby. Chapter 6 also details a prevention programme for women at risk of postnatal depression.

The first scheme, based in south Manchester, was designed to give social, psychological and practical support during pregnancy to women who were thought to be at risk of having a low birthweight baby. It was hypothesized that this would reduce stress and thereby improve the health and well-being of the women and their babies. The source of this support was a family worker – a mature, experienced woman who helped with domestic chores and child care, when there were older children in the family, gave practical advice, emotional support and basic one-to-one health education. She was not necessarily professionally qualified but received regular training and liaised with midwives, health visitors and social workers. The use of a family worker was based on a French scheme which succeeded in reducing very low birthweight delivery by 50% through the use of family workers, financial compensation for leave of absence from heavy physical work, and increased domiciliary midwife support (see Newton, 1988).

The second scheme, based in Rochester, used midwives rather than family workers to visit subjects regularly pre- and postnatally (Olds et al., 1986). Subjects who received these visits were more likely to be aware of community services, attend antenatal classes and improve their diet than a control group of women who did not receive these extra visits. This indicates that the health education component of the scheme had been successful. The subjects' partners were more interested in the pregnancy. The subjects had better relationships with family and friends and they were more likely to have a supportive companion with them in labour. It seems therefore that the increased professional support these women received facilitated the development of a stronger personal support network. Thus this scheme may have owed its success to the increased support given by family and friends as well as to the direct input of the midwife visitors.

The results of the Rochester study showed that adolescent mothers who had received the visits had babies 395 g heavier on average than those of comparable subjects who had not received extra visits. Midwife-visited smokers had a 75% reduction in preterm labour. The scheme was successful in moderating rates of low birthweight and prematurity in certain vulnerable subjects.

A recently published study carried out in the Midlands and south of England used research midwives to visit women at risk of having a low birthweight baby (Oakley et al., 1990). The midwives visited 254 such women at home at least three times during pregnancy and provided a 24-hour-a-day contact phone number. The midwives did not provide health education or clinical care but attempted to respond in a sympathetic way to whatever questions and needs the women had. These women were compared with a control group of women who received routine antenatal care. The results showed that the supported group fared better on 13 of the 15 fetal, infant and maternal outcomes measured. As with the Rochester study, the provision of professional support was associated with increased family support. The supported women's partners helped more with shopping, cooking, housework and child care than did the partners of the women in the control group.

These schemes are relatively costly and resource-intensive, though comparison with the cost of intensive neonatal care could render them financially viable. The basic premise of the Rochester and Manchester schemes was to provide practical and emotional support along with one-to-one health education. The study carried out by Oakley and colleagues concentrated on providing social support and contact. These provisions could be incorporated into routine antenatal care, so that some of the benefits of programmes like these can be accessed by all women who require extra professional support during pregnancy.

A preliminary study of the relationship between community midwives and parturients found that most mothers wanted a close, confiding, personal, trusting relationship with their midwife and that when this was provided they experienced a great deal of psychosocial support (Wilkins, 1990). The increased provision of community midwifery and team midwifery services may allow the professionals involved more easily to incorporate social support and one-to-one health education into their antenatal care. However, hospital-based services can also provide these if they adhere to the principles involved.

Overview and summary

Pregnancy is a time of considerable happiness and well-being for many families. However, most mothers-to-be also experience feelings of worry, anxiety and occasional depression. These are probably part of the normal process of adjustment to the fundamental physical and psychological changes which occur during pregnancy and after birth, though an increased provision of sensitive psychological care and an emphasis on empowering the mother-to-be may partially alleviate these negative aspects of adaptation.

Some women experience very high levels of anxiety and distress during pregnancy and these can affect the well-being of the fetus and may precipitate premature delivery. They make pregnancy a nightmare for the woman herself and are likely to interfere with her relationship with her partner, family and friends. They are also associated with the occurrence of postnatal depression.

There are many reasons why women suffer from excessive anxiety during pregnancy. Modern screening methods can be very reassuring when the results show that the pregnancy is progressing normally and the fetus is developing optimally. However they may give rise to intense anxiety when the pregnancy is at risk or the results apparently show abnormality. Women who have previously experienced fertility problems, perinatal loss or handicap are likely to be very anxious during their subsequent pregnancy, as are women who are currently experiencing high levels of stress, for instance because of housing or financial problems.

A breakdown in the marital relationship is a potent source of maternal stress whereas a sympathetic and supportive partner can do much to alleviate anxiety and distress and thus improve well-being during pregnancy for both the mother and the fetus. The father-to-be may have some difficulty in adjusting to his partner's pregnancy and to the prospect of fatherhood, and some men exhibit an increased rate of physical and psychological disorder at this time. The relationship between a couple changes during pregnancy, with the woman typically becoming more dependent on her partner for practical and emotional support and the man providing more nurturance. The sexual relationship changes as well. These changes may create a new and uncomfortable balance within the partnership, with both partners experiencing some unfulfilled needs, particularly where there are other children to be cared for. Male concerns about pregnancy often relate to a perceived loss of closeness in the couple which could be alleviated if they understood more about how the dynamics of the family alter during pregnancy and postnatally.

Many women receive adequate practical and emotional support during pregnancy from their partners or from other primary carers such as their mother, sister, or a close friend. Neighbours, colleagues, family and friends also provide a supportive network of people who can help the mother-to-be, and also her primary carers. Some mothers are unsupported, even if they have husbands and family close at hand. These women, along with those who are experiencing a highly stressful pregnancy, need to be provided with extra support from the health professionals who care for them during pregnancy. Clear, accurate, comprehensible information; positive information and reassurance; respect, sympathy, understanding and comforting – all these components of psychological care need to be given to every pregnant woman, and if possible to the father-to-be as well. The unsupported woman, the 'at-risk' woman, the very anxious woman needs this psychological care even more, along with practical support and the best health care and education available.

The midwife or health visitor who provides this kind of psychological care needs looking after as well. S/he needs to acknowledge that there are things which can be done to help the mother and father-to-be during pregnancy and should strive to do them if possible or to get someone else to do them if her/his time and energy are over-committed. But s/he also needs to recognize that some stress and anxiety in pregnancy is inevitable and that some problems are unsolvable (at least by health care professionals). Even when nothing can be done to alleviate a problem, providing a listening ear and a comforting shoulder can be very helpful. Just listening to fears, worries and problems and not seeking to obliterate or solve them but to facilitate their ventilation is a crucial part of psychological care. But it can be stressful for the listener, so the midwife or health visitor who provides this type of psychological care needs to be supported by her or his colleagues and needs to acknowledge her or his own limits.

Further reading

Lewis C. (1986). *Becoming a Father*. Milton Keynes: Open University Press.
Newton R. (1988). Psychosocial aspects of pregnancy: the scope for intervention. *J. Reprod. Infant Psychol.*, **6**, 23–39.
Oglethorpe R. J. L. (1989). Parenting after perinatal bereavement – a review of the literature. *J. Reprod. Infant Psychol.*, **7**, 227–45.
Richards M. P. M. (1989). Social and ethical problems of foetal diagnosis and screening. *J. Reprod. Infant Psychol.*, **7**, 171–87.
Wolkind S., Zajicek E. (1981). *Pregnancy: A Psychological and Social Study*. London: Academic Press.

References

Bibring G. L. (1959). Some considerations of the psychological processes in pregnancy. *Psychoanal. Study Child*, **14**, 113–21.

Blake-Cohen M. (1966). Personal identity and sexual identity. *Psychiatry*, **29**, 1–14.

Bodegard G., Fyro K., Larsson A. (1983). Psychological reaction in 102 families with a newborn who has a falsely positive screening test for congenital hypothyroidism. *Acta Paediatr. Scand.*, suppl. **304**.

Brown G. W., Harris T. (1978). *Social Origins of Depression*. London: Tavistock.

Chamberlain R., Chamberlain G., Howlett B., Claireaux A. (1975). *British Births 1970. Volume 1. The First Week of Life*. London: Heinemann Medical Books.

Condon J. T. (1987). Psychological and physical symptoms during pregnancy: a comparison of male and female expectant parents. *J. Reprod. Infant Psychol.*, **5**, 207–13.

Cox J. L. (1989). Postnatal depression. In *Clinical Obstetrics and Gynaecology. Volume 3, part 4. Psychological Aspects of Obstetrics and Gynaecology* (Oates M., ed.). London: Baillière Tindall.

Currer C. (1986). Health concepts and illness behaviour: the care of Pathan mothers in Britain. Unpublished PhD thesis. University of Warwick.

Deutsch H. (1947). *The Psychology of Women*. New York: Grune and Stratton.

Doering S. G., Entwisle D. R., Quinlan D. (1980). Modeling the quality of women's birth experience. *J. Health Social Behav.*, **21**, 12–21.

Elliot S. A., Rugg A. J., Watson J. P., Brough D. I. (1983). Mood changes during pregnancy and after the birth of a child. *Br. J. Clin. Psychol.*, **22**, 295–308.

Elliot S. A., Sanjack M., Leverton T. J. (1988). Parents groups in pregnancy. In *Marshalling Social Support* (Gottlieb B. H., ed.). London: Sage Publications.

Fairweather D. V. I.(1968). Nausea and vomiting in pregnancy. *Am. J. Obstet. Gynecol.*, **102**, 135–75.

Farrant W. (1980). Stress after amniocentesis for high serum alpha-feto-protein concentrations. *Br. Med. J.*, **281**, 452.

Fearn J., Hibbard B. M., Laurence K. M. et al. (1982). Screening for neural tube defects and maternal anxiety. *Br. J. Obstet. Gynaecol.*, **89**, 218–21.

Gannon K. Psychological factors in recurrent miscarriage: a review and critique. *J. Reprod. Infant Psychol.*, in submission.

Garcia J. Oakley A., Rajan L., Robertson P. (1990). Support from family and friends. *J. Reprod. Infant Psychol.*, **8**, 250.

Gerda C., Dawe S. (1990). Establishing a liaison and outreach service for pregnant opiate users. Paper presented at the Fifth International Conference of the Marcé Society. University of York, England.

Goodenough T. (1990). Mothers' and midwives' perceptions of support in late pregnancy and early parenthood. *J. Reprod. Infant Psychol.*, **8**, 250–1.

Green J. M. (1990). Is the baby alright and other worries. *J. Reprod. Infant Psychol.*, **8**, 225–6.

Green L., Gossop M. (1988). The management of pregnancy in opiate addicts. *J. Reprod. Infant Psychol.*, **6**, 51–7.

Hall M., Chang P. G., MacGillivray I. (1980). Is routine antenatal care worthwhile? *Lancet*, **ii**, 78–80.

Helper M. M., Cohen R. L., Beitenman E. T., Eaton L. F. (1968). Life events and acceptance of pregnancy. *J. Psychosom. Res.*, **12**, 183–8.

Hiller C. A., Slade P. (1989). The impact of antenatal classes on knowledge, anxiety and confidence in primiparous women. *J. Reprod. Infant Psychol.*, **7**, 3–13.

Hwang P. (1988). Swedish fathers and childbearing. Paper presented at the Fourth International Conference of the Marcé Society, University of Keele, England.

Illsley R., Mitchell R. G. (1984). *Low Birth Weight: a Medical, Psychological and Social Study*. Chichester: Wiley.

Istvan J. (1986). Stress, anxiety and birth outcomes: a critical review of the evidence. *Psychol. Bull.*, **100**, 331–48.

Janis I. L. (1958). *Psychological Stress*. New York: Wiley.

Johnston M. (1982). Recognition of patients' worries by nurses and other patients. *Br. J. Clin. Psychol.*, **21**, 255–61.

Kehrer B. H., Wohin C. M. (1979). Impact of income maintenance on low birthweight: evidence from the Gary experiment. *J. Human Res.*, **14**, 434.

Kirkham M. (1989). Midwives and information giving during labour. In *Midwives, Research and Childbirth. Volume 1* (Robinson S., Thomson A. M., eds). London: Chapman and Hall.

Kumar R., Brant H. A., Robson K. M. (1981). Childbearing and maternal sexuality: a prospective study of 119 primiparae. *J. Psychosom. Res.*, **25**, 373–83.

Kumar R., Robson K. (1984). A prospective study of emotional disorders in childbearing women. *Br. J. Psychiatry*, **144**, 35–47.

Lederman R. P., Lederman E., Work B. A., McCann D. S. (1978). The relationship of maternal anxiety, plasma catecholamines and plasma cortisol to progress in labour. *Am. J. Obstet. Gynecol.*, **132**, 495–500.

Lewis C. (1986). *Becoming a Father*. Milton Keynes: Open University Press.

Ley P. (1982). Giving information to patients. In *Social Psychology and Behavioral Medicine* (Eiser J. R., ed.). Chichester: Wiley.

Lilford R. J. (1989). 'In my day we just had babies.' *J. Reprod. Infant Psychol.*, **7**, 187–91.

Luke B., Dickinson C., Petrie R. H. (1981). Intrauterine growth: correlations and maternal nutritional status and rate of gestational weight gain. *Eur. J. Obstet.*, **123**, 113–21.

MacCarthy D. (1969). The repercussions of the death of a child. *Proc. R. Soc. Med.*, **56**, 774–6.

Mandell F., Wolfe L. (1975). Sudden infant death syndrome and subsequent pregnancy. *Pediatrics*, **56**, 774–6.

Marteau T. (1990). The antenatal clinic as a tower of Babel: doctors and women discussing amniocentesis. *J. Reprod. Infant Psychol.*, **8**, 225.

Newton R. W. (1988). Psychosocial aspects of pregnancy: the scope for intervention. *J. Reprod. Infant Psychol.*, **6**, 23–39.

Newton R. W., Hunt L. P. (1984). Psychosocial stress in pregnancy and its relation to low birth weight. *Br. Med. J.*, **288**, 1191–4.

Niven C., Gijsbers K. (1984). Obstetric and non-obstetric factors relating to labour pain. *J. Reprod. Infant Psychol.*, **2**, 61–78.

Niven C., Wiszniewski C., AlRoomi L. Attachment in mothers of preterm babies. *J. Reprod. Infant Psychol.*, in press.

Norbeck J. S., Tilden V. P. (1983). Life stress, social support and emotional disequilibrium in complications of pregnancy: a prospective multivariate study. *J. Health Social Behav.*, **24**, 30–6.

Nuckolls K. B., Cassel J., Kaplan B. H. (1972). Psychosocial assets, life crises and the prognosis of pregnancy. *Am. J. Epidemiol.*, **95**, 431–41.

Oakley A. (1988). Is social support good for the health of mothers and babies? *J. Reprod. Infant Psychol.*, **6**, 3–21.

Oakley A., Macfarlane A., Chalmers I. (1982). Social class, stress and reproduction. In *Disease and the Environment* (Rees R. A., Purcell H., eds). Chichester: Wiley.

Oakley A., Rajan L., Grant A. (1990). Social support and pregnancy outcome. *Br. J. Obstet. Gynaecol.*, **97**, 155–62.

Office of Population Censuses and Surveys (1987). Infant and perinatal mortality 1985. *Monitor*, February.

Oglethorpe R. J. L. (1989). Parenting after perinatal bereavement – a review of the literature. *J. Reprod. Infant Psychol.*, **7**, 227–45.

Olds D. L., Henderson C. R., Tatlebaun R., Chamberlain R. (1986). Improving the delivery of pre-natal care and outcomes of pregnancy. A randomised trial of nurse visitation. *Pediatrics*, **77**, 16–28.

Phoenix A. (1991). *Young Mothers?* Cambridge: Polity Press.

Reading A., Cheng Li C., Kerin J. F. (1989). Psychological state and coping style across an IVF treatment cycle. *J. Reprod. Infant Psychol.*, **7**, 95–105.

Riley D. Antenatal care and outcome of pregnancy in opiate addicts. *J. Addict.*, in press.

Robinson J., Hibbard B. M., Lawrance K. M. (1984). Anxiety during a crisis: emotional effects of screening for neural tube defects. *J. Psychosom. Res.*, **28**, 163–9.

Scott-Heyes G. (1983). Marital adaptation during pregnancy and after childbirth. *J. Reprod. Infant Psychol.*, **1**, 18–29.

Scott-Heyes G. (1984). Childbearing as a mutual experience. Unpublished D. Phil thesis. New University of Ulster.

Sharp D. J. (1989). Emotional disorders during pregnancy and the puerperium – a longitudinal prospective study in primary care. *Marcé Soc. Bull.*, Spring.

Shereshevsky P. M., Yarrow L. J. (1974). *Psychological Aspects of a First Pregnancy and Early Postnatal Adaptation*. New York: Raven Press.

Stevens R. J., Becker R. C., Krumpos G. L. et al. (1988). Postnatal sequelae of parental smoking during and after pregnancy. *J. Reprod. Infant Psychol.*, **6**, 61–81.

Tsoi M. M., Hunter M. (1987). Ultrasound scanning in pregnancy: consumer reaction. *J. Reprod. Infant Psychol.*, **5**, 43–8.

Tylden E. (1990). Post-traumatic stress disorder in obstetrics. Paper presented at the Fifth International Conference of Childbearing and Mental Health, Marcé Society, University of York, England.

Van den Akker O., Sweeny V., Rosenblatt D. (1990). Psychological factors associated with pregnancy and the postnatal period in women at risk for preterm labour/delivery. *J. Reprod. Infant Psychol.*, **8**, 296–7.

Wainwright W. H. (1966). Fatherhood as a precipitant of mental illness. *Am. J. Psychiatry*, **123**, 40–4.

Watson J. P., Elliot S. A., Rugg A. H., Brough D. I. (1984). Psychiatric disorder in pregnancy and the first postnatal year. *Br. J. Psychiatry*, **144**, 453–62.

Wilkins R. (1990). Relationships between mothers and their community midwives. *J. Reprod. Infant Psychol.*, **8**, 251.

Wolkind S., Zajicek E. (1981). *Pregnancy: A Psychological and Social Study.* London: Academic Press.

Yamamoto K. J., Kinney D. K. (1976). Pregnant women's ratings of different factors influencing psychological stress during pregnancy. *Psychol. Rep.*, **39**. 203–14.

2 Birth

Stress and anxiety in childbirth

Childbirth is inherently stressful for mothers and babies. The physical stresses placed on both are tremendous. That short journey from the uterus to the outside world is the most dangerous we humans ever undertake and even the most straightforward of births involve real risk. Though the baby is the partner most at risk, s/he is fortunate because s/he doesn't know it. The mother at this time does the worrying for both herself and her child – a process she will repeat many times before the child is safely reared to maturity!

As in pregnancy, excessively high levels of stress and anxiety during childbirth can harm both the mother and the baby. For the mother, they can transform one of the most potentially rewarding experiences of her life into a terrifying and traumatic experience (which can have long-lasting effects, see Chapter 3). Very high levels of stress and anxiety are likely to result in raised maternal blood pressure with the accompanying risks of fetal asphyxia (Ascher, 1978) and catecholamine elaboration (Fox, 1979). Anxiety levels during the active phase of the first stage of labour have been found to correlate with plasma adrenaline levels which in turn were associated with lower uterine contractile activity and prolonged first-stage labour (Lederman et al., 1978). High plasma cortisol levels attributed to psychological stress have also been associated with a longer first stage of labour (Burns, 1976).

Excessive stress and anxiety during childbirth can be influenced by a large number of factors. Any factors which make the baby very precious or put the baby's or mother's well-being at risk will be likely to increase the mother's anxiety during the birth, so a history of infertility or reproductive loss, a previous stillbirth or neonatal death, or a possibility of handicap in the baby or damage to the mother are all likely to be associated with higher than normal levels of anxiety.

Previous bad birth experiences will affect the mother's and father's feelings during labour. For instance, subjects participating in a 5-year follow-up study of labour pain reported that their memories of labour pain 'all came back' the moment they went into labour again (Niven, 1988).

All mothers-to-be suffer some anticipatory anxieties about childbirth. These worries centre on the threat of harm to or loss of the baby, the threat of personal harm and death (Astbury, 1980) and on pain (see Pain in childbirth, below). Worrying about potential stressors in advance probably constitutes a normal, healthy method of preparing for a stressful event (Janis, 1958). However, anything which acts to confirm these worries during the birth will increase concurrent anxiety, and this increase in anxiety during the birth may be neither healthy nor helpful.

One way of minimizing the anxiety and stress that mothers experience during childbirth is to provide sufficient information to obviate unnecessary worries and to reassure the woman that her experience is normal rather than abnormal. (The effectiveness of antenatal classes in doing this is dealt with later in this chapter.) A study carried out in the north of England by Kirkham (1989) looked at information given by midwives in a consultant unit, a general practitioner unit and, in a minority of cases, during home confinements. It found that for many parturients, information was what they wanted most from their midwives. Though it was sometimes conceded that there were women who didn't want to know, none of the 113 subjects placed themselves in that category. Instead, like recipients of other forms of health care (Ley, 1982), they wanted to know everything – the bad things as well as the good things. They wanted to know if their labour was not progressing normally so they could prepare themselves for what might happen – forceps, section, etc. – and so they weren't left to guess 'from looking at their faces' that something was wrong, and to fear the worst.

The author noted that in the consultant unit she saw 'information being given by midwives to labouring women, results of examinations carefully explained and women told what to expect for the rest of their labour' but also 'little consistency in the giving of information and much (good news as well as bad) that was not given' (Kirkham, 1989, p. 112). 'Omitting to give information was not seen as bad care, comparable to the omission of more visible forms of care. . . . Indeed it seemed to be considered wiser to omit information as a precaution against saying the wrong thing.' (p. 125). Kirkham notes the inhibitory effects of the presence of senior staff who are presumed to have the responsibility for conveying information to the parturient. If, as often occurs, they do not provide adequate or understandable information, the mother can be left in total ignorance of what is happening to her and her baby.

While my own experience as a researcher working in a labour ward certainly confirmed that labouring women desire as much information as possible, it did not generally conform to such a negative view of midwives as information givers. However, my research was not directed towards monitoring midwife–parturient communication, nor was I (unlike Kirkham) a senior midwifery sister, so the midwives I observed may have been less inhibited by my presence. The unit where I carried out my research into labour pain was a consultant unit where the midwives had a (perhaps unusual) degree of autonomy. It may have more closely resembled the general practitioner units which Kirkham also studied where she found that 'women were given more information with which to orient themselves to their labour. . . . They were also more likely to ask questions and have them answered' (p. 133). She also found that in the small number of home confinements studied, the midwives treated the mothers more like colleagues and provided information and support which enabled them to make informed decisions about clinical matters such as when to have their membranes ruptured. In fact, Kirkham comments that these women were able to make decisions in their own homes which were impossible for most midwives to make in consultant units – a fine example of empowering the parturient. These observations provide good arguments for community-based care and midwife autonomy. They should also help all midwives to analyse and improve their information-giving behaviour.

Kirkham's study also showed that women of a higher social class were given more information by midwives than women of a lower social class, who in fact were often the ones who knew and understood less about childbirth and its accompanying medical and technical procedures. They therefore required more information, not less. Studies of working-class parturients have shown that their attitudes to labour are somewhat different from those prompted as typical – which are sometimes just typical of the middle class. For instance, a study of working-class women in Glasgow found that the great majority of the 80 subjects viewed childbirth as merely 'a hurdle to be surmounted on the way to motherhood' rather than a potentially positive experience (McIntosh, 1989, p. 193). They were concerned about labour pain, particularly about the possibility that they might break down or lose their composure during labour because of its effects, and they therefore appreciated any procedures which would allow labour to be over as quickly and painlessly as possible. This finding was supported by a study by Woolet et al. (1983) carried out among working-class women in London and by Woolet and Dosanjh-Matwala (1990) amongst women of Asian background living in London.

The information and reassurance that these women would require might therefore be different from that required by a middle-class woman who was anxious to have as natural a childbirth as possible. However, categorizing people by social class is always dangerous as it leads to a tendency to ignore each person's individuality. An important minority of McIntosh's subjects were unhappy about interventions, particularly about epidural anaesthesia (though it was very popular with the majority of subjects), induction of labour by artificial rupture of the membranes (ARM) and the use of forceps. They also reported that they were dissatisfied with a lack of information about what was happening to them and being done to them during labour and delivery. 'They should tell you a lot more aboot what's goin' on. You're kept in the dark all the time and ye just worry and imagine things. Yer imagination runs away wi' you and ye think o' the worst' (subject of McIntosh, 1989, p. 205).

These reports clearly echo Kirkham's findings, as do the results of a number of studies which consistently show that the consumers of maternity care desire more information (e.g. Garcia, 1982; Williams et al. 1989). The kind of information and reassurance which a parturient requires can only be accurately gauged by staff who understand her view of childbirth, her wishes and her worries. These can only be ascertained by asking her, and listening to her answers.

Attempts at reassurance were also described in Kirkham's study. Sometimes these consisted of a denial of the woman's apprehensions, sometimes of a ritual process which seemed to do more to reassure the midwife than the parturient, e.g. 'Student midwife after insertion of epidural: "That's not bad is it. It's never as bad as you think it is" . . . Mrs. 86 does not answer' (p. 130). She also gives examples of staff speaking for parturients who are perfectly capable of speaking for themselves.

Sister A: Do you want a little drink?
Sister B: I think she should. She's very dry.
Sister A gets water. Mrs B6 drinks.
Sister B: That's better (Kirkham, 1989, p. 131).

These excerpts, the latter of which is a perfect example of depowering the parturient, make me laugh guiltily as I'm sure they make any honest nurse or midwife laugh as s/he recognizes her/himself. The point of describing them here is to allow us all to recognize the bad communication habits we can get into, so that the next time we are inclined to use them, we'll stop and think, and try to communicate more effectively.

Pain in childbirth

The anticipation of labour pain causes intense anxiety for many women (Astbury, 1980; McIntosh, 1989; Woolet and Dosanjh-Matwala, 1990). Pain in labour, as with all types of pain, can act as a major stressor (Melzack and Wall, 1988) and a number of studies have found a relationship between high levels of pain in childbirth and assessments of stress or anxiety (e.g. Niven and Gijsbers, 1984; Reading and Cox, 1985). Intense pain is associated with reflex increases in blood pressure, oxygen consumption and catecholamine release, all of which can adversely affect uterine blood flow (Bonica, 1984) so high levels of labour pain are not only undesirable in themselves but may also adversely affect the baby. They will usually influence analgesic requirements which may also affect the condition of the baby at birth (Brazelton, 1961).

Of course levels of pain may be exacerbated by anxiety as well as being the cause of it. Common experience teaches us that if we are anxious, tense or frightened when we are hurt, we are liable to feel more pain than if we are relaxed, calm and unworried. Research into the effects of anxiety on postoperative pain has often, though not invariably, found a positive association between these two variables (see, for instance, Ray and Fitzgibbon, 1981). These studies assessed anxiety before surgery and related it to pain levels after surgery so there was some basis for suggesting that it was the high anxiety which caused the high pain, not the other way round. In childbirth we are concerned with anxiety and pain which occur at the same time so it is more difficult to tease out the direction of the effects. The midwife's concern should be to ensure that each does not exacerbate the other, to the detriment of mother and baby.

Normal labour typically involves pain, even for confident unworried parturients. It emanates from dilation of the cervix and contraction of the uterus in the first stage of labour, and from contraction of the uterus, distension and traumatization of the vagina and perineum and traction and pressure on pelvic nerves, organs and fascia during the second stage (see Bonica, 1984). The intensity of labour pain is on average severe, as can be seen from Figure 2.1 where it is compared with pain from a number of other clinical and traumatic conditions.

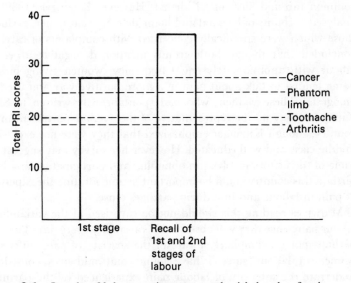

Figure 2.1 Levels of labour pain compared with levels of pain associated with other clinical and traumatic conditions (PRI = Pain Rating Index) (Niven and Gijsbers, 1984)

However, the intensity of labour pain varies widely. For instance, Nettlebladt and colleagues (1976) working in Scandinavia found that 28% of their labouring subjects suffered moderate pain, 37% severe pain and 35% intolerable pain. Melzack and colleagues, who have carried out a series of studies on labour pain in Canada, report that approximately 10% of primiparous subjects have mild or very mild pain, 30% moderate pain, 38% severe pain and 24% very severe pain (see Melzack, 1984). In a study which I carried out in Stirling in Scotland, I found that approximately 8% of subjects had very little pain in labour, whereas 16% rated it as being 'as bad as I could possibly imagine' (Niven and Gijsbers, 1984; Niven, 1986).

All these studies were carried out in hospital settings and it may be that labour pain is less intense when women give birth in familiar surroundings and are accompanied by staff with whom they have established a close relationship. Delivery at home is however nowadays so rare in this country that it is impossible directly to compare those giving birth at home, who differ from the majority of parturients in a number of important ways, with those giving birth in hospital. Comparison of pain experience would need to be carried out in a country like the Netherlands where home delivery is still relatively common (around 36% of all births). However Kitzinger (1989) has analysed accounts of hospital and home delivery sent to her, excluding those which were specifically concerned with complaints of care. She concluded that though both groups mentioned negative aspects of labour with approximately equal frequency, women giving birth at home tended to talk about pain in a more positive way and used less analgesia. These women, who had spontaneously written to Sheila Kitzinger, may not be representative of the average parturient in this country, though Kitzinger emphasized that they were not exclusively middle class and well educated. However her survey may suggest that some of the factors involved in obtaining and participating in a home birth in this country could be important in ameliorating the experience of pain in labour and in reducing analgesic use.

Midwives reading this should not be surprised at the variability in labour pain since they will observe this variability every day. They may perhaps not be completely aware of the severity of pain suffered by women in labour since I have found that midwives consistently underrate the intensity of labour pain experienced by the parturient they are attendant upon, though they agree that labour is usually 'severely painful' (Niven and Gijsbers, 1984; Niven, 1991). This, like the tendency towards self-reassurance described above (see Stress and anxiety in childbirth), may be an unconscious self-protecting mechanism which prevents the midwife from acknowledging just how much pain the mother in her care is suffering. Such consistent underrating of labour pain may however make the midwife less sympathetic then s/he should be towards the parturient in her/his care, and thus may interfere with the relationship between them.

Factors which will affect the amount of noxious (potentially pain-producing) stimulation occurring in labour, such as the dimensions of the birth canal relative to the size and position of the baby, or the duration of labour, will affect the amount of pain a parturient experiences. Bonica and Akamatsu have shown that the rate of dilation of the cervix is closely related to the degree of pain women experience (see Bonica, 1984) so that a short first stage of labour with a rapidly dilating cervix should theoretically involve more pain per contraction than a longer first stage. Midwives will often have observed this effect after an ARM is performed or when a Syntocinon infusion is suddenly increased and the intensity of pain the mother experiences rapidly intensifies.

However, the duration of labour is not always negatively correlated with the intensity of pain overall. For instance, Reading and Cox (1985) in their London-based study found no relationship between duration and pain. Wuitchik et al. (1989), working in Canada, found that women who reported intense pain during the latent phase of labour (defined as between the onset of labour and cervical dilation of 3 cm) had significantly longer latent and active phases, i.e. there was a positive correlation between duration and pain intensity. They attributed this relationship to possible increases in catecholamine and cortisol levels which are activated by the subjects' distress in latent labour and which subsequently attenuate uterine activity. In my own study I found a complex relationship between duration, parity and pain (Niven, 1986). The duration of the first stage of labour was positively correlated with levels of labour pain recorded after labour was over, that is, when subjects looked back over their entire labour. This effect was only statistically significant in multiparous subjects and may have reflected their distress at the unexpectedly prolonged repetition of painful contractions, since multiparous women generally expect to have shorter labours than primiparous ones and longer labours are generally experienced as more distressing (Morgan et al., 1982). However, pain assessments taken during the active phase of labour immediately following a contraction, correlated negatively, though non-significantly, with pain, giving some support to Bonica's theory that short labours involve greater dilation per contraction and therefore more pain per contraction. A shorter second stage was associated with higher levels of pain in both primiparous and multiparous subjects, though again the effect was stronger in multiparous women, probably reflecting the greater trauma associated with a rapid delivery.

Thus the relationship between duration of labour and levels of pain is complex and probably depends on psychological factors as well as on physiological or obstetric ones. There is more consensus about the amount of distress associated with duration, the majority of studies showing that a longer labour is perceived as more stressful (Wolkind and Zajicek, 1981; Morgan et al., 1982; Niven and Gijsbers, 1984). There may therefore be advantages in reducing the duration of labour where possible. Wuitchik's findings suggest that this might be achieved by ameliorating excessive pain and anxiety in latent labour and Klaus and colleagues (1986) have shown that the provision of continuous emotional support from a *doula* is associated with significantly shorter labour (see Social support in childbirth, this chapter). However most policies which aim to shorten labour usually involve the use of induction techniques (e.g. O'Driscoll et al., 1973) which may have less positive psychological effects.

ARM is described by many parturients as 'nasty' and as a procedure which they would not wish to be repeated (Cartwright, 1979). It was found to be deeply unpopular with many of McIntosh's Glaswegian working-class subjects who, you will remember, generally welcomed obstetric interventions. They described it as a sort of violation. I found it to be significantly associated with higher levels of pain recorded during the first stage of labour (after ARM had been performed) for both primiparous and multiparous subjects. The relationship between ARM and levels of labour pain may also be due to physiological effects in that it increases the strength of each contraction and thus the rapidity of cervical dilation which in turn may increase pain (Bonica, 1984; see above). However it was evident in my study that the relationship between ARM and levels of labour pain was not due to the shorter duration of ARM labours but seemed to have more to do with the sudden onset of intense contractions – to 'things starting with a bang' . . . which takes the parturient by surprise and prevents her coping with labour pain successfully. Women who experience a slow build-up of contraction strength are better placed to utilize relaxation, distraction or breathing exercises in coping with the accompanying pain. Women whose contraction pattern suddenly changes can be swamped by an unexpectedly painful contraction following ARM and subsequently find difficulty in recovering the concentration, motivation and confidence to cope with the next one (see Niven and Gijsbers, 1984).

A huge number of factors associated with labour pain have been reported. Apart from the effects of duration and ARM discussed above, studies have confirmed that obstetric factors such as parity are associated with pain, with multiparous women having less pain than primiparous women (Melzack, 1984; Niven and Gijsbers, 1984); that the weight of the baby is positively correlated with pain (Melzack, 1984; Niven and Gijsbers, 1984); and that the weight of the mother relative to her height is also positively correlated with pain levels during childbirth (Melzack, 1984). Wuitchik et al. (1989) found that high pain levels during latent labour were associated with an increased incidence of Caesarian section – women who reported severe pain, rated as 'horrible or excruciating' on the Present Pain Index of the McGill Pain Questionnaire (see Melzack and Wall, 1988) between the onset of labour and 3 cm cervical dilation had a 26% incidence of Caesarian section whereas no women who rated their pain as merely 'discomforting' at that time went on to have a section. The authors suggest that this relationship is due to the effect of intense pain and distress early in labour on catecholamine levels which subsequently disrupt efficient uterine activity (see also previous section on Stress and anxiety in childbirth). In the Stirling study, an association was found between high levels of pain in the first stage of labour and significantly lower Apgar scores at 1 min (Niven, 1986). This relationship may have also been due to the effects of distress on maternal catecholamine levels, which in turn affected the baby's condition at birth. Fortunately these effects did not persist.

Melzack and colleagues, working in Canada, found significant associations between young maternal age, low social class and high levels of pain (see Melzack, 1984). In my Scottish Stirling-based study I found no significant correlations between these factors. This may have been due to differences in the populations studied. Though both studies used broadly similar subjects who were representative of the reproductive population as a whole, Melzack's subjects were drawn from a big city (Montreal) whereas mine were from a more mixed rural and urban community where the extremes of poverty and privilege are less apparent. There was no strong association between low social class and the incidence of obstetric complications in my study, a relationship which is often found in large urban studies (see Oakley et al., 1982) and which may account for some of the increase in anxiety and pain which these urban subjects may suffer.

Some of the characteristics of labour pain itself may make it more distressing or difficult to cope with. Melzack and Schaffelberg (1987) interviewed a representative sample of women giving birth in a large general hospital in Canada and found that 33% of the sample had continuous severe low back pain as well as contraction pain localized both to the abdomen and to the back. This continuous pain was described as 'unrelenting' and 'exhausting'. It seemed to be particularly hard to endure since it was unexpected, and 'rode on top' of contraction pain so that the women had to cope with two co-occurring pains rather than just one.

Ron Melzack together with Patrick Wall developed the vastly influential 'gate theory' of pain. In their conceptualization of the nature of pain, they suggest that pain has sensory, affective and evaluative components. The affective component of pain represents the horrible, distressing and undesirable qualities of pain rather than its spatial and temporal sensory qualities. For example, subjects responding to the McGill Pain Questionnaire (MPQ), developed by Melzack and Torgerson, can select descriptors relating specifically to the affective dimension of pain such as 'terrifying, torturing, cruel or wretched'. (For material related to the gate theory of pain and to pain components and assessment, see Melzack and Wall, 1988.) Women in labour usually score highly on all components of the MPQ except for the affective section (Melzack, 1984; Niven, 1986). These comparatively low affective scores presumably reflect the essentially joyful nature of childbirth, despite the pain and anxiety suffered (compared with for instance cancer pain which is of similar intensity but has a higher affective component). However high affective scores are reported by some parturients and have been found to be associated with some of the factors discussed in this chapter, for example persistent negative attitudes to pregnancy and the unsuccessful use of pethidine early in labour (Niven, 1986). The relationship found in my study between high levels of pain in the first stage of labour and low Apgar scores in the baby was most marked on the affective dimension of pain, so it is likely that these women were particularly distressed during the first stage of labour, which resulted in raised catecholamine levels which may have subsequently affected the condition of their baby at birth. Many of the psychological variables I studied related most strongly to levels of affective pain, e.g. antenatal training, positive perceptions of staff control, welcomed presence of the father at the birth, so this dimension of pain experience seems particularly relevant to the psychological domain.

A variety of psychological factors including expectations of birth, antenatal education, the use of coping strategies and the provision of social support are discussed in the following sections of this chapter. These have been shown to be related to pain in labour as well as to anxiety and stress (Astbury, 1980; Melzack, 1984; Niven and Gijsbers, 1984; Niven, 1986). The desirability of pregnancy has generally been found to correlate negatively with labour pain (e.g. Eysenck, 1961; Niven, 1986). However Astbury (1980) who assessed desirability in the third trimester when negative attitudes towards the baby are generally more stable (see The mother's adjustment to pregnancy, Chapter 1) found no relationship between unplanned pregnancy or negative attitudes towards the baby and subsequent levels of pain in childbirth.

Studies which have examined the relationship between personality factors and the experience of pain in childbirth have reported inconsistent findings. Eysenck (1961) in an English study found that subjects who scored highly on a measure of extroversion reported higher levels of labour pain than those scoring more highly on a measure of introversion. Reading and Cox (1985), also utilizing English subjects, found that extroverts had significantly higher levels of pain on one measure of pain but significantly lower levels on another. An anxious personality is one which predisposes the subject to respond to stressful events with high levels of anxiety (a personality type known in psychological jargon as trait anxiety) or with emotional over-responsiveness, high levels of arousal and autonomic reactivity (in the jargon, neuroticism). Reading and Cox (1985) found that neurotic subjects had higher levels of labour pain whereas Scott-Palmer and Skevington (1981) found it was related to lower levels of pain. Astbury (1980) found that trait anxiety was not related to higher levels of pain. The reasons for these inconsistencies are partly methodological. The timing of the assessments of personality varied between studies, and the meaning that they had for the subjects may have markedly affected the results obtained. The inconsistent findings may also be due to the fact that women in childbirth do not necessarily demonstrate their normal personality. The cowardly can be unexpectedly brave, the strong surprisingly weak, the outgoing unusually quiet and the polite devastatingly rude. The demands of giving birth are exceptional and they bring out exceptional characteristics in those who go through it. The midwife is better off assessing each woman's individuality as it unfolds before her/him during labour and delivery, than attempting to prejudge her personality.

In our culture it is normal for parturients to be offered pharmacological analgesics to relieve the pain of labour. While some women may be able to endure labour pain without the help of pethidine, Entonox or epidural anaesthesia, or may experience so little pain that analgesics are not needed, the levels of pain suffered by most parturients (see above) necessitate some amelioration. The use of pethidine has been considerably curtailed since the effects it can have on the baby at birth have become apparent (see Bonica, 1984). Therefore in units where it is used, the amount that can be given is strictly limited. For instance, in my Stirling study, around 20% of the subjects received no pethidine at all in labour. Sixty per cent received pethidine during the active phase of labour and 20% during early labour, most of whom received repeat doses later. The subjects who received no pethidine had the lowest levels of pain, so use versus non-use was apparently determined by need, with women who could avoid its use doing so (Niven and Gijsbers, 1984; Niven, 1986). A similar finding is reported by Brewin and Bradley (1982) in a study based in an English maternity unit. The Stirling subjects who had high levels of pain early in labour received the largest amount of pethidine in total, with doses given early on and repeated, usually only once, during active labour. Unfortunately, these subjects, who were characteristically young, inexperienced and anxious, continued to have intense pain despite the potent effects of the drug and recorded the highest levels of pain throughout labour and delivery. The necessary restrictions on the use of pethidine may have made it relatively ineffective in controlling their intense pain and anxiety; only 54% of these subjects reported that it gave them any relief from pain. A proportion (unfortunately not quantified) of McIntosh's subjects were dissatisfied with the effects of pethidine; some reported that it hadn't worked and some that it had worked too well, leaving them dopey – 'See that pethidine, it knocked me oot' (McIntosh, 1989, p. 201) – a complaint echoed by some of my subjects as well. Slade et al. (1990) found that women who received pethidine were less satisfied with their birth experience. However 68% of my subjects who received pethidine only in active labour said that it was effective in reducing their pain.

Entonox, along with pethidine, was widely used in the Stirling unit at the time of my study. Unlike pethidine, its administration is totally under the control of the parturient and her attendant midwife. Some midwives encouraged the women they were attending to use Entonox early on in the active phase of labour if they had significant pain at that time. This approach seemed to be particularly effective as these subjects assessed their labour overall as being less painful than that of subjects who had received Entonox later in the first stage or in early second-stage labour. Furthermore, 91% of 'early Entonox' subjects reported that its use had been beneficial whereas only 73% of 'later Entonox' subjects reported as positively. However, it is possible that the effect seen in this instance is a midwife effect rather than an Entonox effect, since this pattern of analgesic administration was peculiar to one or two midwives whose standards of psychological care were (in my opinion) particularly high.

Even though the traditional obstetric analgesic regimen of pethidine and Entonox may be regarded as satisfactory by a majority of parturients, the hope of painless childbirth is not usually fulfilled. Epidural anaesthesia can fulfil this hope although studies carried out in London have shown that despite adequate pain relief, levels of maternal satisfaction with epidural anaesthesia is low when their use is associated with the need for assisted delivery (Morgan et al., 1982). Slade et al. (1990), in the preliminary analysis of a recent English study, also found that the use of epidural anaesthesia was associated with low satisfaction with childbirth. In a series of studies carried out in Canada, Melzack and colleagues demonstrated that epidural anaesthesia is not always effective (see Melzack, 1984). In one study it was found to be ineffective in 10% of cases and, in another, in 33% of cases. The unusually high percentage of failures in the second study was attributed to the inexperience of the anaesthetists, several of whom were just beginning their residency. Women who experience epidural failure are likely to be deeply distressed as well as in severe pain since they have been led to expect complete relief from labour pain. However, in skilled experienced hands, where epidural failure is minimized and the association with assisted deliveries is reduced, epidural anaesthesia offers welcome relief from labour pain for those who require it. It may be particularly useful for women who for either physiological or psychological reasons are experiencing very high levels of labour pain.

All parturients should be offered the opportunity to use pharmacological analgesia in childbirth, whether they ask for it or not (some don't like 'to bother you') and whether they look like they need it or not. Assessing pain is notoriously difficult and assessing labour pain doubly so, since childbirth involves a lot of grunting, grimacing and vocalizing, just as pain does – it is therefore easy to confuse the two. A study in France noted a correspondence between parturients' behaviour during and between contraction and their reports of the intensity of their pain (Bonnel and Boureau, 1985) but I found that midwives silently observing the behaviour of British subjects in labour could not accurately rate the amount of pain they were suffering; incidentally, neither could I (Niven, 1987)! So you should never take the risk that the parturient is suffering in silence unbeknownst to you.

On the other hand, many women will want to try to cope with labour pain through the use of psychoprophylactic techniques (psychological analgesia) rather than pharmacological analgesia. They may feel pressured into accepting analgesics against their wishes if asked every 5 min 'Do you want something for your pain now' (McIntosh, 1989), so a fine line has to be drawn between offering analgesia and forcing it on an unwilling recipient. The worst culprits I have ever observed in this regard are consultants caring for doctors' wives. I've seen them even draw up the pethidine that had been refused so that not a minute would be wasted in administering it 'if you change your mind'. It's done out of concern for the woman's possible distress but may also be a symptom of that not uncommon phenomenon in maternity care – obstetrician's distress.

Any factor which relates to very high levels of pain in childbirth should signal the need for especially effective pharmacological analgesia. Although it is obviously desirable to reduce all components of pain in childbirth, it might be considered more important to reduce those which are most distressing – the affective components (see above) – so factors which have been associated with high levels of affective pain should be particularly salient to the staff planning the provision of adequate analgesia in labour. Currently it seems that epidural anaesthesia offers the best chance of reducing intense labour pain to minimal levels. However, some parturients do not require this level of anaesthesia and some do not want it, so the provision of pethidine, Entonox or alternative means of pain control such as acupuncture (Skelton, 1984) or transcutaneous electrical nerve stimulation (Melzack and Schaffelberg, 1987) should be considered. Many parturients prefer to use their own forms of psychological analgesia or pain-coping strategies instead of, or as well as, any of the methods so far described. These will be discussed in the following sections.

Preparation for childbirth

Childbirth has always been a complex, mysterious event which involves pain and stress and therefore gives rise to anxiety. In the past when births were more plentiful and normally took place at home, a certain amount of information about its mysteries would be gleaned from everyday experience and from the 'old wives' who attended the birth. Nowadays in our society birth is an infrequent event and the vast majority of births take place in hospital, so information about childbirth has to be transmitted formally. Although books and pamphlets provide some information, probably the main route for the transmission of information which aims to prepare women for childbirth is through antenatal education.

Various forms of antenatal preparation exist in this country as elsewhere but all aim to address the twin concerns of anxiety and pain in childbirth. Preparation for parenthood – for infant care and child-rearing – is usually also provided but is not dealt with in this chapter; Chapter 6 discusses some aspects of preparation for parenthood. In the UK, antenatal classes provided by the NHS have primarily evolved from Grantly Dick-Read's pioneering work in educating women about the mechanisms of pregnancy and childbirth, and preparing them to use relaxation and breathing techniques during labour and delivery (Dick-Read, 1942). The relief of fear and anxiety during childbirth was central to his thinking since he believed that pain in labour was primarily caused by tension – a largely unwarranted belief (Bonica, 1984). 'Childbirth without fear' was his aim; an aim which if fulfilled can certainly be beneficial to the parturient in relieving the stress and anxiety of labour as well as modulating the pain. The Lamaze method of prepared childbirth training (PCT), which is dominant in North America, aims to produce 'childbirth without pain'. It has evolved from the Russian and French schools of psychoprophylactic training and utilizes more intensive education in methods of pain control. National Childbirth Trust classes run in this country utilize many of the Lamaze techniques. Beck et al. (1979), who have reviewed the historical development of preparation for labour, however conclude that there are few substantial differences between the two approaches, both of which provide 'accurate information regarding the processes of pregnancy, labor and delivery; training in relaxation and in the use of breathing techniques' (Beck et al., 1979, p. 252).

The provision of accurate information should relieve some of the anxieties women experience during childbirth as it should normalize their experience, i.e. allow them to realize that what they are experiencing is normal and healthy and does not signal that something is wrong. It should also help them to cope with the physical and psychological demands of childbirth by providing them with information which will allow them to prepare themselves for the realities of the situation. Research studies which have looked at the effects of information in preparing subjects for other painful and stressful events such as surgery have generally, though not invariably, shown that prepared subjects experience less pain and distress and recover more quickly. (These studies have been reviewed by Tan (1982) and the reader is directed to this paper for details of methodology and results.) For instance, Johnson et al. (1978) provided accurate information to patients about to undergo cholecystectomy and found that these subjects had a reduced hospital stay and improved recovery on return home. Subjects who were additionally provided with coping information had reduced use of postoperative medication and increased ambulation. Similarly the prepared parturient should have fewer anxieties and be better able to cope with childbirth. She should be less stressed and should experience less pain than a parturient who is unprepared. She should also be more knowledgeable.

Education in the use of relaxation techniques should reduce pain in childbirth since research has shown that relaxation modulates pain of other kinds. For instance, a study that I carried out along with Isobel Garden showed that teaching women to use relaxation techniques was more effective than teaching them to use a variety of cognitive coping strategies (distraction, imagery etc.) in reducing their dysmenorrhoea, a pain which though generally not as severe as labour pain has some affinity with it (Niven and Garden, 1986). Relaxation techniques have also been shown to be effective in reducing stress (see Tan, 1982). The use of Lamaze breathing techniques was assessed by Worthington (1982) using an experimentally induced pain stimulus rather than a 'real-life' pain. They found that it was more effective in reducing this pain than any of the other components of the Lamaze method. The use of these techniques in childbirth is therefore likely to be similarly effective.

Participation in antenatal classes should theoretically result in an increase in knowledge about childbirth, and a reduction in pain and distress in labour. However, research findings have yet to establish conclusively that participation has such effects. Many of the studies published in this area concern American data (see Beck et al., 1979 and

Tan, 1982 for reviews) and many (not just the American ones) have methodological problems which prevent us drawing firm conclusions about the success of PCT classes. For instance, most studies find that women who choose to attend PCT classes are older and of higher social class and education level. These factors by themselves are associated with improved obstetric outcome, so the benefits which have been found to be associated with PCT in some studies such as lower induction rates or fewer assisted deliveries could be due to their effects rather than to the consequences of the preparation. In the UK, where classes are free and widely available, it might be hoped that antenatal classes would be attended by a broader cross-section of the reproductive population. This is not so. A study of antenatal class attendance in 1115 London parturients (Jones and Dougherty, 1984) found that frequent attenders were more likely to be primiparous, Caucasian (but not Irish), older, married or cohabiting, professional or skilled, non-smoking women. In my Stirling study, class attendance was strongly related to older age and higher social class (Niven, 1986). A few studies have attempted to allocate class attendance on a random basis so that attenders and non-attenders would be matched for class, age, parity etc. However drop-out rates varied between classes so at the end of the study, the inequalities were still evident. Despite these difficulties some consistency of outcome is found, in that class attenders report increased maternal satisfaction with childbirth and decreased use of analgesics. Jones and Dougherty (1984) found that antenatal class attenders were less likely to have elective sections or forceps delivery, even when the effects of age, class, etc. were controlled statistically.

A study carried out in the north of England (Hiller and Slade, 1989) examined primiparous women's knowledge about pregnancy, labour and the care of a baby and their confidence in their ability to cope with childbirth and the care of their baby. Concurrent anxiety was also measured. These factors were rated before attendance at NHS hospital-based and community-based antenatal classes, and after. A significant increase in knowledge was found after classes along with considerable increase in confidence in coping with childbirth and the care of the baby. The amount of knowledge the women had was not initially correlated with their confidence. But after participating in the antenatal classes, these two factors correlated significantly. The women who had the most knowledge were most confident about their ability to cope with labour. Although the subjects' general anxiety fell somewhat after classes, their anxiety about pregnancy as such was not reduced and the reduction in anxiety was not related to their increased knowledge. Another British study which assessed anxiety in women in the 39th week of their pregnancy found no difference in anxiety about the birth between subjects who were attending antenatal classes and those who were not (Brewin and Bradley, 1982); however class attenders felt that they would be more able to 'help reduce discomfort during labour' than non-attenders.

It seems therefore that antenatal preparation is not effective in reducing anticipatory anxiety about childbirth, perhaps as Astbury (1980) suggests because fears and worries about childbirth are very deep-seated and resistant to change by rational conscious means. They may in fact be performing a useful function in generating 'worry-work' (Janis, 1958) which will help the mother-to-be prepare herself for the inevitable stress of childbirth. The results of Hiller and Slade's (1989) study suggest that NHS antenatal classes succeed in educating pregnant women about childbirth and, along with those of Brewin and Bradley, that they increase women's confidence in their ability to cope with it. However, they do not tell us whether or not this knowledge and confidence affect the women's experience once they are actually in labour.

A study carried out in Australia (Astbury, 1980) found that primiparous subjects who had attended antenatal classes had, like Hiller and Slade's subjects, more knowledge of childbirth and were more likely to have formed expectations of childbirth than had untrained women. However, their expectations did not turn out to be more accurate when compared with their actual experience of childbirth: 68 out of 90 women found that labour was not what they expected it to be, 37 of whom had attended classes and 31 of whom had not. McIntosh (1989) working in Glasgow similarly found no relationship between the accuracy of expectations and antenatal class attendance. The class attenders in Astbury's study also reported having been as fearful as the non-attenders during the birth and having had as much pain. Both class attenders and non-attenders who had inaccurate expectations of birth had significantly more severe pain in childbirth than those whose expectations were accurate. This relationship was not simply due to those women whose labours had been worse than expected but to the gap between expectation and experience (Astbury, 1980). I found a similar association between inaccurate expectations of birth and higher levels of pain, and a similar lack of association between antenatal class attendance and the stressfulness of birth (Niven, 1986).

I did find that women who had attended classes had more positive expectations of the birth, which were generally but not invariably associated with lower levels of pain (Niven and Gijsbers, 1984; Niven, 1986). Preliminary analysis of an English study which compared expectations and experience of childbirth (Slade et al., 1990) suggests that though subjects' expectations of childbirth were generally over-optimistic, those who had attended antenatal classes had more realistic expectations, especially with regard to the intensity of pain. This study, being the most recent of those described here, may be reflecting a changing emphasis in antenatal education towards increased realism. Slade and colleagues also found a relationship between positive expectations and positive experiences, as did Byrne-Lynch (1990) who looked at expectations of self-efficacy – the belief that you will be able to cope effectively with the various aspects of childbirth. Thus the generation of positive but realistic expectations which encourage the woman to feel that she will be able to cope with the realities of childbirth seems to offer the best kind of preparation for childbirth.

Most research suggests that though antenatal education provides information that is accurate in medical and biological terms, it is not accurate in experiential terms, at least as far as the majority of women are concerned. A number of studies have shown that information which graphically describes the typical sensations perceived by a subject undergoing a distressing procedure such as endoscopy (sensory infor-mation), along with the provision of instructions on how to cope with the procedure, is more effective in reducing distress than the provision of general information on what's to be done, why it's to be done and how it's to be done (see Johnson et al., 1978). This is because sensory information allows the subject to normalize his or her experience.

The results of Astbury's, McIntosh's and Niven's studies suggest that antenatal education does (or did) not provide this kind of information. For instance, a number of subjects in my study thought they were dying because their labour pain was so unexpectedly severe. Instead antenatal preparation may seek to reduce the anticipatory anxiety of mothers-to-be and thus minimize their pain and distress in labour by being euphemistic, optimistic and reassuring in their descrip-tions of childbirth. Antenatal educators may also avoid the discussion of complications of birth such as assisted delivery on the grounds that this will increase the anxiety of a substantial number of mothers who will not encounter these difficulties. This reassuring approach does not seem to be effective, as there is no strong evidence that attendance at antenatal classes reduces fear and anxiety during labour (Astbury, 1980; Niven and Gijsbers, 1984).

I have every sympathy with antenatal educators who seek to reassure pregnant women rather than inform them graphically about what is to come. There are studies which show that the mention of the word 'pain' makes it more likely that subjects will report a mild electric shock to be painful (see Tan, 1982), so it could seem sensible to avoid describing childbirth as painful. However these studies dealt with minimal levels of noxious stimulation which *could* be perceived as painless. This is not usually the case in childbirth where levels of noxious stimulation are very high and levels of labour pain rank 'among the most intense pains recorded' (Melzack, 1984, pp. 323–4).

The adverse effects of raising anxiety levels in pregnant and labouring women must also be taken into account. However, the material presented in Chapters 1 and 2 makes it clear that all women worry about childbirth, so a frank antenatal trainer is not going to create anxieties which do not exist already. S/he may however temporarily suppress them and create a reassuring vision of childbirth which is unlikely to be fulfilled. Lumley and Astbury (1980) report that in certain circumstances untrained women have more realistic expectations of childbirth than trained ones. McIntosh found that his working-class subjects who got most of their information from family and friends rather than from books and classes had very negative expectations but seemed to benefit from these come the birth, as the majority found labour to be better than expected and were pleasantly surprised. So even pessimistic expectations of childbirth may be beneficial in the long run. Astbury (1980) has suggested that pregnant women should be encouraged to ventilate their fears and anxieties about childbirth during their antenatal classes, a process which is likely temporarily to increase their anxiety as the fears of others are added to their own anxieties. However, this would allow the antenatal trainer to address the specific anxieties of her/his students and allow the students to give one another mutual support of the 'we're all in this together' variety.

It must be acknowledged that it is difficult and distressing for antenatal trainers to be completely frank about the experience of childbirth and its accompanying risks, pain and indignity. I find it disturbing when every time I give a talk about labour pain, I get half-way through describing the finding depicted in Figure 2.1 and look up and meet the white face of someone at the back. Then I notice her bump! It's awful, but I do it deliberately now because I have gone into a postnatal ward so often and been met with the heartfelt plea – 'Why didn't anyone tell me what it would be like?' Perhaps because I and others have publicized these data and these views, antenatal educators are becoming more realistic in their descriptions of labour pain, producing the effect which Slade and her colleagues in their 1990 presentation have reported – that they found parturients' expectations of pain to be generally accurate.

However it still seems that some women have very unrealistic expectations of childbirth, perhaps because of the kind of antenatal preparation they have been provided with, or because of a personal tendency to prepare for stressful events by denying their stressfulness (see below). When these overoptimistic expectation are unfulfilled, these women are angry – they blame their failure to have the kind of birth they planned on their antenatal educators, on maternity staff, but worst of all, on themselves. Stewart, a Canadian clinician, has described how these women may end up depressed, even suicidal, losing interest in sex and their marriage because they feel guilty, angry and a failure (Stewart, 1982). These women are of course the exception but many women feel that they were not adequately prepared for childbirth and so the need for more efficient preparation is clear.

The need may be clear but the possibility of fulfilling that need is not. Childbirth is an immensely complex physiological, psychological and emotional experience and the meaning of that experience has great personal and cultural significance. Therefore every woman's experience will be different. Childbirth experiences vary much more than experiences of surgery, or of medical procedures such as endoscopy which have served as the models for effective information-giving. It is difficult, if not impossible, to give entirely accurate information about childbirth which will allow every woman to experience a birth which she correctly anticipates. Research into preparation for surgery also indicates that there are some people who will avoid such information even if it is clearly and directly presented to them. These people, 'deniers' as they are termed, do not actively seek information spontaneously, so they may not attend antenatal classes, as a recent study carried out in London suggests. Michie (1990), in a study of attitudes towards antenatal class attendance, found that the best predictor of non-attendance was an avoidant coping attitude – those who did not go to classes were more likely to be deniers.

If information is presented to deniers, they do their best to ignore it, by not listening to the information, or not remembering or believing what they've been told. I'm sure you all recognize this type of person, as well as the 'vigilant' person, who goes to the other extreme and demands every last piece of information from each member of staff and from books, articles and fellow sufferers as well! Janis (1958), in an early study, found that people who prior to surgery were neither notably vigilant nor denying coped better following surgery than did those who fell into either of the more extreme categories. He hypothesized that this was because the deniers experienced too little anxiety prior to surgery and thus did not engage in preparatory 'worry-work', while the vigilant group sought information because they were highly anxious. The people who lay midway between these two groups benefited from accepting and thinking about a moderate amount of information and by preparing themselves for the stress and distress of surgery without 'catastrophizing' about everything that might go wrong. However more recent research suggests that some deniers may be as anxious as subjects who are vigilant but that they cope with their anxiety in a different way – by avoiding thinking about it. These deniers probably cope best if they are not subjected to anxiety-provoking information. On the other hand some so-called deniers seem to be genuinely not anxious (rather than denying their anxiety). These subjects, who also do not seek information, tend to recover better from surgery than either vigilant or neutral (neither denying nor vigilant) subjects (Johnston and Carpenter, 1980).

Any professional who is involved in preparing women for childbirth, whether at antenatal classes or through individual care before and during labour, has carefully to weigh the results of the research I have presented so far. You have to consider the nature of the woman you are giving information to – is she vigilant, a denier, an in-betweener, or some category of person that researchers haven't yet got around to labelling? The best way of finding this out is by asking the woman what kind and amount of information she requires. If you provide a standardized form of information, the denier probably won't listen to you, and the information will go in one ear and out the other. In these circumstances you have to accept that this is the denier's own way of coping and that it is probably the best way of coping for her. The vigilant woman will seek out the information she craves anyway, so if you don't provide the amount and quality of information required, she will get it elsewhere. This means that you, as information giver, do not have absolute control over the quality and quantity of information conveyed. The recipient of preparatory information is not passive, she actively regulates the flow of information which she receives and generally regulates it to her advantage – postoperative recovery may be poorer in extremely vigilant subjects and in some cases also in deniers, but preoperatively, deniers benefit from reduced anxiety and post-operatively, the highly anxious vigilant subject probably benefits from the subsequent 'better-than-expected' phenomenon.

You also have to consider the best kind of information to give, so that those people who do want information will be provided with the most helpful variety. A lot of information which is given about childbirth is procedural and research suggests that this is less helpful than sensory information combined with coping instructions (Johnson et al., 1978). The use of sensory information could be emphasized in antenatal education so as to make the anticipated experience more realistic.

Sensory information describes, in language the subject can under-stand, the sights, sounds, smells, tastes and tactile sensations involved in an experience. For instance, preparation for endoscopy would detail the taste of the tube, the sudden onset of retching when the tube goes over the back of the throat, the feeling of fullness in the throat, etc. It allows patients to anticipate these sensations so they don't think that the endoscope will burst their throat or that they are the only person who feels sick. Preparation for orthopaedic cast removal describes the sound of the saw, the smell of the dust, the feeling of heat etc., so that children undergoing this procedure don't think that their leg is going to get cut or, misinterpreting the dust for smoke and feeling the heat on their leg, that they've been set on fire.

The provision of sensory information about childbirth would need to concentrate on the sensations of contractions during each of the stages of labour. This kind of information, sometimes based on informative descriptions which are contained in the copious literature on childbirth (e.g. Oakley, 1979), is often given to mothers-to-be. Sensory informa-tion on childbirth would also need to describe the pain which women may have, including its intensity, its nature, its distribution (front/back/down legs), how it changes from one stage to another and how analgesia may affect it. In my experience, this is not often provided. Papers by Bonica, Melzack and colleagues, Niven and Gijsbers, and Oakley, listed in the reference section, give information about labour pain which could form the basis of such a description. The sensations accompanying common midwifery and medical procedures such as vaginal examination, ARM, episiotomy and stitching would need to be detailed as well. Many antenatal educators do not have the necessary information on which to base these descriptions. This would therefore first have to be collected from labouring women. This in itself is likely to be an informative procedure for any midwife or antenatal educator. The literature on preparation for surgery shows that most preparation is done shortly before surgery, e.g. the night before. Sensory information is often most effective when it is provided immediately before or during the distressing procedure, such as just before endoscopy or during cast removal. Information which is given weeks before an event, as antenatal information often is, can be forgotten or distorted by memory so that it is not accessible at the time it is needed. Information given at the time is accessible. It can be more easily tailored to the circumstances of the individual person and is likely to be more effective in normalizing the experience. If sensory information about childbirth, for example about the manner in which the pain may increase in intensity or change in nature, is given when the mother is in early labour, and information about the typical sensations experienced during procedures such as ARM or forceps delivery is given at the time when they are performed, this is likely to be more helpful than if it were given during antenatal classes when it might increase anxiety unnecessarily or be forgotten in the interim. Sensory information given at the time of birth would become the prerogative of the attendant midwifery staff. So midwives who are not inolved in formal class-based antenatal education would be centrally involved in individual preparation for childbirth; they would be *intranatal* educators. This would allow them to reinforce helpful information which had been given at antenatal classes or obtained from books, pamphlets and television. They could ameliorate the worst excesses of faulty or alarmist information (the infamous 'old wives' tales) and, most importantly, they could tailor the information being given precisely to the needs of the individual parturient. In this way women who had gone to antenatal classes and those who had not could both benefit from helpful information. The current move towards involving more midwives in antenatal preparation and towards continuity of care and team midwifery will, if implemented, facilitate such a combination of ante- and intranatal education.

I observed just such a combination in my study when I examined the use of breathing exercises during labour and related them to attendance at antenatal classes. As breathing exercises are taught at these classes, I expected to find a clear relationship between class attendance and the use of exercises. I found no such effect – women who had been to classes and women who hadn't were equally likely to use these exercises. This was because women who hadn't attended classes were taught the exercises by their attendant midwife during the early stages of labour. Women who had attended classes were also frequently reminded of these techniques by their midwife, so both groups bene-fited from this form of intranatal education.

Provision of this kind of information is termed 'coping instruction' and it forms the second important aspect of preparation using sensory information. It is unhelpful to describe the sensory nature of a distressing experience to the person about to experience it, unless you also provide the person with help in coping with that experience. Telling mothers-to-be that labour is going to be hard work and is usually intensely painful isn't going to be much use unless you also tell them of ways that you and they can relieve the pain and put the hard work to good effect. Antenatal classes typically place great emphasis on coping instructions of this type, discussing the ways that staff can help parturients during labour and delivery and the analgesics which are available, and the ways that the parturients themselves can help to make labour and delivery more efficient and less painful. Attendance at antenatal classes seems to be effective in encouraging the general belief that 'I can cope with labour' and that 'the staff will help me to do so'. Hiller and Slade's (1989) study (see above) showed that women who had attended classes were more confident in their ability to cope with childbirth. My Stirling study (Niven, 1986) found that women who had attended classes were more likely to feel that maternity staff who cared for them during labour were competent and trustworthy.

A number of studies of PCT have shown that it is associated with reduced analgesic use during childbirth (see review by Beck et al., 1979). This may be due to the information conveyed about obstetric analgesics in these classes which sometimes tends to discourage their use (Melzack, 1984) or to the subjects' experience of pain which has been reduced through training in psychoprophylaxis – relaxation and breathing exercises – and thus requires less pharmacological pain relief.

In his Canadian studies, Melzack found that women who had attended PCT classes had significantly lower levels of labour pain compared with those who had not gone to these classes. Though the vast majority of his subjects (PCT and non-PCT) used epidural anaesthesia, women who had attended classes tended to use it later in labour, especially when their PCT educator had strongly encouraged her students to forgo it (Melzack, 1984). Thus it seems that his PCT subjects did generally have lower levels of labour pain. However the intensity of their pain was such that though they deferred accepting an epidural, they eventually sought to relieve their pain in this way, despite in some cases having been warned off its use. So though PCT appeared to be related to lower levels of labour pain, it was not related to painless childbirth. Reading and Cox (1985), in a London study, found no association between antenatal class attendance and lower levels of labour pain recorded after the birth. I found that women who had attended antenatal classes in the current pregnancy had lower levels of affective pain recorded during the active phase of the first stage of labour, even when the effects of age, class and more positive expectations of birth were statistically controlled. Women who attended classes were marginally more likely to use Entonox than women who had not attended classes but there were no significant differences in pethidine use. These results would indicate that antenatal education was effective in reducing labour pain and that this effect was not solely due to the relationship between class attendance and variables which independently affected obstetric outcome or pain levels (Niven and Gijsbers, 1984; Niven, 1986).

Thus, although antenatal class attendance seems to offer some benefits, these appear to be limited. Pain and stress in labour are reduced to some extent in women who attend classes, but this reduction does not result in a painless or stress-free childbirth. Anticipatory anxiety is not apparently lowered. Antenatal education generally seems to provide accurate procedural and obstetric information, but parturients might benefit more from the provision of accurate experiential information of a sensory nature. Such provision might make expectations of childbirth more realistic. However, it is unlikely that entirely accurate expectations of childbirth can be created and it is debatable whether or not the creation of such accurate expectations would invariably be helpful. People have different ways of coping with the anticipation of a stressful event such as childbirth. Some people want to receive as much information as possible, while others attempt not to think about what's coming. The professional who aims to prepare women for childbirth thus has to take into consideration the wishes of the mother-to-be regarding the nature and amount of information which is conveyed. This difficult and delicate task may be easier to accomplish if antenatal education is combined with one-to-one, intranatal education. The provision of intranatal education would ensure that all parturients, not just those who choose to attend antenatal classes (typically the more advantaged members of the reproductive population), could be adequately prepared for childbirth.

Coping with childbirth

The beneficial effects of antenatal education may be due to the use of coping strategies such as relaxation which are taught at the classes. I examined the use of coping strategies in detail in 50% of my subjects (50% = 51 subjects). Thirty-five per cent of these subjects used relaxation strategies during labour. These subjects had significantly lower levels of labour pain when compared with subjects who had not used relaxation strategies. The strategies they used involved techniques which are taught in antenatal classes – the deliberate tensing and relaxing of various muscle groups, concentration on slow, regular breathing and on relaxing images – but there was only a marginal association between the use of relaxation during labour and attendance at antenatal classes. Women who attend antenatal classes will not necessarily learn the techniques taught there, nor use them once they are in labour. A number of subjects who had been taught how to relax when they were healthily pregnant, in no pain and under little stress (during antenatal education) found it impossible to relax during labour. Relaxing in labour was easier for multiparous subjects and also for women who routinely used relaxation as a way of coping with pain and stress unassociated with childbirth. These women had practised relaxing when they were in pain or under stress and had thus developed and refined their ability to cope using some form of relaxation (not necessarily the form taught in classes). They had also proved to themselves that relaxation works, something that women who had merely learned the techniques at antenatal classes could not be sure of.

A Czechoslovakian study which used systematic desensitization techniques (Kondas and Scetnicka, 1972) found that these were more effective in reducing anxiety and pain in labour than routine psychoprophylactic education (the kind usually taught in antenatal classes). Systematic desensitization involves subjects imagining themselves in anxiety-provoking situations (in this case related to labour) while practising relaxation strategies. Subjects who have been trained to relax in this way have, like subjects who use relaxation to cope with everyday pains and stresses, had the opportunity to practise relaxing while experiencing tension. This brings their educational situation closer to the childbirth situation and makes that education more effective.

Routine psychoprophylactic education typically involves the use of breathing exercises as well as education in relaxation. The use of breathing exercises as taught in British antenatal classes was associated with a significant reduction in affective pain as well as in subjects' overall evaluation of the pain of labour and delivery. Seventy-eight per cent of subjects used these techniques at some point during labour and, as discussed above (see Preparation for childbirth), this number included parturients who had been taught the techniques at antenatal classes, as well as those who were instructed in their use by their attendant midwife (Niven, 1986; Niven, 1991).

Other techniques used by subjects to cope with labour pain included distraction (concentrating on something other than the pain, e.g. counting the ceiling tiles in the labour room), the use of imagery (concentrating on a vivid image, often of the baby) and thinking very positively about the pain of contractions as signalling healthy and efficient progress of labour. Distraction techniques were used by 69% of subjects and were associated with some reduction in labour pain; imagery was used by 34% of subjects but was not associated with lower levels of pain, and thinking positively about labour pain (known as 'reversing the affect' of pain) was used as a deliberate coping strategy by 22% of subjects who had very significantly lower levels of labour pain (Niven, 1986; Niven and Gijsbers, in press). The use of these coping strategies has been tested in other clinical and experimental studies and has been shown to be effective in reducing some kinds of pain (see Tan, 1982). It is therefore more likely that, as the results of the Stirling study indicate, some of these strategies are effective in ameliorating labour pain than that women who experience lower levels of pain during childbirth are more able to relax, take their minds off the pain, and think of it positively. However, the use of such strategies does not ensure painless childbirth, as can be seen from Figure 2.2 where the level of pain associated with the use of these strategies is depicted. Comparison with levels of pain depicted in Figure 2.1 show that levels of labour pain are still high.

Some antenatal teachers will include instruction in the use of coping strategies such as distraction and reversal of affect in their antenatal classes. Others will not. Many of my subjects who used these strategies during labour had evolved them spontaneously or had used them

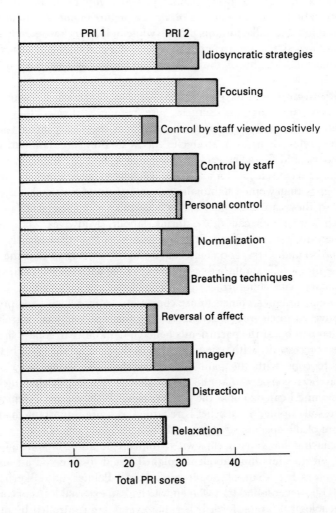

Figure 2.2 Levels of labour pain associated with the use of various coping strategies (PRI = Pain Ranking Index: PRI 1 = Pain Ranking Index related to first stage; PRI 2 = Pain Ranking Index related to first and second stages)

previously to cope with other kinds of pain and stress. Subjects also evolved a whole range of other strategies which could not easily be categorized, e.g. a concert pianist played symphonies in her head during labour; a mother of four brought a picture of one of her children in with her and talked to this picture while in labour; a woman lent up against a wall 'to gain strength' early in labour and later lent up against her husband. Many of these coping strategies had been used previously.

Other researchers have found that subjects, for instance coping with the pain and stress of surgery, use coping strategies they have generated themselves in preference to ones they have been taught. They prefer their own strategies because they are familiar, well rehearsed and fit their overall coping style (see Tan, 1982). It would therefore seem sensible for antenatal teachers to incorporate the coping strategies that women habitually use into their educational programmes so they can form part of the repertoire of coping strategies on which parturients can draw during labour. Midwives who attend women during childbirth could also ask them how they usually cope with pain and stress, and could suggest to the parturient that she tries to use these well established techniques to cope with the pain and stress associated with childbirth.

By encouraging women to use coping strategies which have proved effective in their previous experience, the antenatal or intranatal teacher can boost the parturient's belief in her ability to cope – she has coped successfully with pain and stress in the past, so she is likely to be able to cope with the pain and stress she is suffering now! Some researchers consider that this belief that 'I can cope', that there is 'something I can do about the pain or stress', is the essential element in successful coping. This belief is regarded as more important than the nature of the specific strategy used.

Believing that you can cope with a difficult situation, or knowing that you can do something about it, might be said to give you a sense of control rather than of helplessness. Scott-Palmer and Skevington (1981) however found that women who had an external locus of control (psychological jargon for a belief that events are controlled by others rather than by the individual him/herself) had lower levels of labour pain than those who had an internal locus of control (who believed that they had personal control over events). So, in this study, having a sense of control appeared to be related to more labour pain rather than less. Some midwives, sceptical about 'bolshie natural childbirth' parturients who seek to have as much personal control in labour as possible, might exclaim 'I told you so!' However, Scott-Palmer and Skevington assessed labour pain hourly and external locus of control subjects had longer labours. They would therefore be likely to be dilating more slowly and, according to Bonica's theories (see Pain in childbirth, earlier), have less pain per contraction and per assessment. The relationship between locus of control and labour pain might therefore have been confounded by duration effects. It might also be confounded by social class and associated variables, since research has established a relationship between social class and locus of control (Phares, 1976).

Brewin and Bradley (1982), who also used British subjects but used a retrospective rather than concurrent method of pain assessment, found that women who expected that they would have more personal control during childbirth (through the use of their own resources) reported less discomfort in labour. This relationship was not apparently mediated by analgesic drugs and appears almost to be the opposite of Scott-Palmer and Skevington's findings. However, they also found that women who expected the staff to have more control over their discomfort in labour had less pain – these women might normally be rated as having an external rather than internal locus of control.

In a study of British subjects which looked at their experience of childbirth rather than their expectations, I found that perceptions of personal control in labour were not associated with either significantly higher or lower levels of labour pain (Niven, 1986; Niven, in press). It seems that the debate over the relationship between personal control and levels of labour pain continues, as a recent conference discussion of this issue demonstrated (Slade et al., 1990).

Brewin and Bradley (1982) state that attendance at antenatal classes was significantly associated with expectations of both increased personal control and increased staff control but it is unclear whether these perceptions were held by one and the same subjects. In my own study I asked subjects about their perceptions of personal and of staff control. They reported a wide range of perceptions relating to the concept of control in childbirth. Some subjects reported that they had felt in control during childbirth; some that the staff had been in control; some that both they and the staff had been in control; and an unfortunate few, that no one had been in control. Some women considered control to be related to control of pain; some that it was related to the progress and outcome of labour (e.g. whether or not an assisted delivery had been necessary); and others that it concerned 'not being out of control', or not 'giving themselves a showing up', as they put it. It seems that issues of control during childbirth are extremely complex and are not adequately assessed by simple measures such as external versus internal locus of control. Women who have attended antenatal classes have been found to benefit from an increased confidence in their ability to cope with childbirth (Hiller and Slade, 1989). This may involve high expectations of personal control and of staff control (Slade et al., 1990 and following section).

Brewin and Bradley found that high expectations of staff control were related to lower levels of pain, both in subjects who had attended antenatal classes and in those who had not. I found that subjects who had perceived that the staff were in control during childbirth did not have significantly lower levels of labour pain. There was no relationship between perceived staff control per se and attendance at antenatal classes.

Perceptions of staff control however could be positive, implying a welcome competence and support, or negative, involving unwelcomed domination and lack of consultation. Over 50% of my subjects perceived the staff to be in control during their labours; 90% of these were happy about this. Subjects who viewed staff control positively had very significantly lower levels of labour pain (see Fig. 2.2). This relationship was in part due to the staff's skilful administration of analgesics, but even when the relationship between pain levels and effective analgesia was controlled statistically, the beneficial consequences of good staff–parturient relations were apparent. Levels of affective pain were particularly strongly related to positive perceptions of staff control.

Subjects who viewed staff control positively were significantly more likely to have attended antenatal classes. Since the same group of midwives cared for class attenders and non-attenders, this suggests that the parturients' positive perceptions of the midwife were not just dependent on the midwives' behaviour. Perhaps antenatal education encourages a more positive attitude towards midwifery staff through the interactions between them and mothers-to-be during their attendance at classes. Certainly Brant (1962) suggested some time ago that continuity of care from pregnancy to childbirth can have beneficial effects on obstetric outcome. That study involved the same midwife caring for the woman during pregnancy and in labour. This did not happen in Stirling but any positive contact that class attenders had with other midwifery staff may have carried over into labour. On the other hand it may be that women who choose to attend classes are more positively disposed towards midwifery staff anyway, with those who dislike hospitals and distrust their staff avoiding classes. They (the non-attenders) may provoke more negative reactions from their mid-wives which will reinforce their distrust and exacerbate the difficulties that the midwives have in relating to them (Niven, 1986; Niven, in press; Niven and Gijsbers, in press).

The results of my study suggest strongly that the relationship between the midwife and the parturient s/he is attendant upon is of importance in modulating the experience of labour pain. I found that subjects who viewed staff control positively used a larger number of coping strategies during their labour and delivery. This suggests that when parturients trust the staff who care for them they are empowered to utilize their own coping resources more effectively. The preliminary results of two recent studies reinforce this contention. A study carried out in Ireland found that women's expectations of self-efficacy in childbirth – their belief that they will be able to cope effectively with the various aspects of childbirth – were related to positive perceptions of staff support (Byrne-Lynch, 1990). And a study carried out in England (Slade et al., 1990) found that satisfaction with the midwife was solely related to the parturient's sense of personal satisfaction with her labour. This in turn was related to the woman's sense of personal control over labour pain; to her ability to control panic; to her use of coping strategies and to their efficacy. It therefore seems that personal control and staff control during childbirth are interwoven and, far from being antagonistic concepts, can be mutually supportive to the benefit of staff and parturient alike.

Social support in childbirth

In the UK, the woman in labour has two main sources of social support – her midwife, and her husband or other chosen birth companion. The research detailed above, which showed that a positive perception of attendant staff was associated with lower levels of pain in childbirth, suggests that social support by midwives may be important in amelio-rating pain and distress at that time. The midwife as we know her/him does not exist in some countries where women in labour are cared for by doctors who are assisted by obstetric nurses. Although the caring, supportive aspects of midwifery may be performed by these nurses, they are not seen as an integral component of their patient care in the way they are here.

Klaus, Kennel and colleagues have examined the effects of providing continuous social support to women in childbirth who are not attended by midwives and do not receive this type of care from obstetric staff. Their original studies were carried out in Social Security hospitals in Guatemala. One group of parturients was provided with a *doula* ('woman's servant' in Greek) – a lay woman who gave constant emotional and physical support to them throughout active labour and delivery. These parturients were compared with another group who received routine care which was given by medical staff assisted by obstetric nurses. They did not receive any continuous staff or family support.

The parturients who were accompanied by *doulas* had significantly fewer perinatal complications, including Caesarian section, and their babies were less likely to be admitted to neonatal intensive care units. In those who had intervention-free childbirth, the duration of labour was significantly shorter if they had been accompanied by a *doula*. Since anxiety in labour can affect uterine efficiency (see Stress and anxiety in childbirth, this chapter) it was suggested that women who had the support of a *doula* were less anxious and so had more rapid and efficient labours and thus were delivered of more healthy infants (see Klaus et al., 1986).

The presence of a constant companion whose role is to concentrate on the well-being of the woman in labour could also affect medical and nursing standards of care. In a further study carried out in a US hospital where modern obstetric practices such as fetal monitoring, induction and augmentation of labour and epidural anaesthesia were widely used, the effects of a *doula* were compared with the effects of a constant but silent observer who gave no obvious support to the labouring woman but monitored her charts and logged her progress. The presence of the observer might thus affect the staff rather than the parturient. A control group who had neither a *doula* nor an observer was also included in the study. This study (Kennel et al., 1988) found that the control group used significantly higher rates of forceps and Caesarian delivery than either of the two other groups. The *doula*-accompanied group had the lowest rate of epidurals, forceps and Caesarians, with the silent observer group coming between the *doula* and control groups.

These results suggest that the presence of any birth companion, no matter how silent, beneficially affects the labour process. It would seem that the major effect of the silent observer would be on the staff who perhaps provided superior psychological and physical care, or were less quick to intervene in labour or delivery. However, the authors note that almost every mother in the observed group commented how much they appreciated 'that woman who stayed in the labor room with me throughout my entire labor and checked my chart to make sure that everything was all right'; so the silent observer may have offered the parturient a subtle but important form of social support without intending to.

The superior results of the *doula*-accompanied group show clearly that these women received an additional benefit from her active support. This support involved explanation, encouragement, reassurance, tactile contact such as hand-holding, brow-mopping and back-rubbing, and a continuous presence which was solely directed towards the physical and emotional needs of the parturient.

The British midwife normally accompanies the parturient throughout labour and delivery and gives practical and emotional support. While s/he is not the exact equivalent of the *doula*, many of the *doula's* functions can be and are performed by good midwives. Klaus and Kennel's research does not indicate which of these functions may be the most important for maternal well-being – the continuous presence, the emotional support, the physical ministrations, the monitoring of progress. Inclusion in a research study could also affect the parturient's experience. It might influence both subjects and staff to 'behave better', interact more positively or report more favourably than they would if the same conditions occurred but were not being studied and recorded. Until further research has been carried out, it is safest to assume that all these factors may be important and to implement as many of the apparently helpful practices as possible.

The parturient's partner or other chosen birth companion can also act as a *doula*. Of course it can be difficult for a man who is about to become a father for the first time to cater to all the physical and emotional needs of his partner in labour; he will be anxious too (see below) and will usually know even less about the normal course of labour and delivery than she will (see Introduction). *Doulas*, though medically untrained, are mature experienced women who accompany a number of parturients in labour and thus become familiar with hospital procedures and the variety of experiences women have in childbirth.

Research carried out in the UK suggests that some fathers do provide a lot of physical and emotional support to their partner during childbirth; rubbing her back, mopping her brow, encouraging her in the use of breathing techniques and pushing efforts and acting as an essential source of knowledge about what is happening during labour and delivery which they can convey to their partner at the time, and recall for her later (Niven, 1985; Lewis, 1986). Many men are constantly present during labour and delivery, though some are asked to go out periodically, e.g. during internal examination, and some are either asked to leave or leave voluntarily when complications develop, just when personal support and comfort may be most needed. Lewis, working in Nottingham, noted that fathers are often used to supplement midwifery care on busy units where the staff cannot be with a labouring woman constantly. They may also be given tasks to carry out which tend to align them more closely with the medical and physiological aspects of the birth than with its personal and psychological aspects, e.g. watching the epidural chart or confirming contraction timing and monitoring (Lewis, 1986). Although these tasks may be spurious and may merely be provided in order to make the father feel he is doing something important, they may divert his attention away from more socially supportive procedures.

The presence of the father at labour and delivery has become an almost automatic part of modern childbirth. Lewis notes that in 1960, 60% of Nottingham births were at home, and fathers attended 13% of these and 8% of all births. In 1980, fathers attended 84% of Nottingham births, 98% of which took place in hospital.

The change in birth practices which has taken place within 20 years, from those in which the father's rightful place during the birth of his child was seen to be 'if not at work, in the local' (Lewis, 1986, p. 57) to those in which his presence at the birth is almost mandatory, is remarkable. This change is apparent even within ethnic groups where the use of female birth companions is traditional. Woolet and Dosanjh-Matwala (1990) found that 78% of Asian fathers were present at some point during the birth of their child. This percentage is comparable to those of non-Asian subjects living in the same part of London (White and Woolet, 1987) and to Bengali subjects living in London (Watson, 1984) but not to Punjabi subjects living in the Midlands (Homans, 1982). Regional, cultural and religious differences may all influence attitudes to the presence of birth companions (Currer, 1986) but the father's presence at the birth seems to be becoming more generally accepted.

The father's own experience of childbirth is discussed below (The father's experience of childbirth). In this current section I want to look at how his presence affects his partner's experience. The move towards accepting and encouraging the father's presence at childbirth has made it less likely that woman will have other birth companions. For instance, Lewis found that when Nottinghamshire women gave birth at home in the 1960s, 15% were accompanied by another woman rather than by their male partners. He notes that many hospitals at the time of his study refused to allow anyone other than the father to be present in the delivery room. However most hospitals are currently more flexible in their approach to the presence of a chosen birth companion, allowing the mother complete freedom to choose the person or people she wishes to accompany her.

Most studies which concern the presence of a birth companion refer to the father's or husband's presence and subsume fathers, husbands and cohabitees under either heading. These studies have consistently shown that parturients are generally positive about his presence. For example, Henneborn and Cogan (1975) working in the USA found that the father's presence was associated with increased maternal satisfaction with the birth experience and Oakley (1979), working in the UK, that most of the pressure to include fathers in labour and delivery came from the expectant mothers. Woolet and Dosanjh-Matwala (1990) found that the majority of their London Asian subjects welcomed their husband's presence at the birth and valued his support. In a study of the effects of the presence of a birth companion (Niven, 1985) I found that the majority of my British Caucasian subjects giving birth in Stirling welcomed the presence of their birth companion (usually but not invariably their partner) very positively, remarking that 'it was comforting', 'he was someone to hold on to (literally and metaphorically)', or even that 'him being there was the only thing that helped', or that 'I fell in love with him all over again'. They also commented on his physical ministrations and occasionally on his help in the use of pain-coping strategies.

However, not all women positively welcome their partner's presence. I found that 16% of women whose partners were with them in labour did not find this helpful. In some cases this was because they were so 'zonked' on pethidine and/or Entonox that they hardly noticed who was with them. But in other cases it was because their partner's presence worried them – the parturient was concerned that he might faint, or get upset by seeing her in pain, or felt that he should be at home looking after the other children. So his presence increased her stress and anxiety rather than reducing it. Some women reported that they preferred to cope with childbirth by themselves as this was the way they normally coped with painful or stressful events in life.

Some of the women who did not welcome their partner's presence during labour were unaccompanied. In other cases, the partner was present, either because he particularly wanted to be at the birth of his child, or because he was encouraged to attend the birth by well-meaning friends, relatives and staff. Woolet and Dosanjh-Matwala (1990) found that a small percentage of the Asian women they studied did not wish their husbands to be present, feeling that they were better supported by a midwife.

Women may suffer less pain in labour when accompanied by their partners because they are less anxious and/or because their partners help them to use pain-coping strategies such as relaxation or breathing techniques. Henneborn and Cogan (1975) found that the husband's presence during childbirth was associated with lower levels of pain, especially when he attended the delivery as well as first-stage labour. However, the presence of a partner does not always affect pain levels in childbirth, with some studies finding no significant relationship between the husband's presence and pain levels in childbirth, e.g. Nettlebladt et al. (1976), and others finding that women report more intense labour pain when their husbands are present than when they are absent (Melzack, 1984). When I analysed the relationship between labour pain levels and the presence of the woman's partner or other chosen birth companion, I found no significant differences in pain levels between the women who had their partners with them and those who did not. However, when the parturient's assessment of his presence was taken into consideration, I found that women who positively welcomed his presence had lower levels of labour pain when compared with all other subjects. This finding was most significant when affective components of labour pain were considered and suggests that it is not the partner's presence per se that is important but the labouring woman's feelings about his presence (Niven, 1985).

Melzack (1984) had found that his subjects reported significantly higher levels of affective pain when their husbands were with them at the time of pain assessment than when they were out of the labour room. It is possible that a considerable proportion of these subjects resented his presence or found it unhelpful and that this accounts for the difference between his findings and my own. Cultural differences and variations in hospital practices may also be involved.

It seems that while many women find it helpful and comforting to have their partner or other chosen birth companion with them during labour and delivery, some women do not. Therefore, looked at from the parturient's point of view, rather than from that of the baby's father, the decision of whether a man is present at the birth of his child or not should depend on the mother's wishes. If his presence will make her more anxious or will interfere with her coping strategies, it should be avoided since it may increase her pain and distress which in turn may affect the baby's well-being (see Pain in childbirth). This view fails to acknowledge the wishes and needs of the father and the ways in which these will interact with those of his partner. When these are taken into consideration, it is obviously best that the father and mother come to a joint decision on whether or not he should be present at the birth. Pressure to attend the birth should not be put on fathers by antenatal or maternity staff. Neither should it be regarded as necessarily the right thing for a 'right-on' caring father to do. Parturients should be encouraged to consider their choice of birth companion in the light of their individual coping needs. Sometimes the best thing a caring father could do is to let someone else act as birth companion, or to leave the woman in labour to cope by herself. Certainly the best support I have witnessed came from a chosen birth companion who was neither the partner of the parturient nor the father of the child. I assume he was selected for his supportive qualities, and he demonstrated them impressively well. Perhaps since he was not so intimately involved in the birth as fathers/partners usually are, he was freer to concentrate on giving care and support to the mother.

Social support in childbirth can be given by a variety of personnel. In this country the midwife is well placed to provide considerable physical and emotional support on a semi-continuous basis. The midwife's role as provider of psychological care to the woman in labour perhaps pre-empts the use of a *doula*, though *doulas* could be used to support women who are particularly vulnerable, such as lone mothers or women who have previously lost a baby in childbirth. The parturient's partner or other chosen birth companion can act as a continuous presence (like the silent observer) and can, under optimum circumstances, provide support which is precisely tailored to the needs of the parturient, since he will know more about her wants, desires, preferences and ways of coping than could any midwife or *doula*. The task of the professionals caring for the family during childbirth is to create these optimum circumstances and to ensure that all support given in childbirth is complementary and not competitive. Sometimes fathers who want to give maximum support to their partner in labour are 'edged out' by midwives who are giving effective psychological care to the parturient. Marshal Klaus (personal communication) observed in an early study of the effect of *doulas* that fathers who accompany women who are also being cared for by *doulas* sit apart from their wives, whereas the *doula* sits close and gives the physical and emotional support. In some circumstances this may be the best situation for the parturient. She has her partner there with her sharing the experience, and she receives good psychological care from an experienced midwife or *doula*. However, the poor father may be left on the sidelines, feeling totally ineffective and useless. *Doulas* are now being trained to encourage the father in the physical and psychological support of his partner and in fact often act as a *doula* for him as well, providing him with the psychological care which enables him in turn to be a more effective supporter of his partner.

Marshal and Phyllis Klaus feel that this combination of *doula* and husband is likely to be much more effective than husband support alone as the husband's own anxiety about the birth and his inexperience and inability to empathize with his partner (because of his gender) make it impossible for him to give the sort of mothering (female comfort, strength and support) that a woman needs during labour (Klaus and Klaus, in press). The female midwife who can similarly utilize the partner's supportive talents as well as her own would therefore be regarded as giving the best care to all the family in labour.

However, I think it is possible for men to give tremendous support to women in labour. I base this belief on my observations of male midwives who worked in the unit where I carried out my study of labour pain. Men are certainly unable totally to empathize with a labouring woman's experience, but this is equally impossible for many female birth attendants even if they are mothers, since the experience of childbirth varies so widely. Male midwives, like female ones and like *doulas*, have witnessed a wide range of different birth experiences and, if sensitive, will have discovered much about the mothers' views of these experiences. Along with their education this will equip them with the necessary knowledge on which to base their provision of psychological support. They are not personally involved in the birth and are therefore unlikely to be unwarrantably anxious about the mother or baby or about their role in childbirth. For these reasons, I would disagree with the view that the best childbirth support is inevitably female. If men strive to overcome the natural disadvantages engendered by their gender, they can be effective psychological carers during childbirth in my opinion. However I would agree that it is very difficult for the woman's partner/father of the baby to have the confidence, knowledge and experience necessary to provide the best support for a woman in labour, and that there can be something especially comforting and strengthening about close, sensitive female support provided at that time.

Some ethnic minority women may prefer to abide by traditional birth practices and be accompanied by female relatives during childbirth. However, the waning of the extended family system may make this difficult and the preferences of the women themselves may be influenced by the dominant culture (see Woolet and Dosanjh-Matwala, 1990). Amongst women who observe purdah the presence of male doctors or midwives goes against all their cultural norms and, though it is tolerated by them, can be regarded as a matter of shame. Currer (1986), for instance, who studied a group of Pathan women living in Bradford, found that they compromised their own beliefs in order to cope with our culture's norms of childbirth. However they 'don't tell their mothers' that they see male doctors, as this would have been regarded as deeply shocking.

The parturient's preference in the choice of birth companion should be regarded as paramount if at all possible. Women who do not have English as their first language need to be accompanied by someone who is fluent in English and in the woman's first language. Woolet and Dosanjh-Matwala found that amongst 19 of their subjects who were not fluent in English, 10 were unaccompanied during delivery. These women tended to be more traditional in their outlook and so were less likely to be accompanied by their husbands. Female relatives were sometimes present in the hospital but were not in the delivery room. Link workers were available in the hospital, but appeared not to have been used. Since three of these women had complex deliveries, the need for effective communication was particularly strong. Staff need to ensure that such women are accompanied by a birth companion/ translator if at all possible. Many of Currer's subjects were not fluent in English, though they spoke at least three languages and so were far more literate than most of us. They understood the difficulties that staff had in trying to communicate with them. Non-verbal communication became very significant in the absence of verbal communication, so that simple behaviours like smiling or touching assumed considerable significance and were greatly appreciated. However some staff seemed to respond to the communication difficulties by ignoring these parturients rather than by utilizing the non-verbal communication patterns that cut across cultural and language barriers.

The father's experience of childbirth

The birth of his child is a significant event for any man whether he is present at the time or not. However, modern obstetric practice has normalized the attendance of the father and most recent British studies show that fathers are present at over 80% of births (Beail and

McGuire, 1982; Niven, 1985; Lewis, 1986). Mothers-to-be are generally keen that their partner should be with them at the birth whereas fathers are more reluctant (Oakley, 1979; Lewis, 1986). Lewis found that 66% of his sample of 100 married men reported that both they and their wives wanted him to be present at the birth of their child. However many of these fathers were in two minds about attending the birth and had only chosen to attend after considerable persuasion. Six per cent of fathers refused to attend the birth, usually citing the risk of embarrassment or of fainting.

Apart from the views of partners, family and friends, the viewing of the 'birth film' at the antenatal class parents' evening seemed to influence the fathers' decisions greatly. For some of the fathers who participated in Lewis's (1986) study, it confirmed their squeamishness and reinforced their decision not to attend the birth, whereas for others it reassured them that they could cope with the realities of birth. Some fathers were 'press-ganged' into attending the birth by hospital staff.

> As soon as I walked into the labour suite [having delivered his wife there] they sort of put a gown on me: there was no 'Are you stopping?' or 'Aren't you stopping?' It was sort of a foregone conclusion that I *was* stopping (Lewis, 1986, p. 64).

Twenty-two per cent of London Asian fathers studied by Woolet and Dosanjh-Matwala (1990) did not want to attend the birth. Although some chose not to attend because of adherence to traditional ideas about woman-centred childbirth practices, the feelings of squeamishness cited by Lewis's subjects were expressed in this group as well. Religious factors did not seem to influence the decision to be present at the birth. Muslim fathers were present as often as Hindu or Sikh fathers. Some Muslim fathers said the Azan (a traditional prayer) in the child's ear after delivery, giving them an additional reason for wishing to be present at that time.

The results of Lewis's study showed that fathers' anxieties about attending childbirth seem to be justified. Sixty per cent of attenders reported that they experienced at least some parts of labour and delivery as distressing. For a minority, the entire process was felt to be completely worrying or upsetting. Only 12 subjects described the birth in exclusively positive terms. The most commonly reported cause of distress was the witnessing of their wife's pain. Other causes included poor communication, where fathers failed to understand the terminology used by medical staff, and sudden exclusion from the labour room when complications (which might be minor) had developed.

Fathers who attended the entire birth were more likely to report the experience in overall positive terms than fathers who had left or were removed before delivery. Fathers who attended the birth felt closer to their child as a result (Lewis, 1986). Being at the birth of their child is an important experience for many fathers. However fathers, like mothers, experience anxiety during childbirth. If severe, this can have lasting consequences with, for instance, the man being reluctant to have a further child (Lewis, 1986). During the birth itself, maternal anxiety can have a direct effect on the baby (see Stress and anxiety in childbirth, this chapter). Paternal anxiety during childbirth, apart from being discomforting to the father, is likely to interfere with the father's ability to help the mother. Caring for fathers during childbirth can therefore affect the entire family.

Since so many fathers attend childbirth, their presence should be put to good use. They have the time and the inclination to support and care for their partners throughout labour and delivery. Unlike obstetric staff they have no other parturients to care for, nor tasks to perform. They can concentrate wholeheartedly on giving good psychological care. Some fathers do this wonderfully (see Social support in childbirth) but many more do not. The reasons for this 'waste of resources' are unclear. Insufficient research has been done in this area. A number of factors already discussed are likely to be involved.

For instance, a father will not be able to comfort or reassure his partner during childbirth if he is highly anxious or distressed himself. He won't be able to explain what's going on to her in language she can comprehend, if he can't understand the jargon that is being used. You might argue here that explanation is the job of the staff not the father, and in principle you would be right. But communicating with women in labour is often difficult, as the processes of childbirth and the effects of analgesic drugs make them drowsy and distanced from events which surround them. At these times, it is often the familiar voice that gets through. Furthermore, Lewis found that the father typically became the essential source of information about what was happening in labour since he could keep track of the sequence of events in a way which was impossible for the mother. This was often of particular importance after the birth when parturients sought to make sense of what had happened, but found it difficult to recall. Providing fathers with clear information will relieve some of their anxiety and allow them to understand what's going on.

Sociological writers have emphasized the low status of the father in childbirth (e.g. Richman and Goldthorp, 1978) which they relate to the absence of any specific role which he can play. Efforts are sometimes made to provide a pseudomedical role for the father which will increase his status and provide him with something definite to do (Brown, 1982). So fathers are asked to watch epidural charts or observe contraction rates on monitors and thus are linked to the 'male' aspects of medicine and technology rather than to the 'female' aspects of caring, nursing and being with women in childbirth. I must admit to some female prejudice here. I cannot stand seeing fathers gazing at monitor screens rather than at their labouring wives. I know that it's probably a lot less anxiety-provoking to look at a machine than at the woman you love, suffering pain and distress. And the mere presence of the father may be comforting to his partner. But I don't think it's what social support is all about.

I agree that fathers should be given a specific role in childbirth. I think it should be to give the woman in labour comfort, support and encouragement. Comfort involves physical comforting – touching, holding, stroking, rubbing backs, mopping brows. A substantial body of research shows that touch lowers heart rate and alleviates distress, communicates caring and can quickly establish a rapport between health professionals and those in their care (e.g. McCorkle, 1974; Drescher et al., 1980). It is therefore very important that women in childbirth – stressed, anxious, often beyond the reach of verbal communication – are touched. Midwives and obstetricians should touch the parturient frequently to reassure and comfort her. But they have tasks to perform which involve less pleasant forms of touch, such as vaginal examination or rupturing of the membranes. The father's touch can be, and should be, exclusively positive.

Support and encouragement for the labouring woman are normally communicated by midwifery and obstetric staff, as well as by the father. However, sometimes they have to communicate negative information, about progress in labour for instance, or give negative feedback, e.g. about pushing wrongly. The father can be positive all the time. Every man will have his own way of telling his partner that he loves her; that she's wonderful; that she's coping magnificently; and that he's with her all the way. These are the feelings that men report having during childbirth (Brown, 1982; Lewis, 1986) and they should be communicated loud and clear to their partners.

Since fathers/partners are also lovers, one would assume that they would know how to communicate positive feelings physically as well as verbally. This is rarely apparent in the labour room where they are usually as discreet and polite as they would be in any other public place. Labour rooms are public places filled with strangers, so polite behaviour might seem to be appropriate. Since the woman in childbirth is engaged in one of the most basic of physical and emotional tasks, I don't think it is appropriate. Therefore fathers at the birth should be encouraged to be somewhat less inhibited with the kisses and cuddles and more generous with the sweet nothings. At the very least they should sit within touching distance and not at the far side of a locker, or a midwife! Of course there will be men who are the opposite of inhibited and there will be women who value discretion above all else, so the behaviour of the father should depend on the wishes of the individuals involved. The provision of increased privacy and the presence of staff with whom the parturient and her partner are familiar and comfortable would do much to encourage fathers and mothers to be more relaxed and uninhibited in their behaviour towards one another during childbirth. This could have many advantages in addition to freeing the father from the constraints imposed by proper public behaviour. Fathers will find it difficult to be positive, comforting and reassuring if they are worried sick. So they need support and reassurance too. They will be more helpful if they know something about the processes of childbirth and about the midwifery and medical procedures which nowadays accompany it. They are likely to feel less distressed about witnessing their partner's pain if they feel that there is something that they can help her to do about it.

There is a current move towards providing antenatal education for fathers-to-be in this country (beyond their token inclusion in the parents' evening). If men attend these classes they could learn more about the processes of childbirth and about the use of pain-coping strategies such as relaxation or breathing techniques. This may allow them to be less anxious and distressed and to help their partner to cope with labour more effectively. However, the literature on antenatal education (see this chapter) suggests that it may not be totally successful in relieving anxiety about childbirth and in promoting the use of coping strategies. So even if men do attend classes, their behaviour in attendance during labour may be largely unaltered.

Men in this country have tended not to attend classes, though the situation may be changing. Lewis (1986) found that only 6% of his male subjects attended antenatal classes. Daytime classes are of course inconvenient for many men to attend, but they also resist going because they and their wives agree that it would be embarrassing. Even parents' evenings, specifically designed for fathers to attend, are regarded as embarrassing, with men 'recoiling in horror at the prospect of having to change a doll's nappy in the presence of others' (Lewis, 1986, p. 40). Those men who do attend parents' evenings do not report that they learn much from them except about the right part of the hospital to deliver their wives to. However the birth film does seem to ease some of their embarrassment about being present at the delivery, and it introduces many men to their first encounter with a newborn baby (Lewis, 1986). Although it may be possible to use the parents' evening to inform fathers about the best ways to help their partners during childbirth, intranatal education may again prove more effective than antenatal education (see Preparation for childbirth, this chapter). It would guarantee that all attendant fathers receive some instruction in how to help their partners during labour and delivery.

No matter how well you educate fathers about how to help their partners during childbirth, there will always be men who are shy, men who are unloving, and men who are not there. In these cases, if an alternative birth companion is not available, the staff should emphasize the psychological aspects of their care. One member of staff might be specifically allocated the *doula* role, especially during delivery when the midwife has to concentrate on obstetric, foot-of-the-bed concerns and the head-of-the-bed tends to get ignored.

Educating fathers to provide high-quality psychological comfort and support may not work. Whether it is the father that exercises these skills or the midwife, or some other person, matters less than that they are exercised by someone, and preferably by as many people as possible.

Overview and summary

All mothers will experience some stress and anxiety in labour but high levels can adversely affect the mother and the baby. They are likely to be associated with any factor which appears to place the mother or baby at risk during childbirth and with traumatic or negative previous experiences. High levels of pain are common in childbirth, though the experience of labour pain varies considerably. A large number of physiological, psychological and pharmacological variables have been related to the nature and intensity of pain in labour.

Antenatal education aims to prepare women for childbirth and to reduce their anxieties and the pain they experience at that time.

Research into the effectiveness of this education is fraught with methodological difficulties but generally indicates that attendance at antenatal classes is associated with some limited reduction in pain and stress in labour but does not reduce anticipatory anxiety. Obstetric and procedural information is acquired by most class attenders but accurate experiential information does not seem to be absorbed. Research indicates that this kind of information is maximally effective in helping subjects to cope with painful and distressing health care procedures such as surgery. It is therefore likely that it would be of considerable benefit to women in labour.

It is difficult to provide preparatory information which will exactly correspond to the childbirth experience of every parturient. Information which is given a considerable time before birth may also be forgotten. Therefore class-based antenatal preparation may need to be supplemented by the provision of individualized information around the time of birth – intranatal as well as antenatal education. The attendant midwife would be well placed to provide such information which could be precisely tailored to the situation, needs and personality of the individual parturient.

Women use a wide range of coping strategies during labour, some of which they were taught at antenatal classes and some of which they acquired through the experience of coping with previous instances of pain and stress. The use of strategies such as relaxation or breathing techniques is associated with some modulation of labour pain. Attendance at classes does not ensure the use of such strategies during childbirth, since some women who attend classes subsequently find it impossible to use the strategies they have been taught at a time when they are suffering intense pain and anxiety. It could be useful if antenatal (and intranatal) trainers incorporated the strategies that women habitually use to cope with pain and stress into their education regimen, so that parturients could utilize strategies with which they were familiar; which were well rehearsed, and which they believed would work. Research indicates that this belief in the efficacy of your coping strategies is particularly important in successful adaptation to pain and stress.

Women who successfully use coping strategies during labour are likely to feel an increased sense of personal control in labour. This sense of personal control has sometimes been contrasted with the belief that the staff are in control during childbirth, with staff control being consequentially downvalued. However, close enquiry into perceptions of control during childbirth reveals that the two concepts are intertwined and suggests that positively perceived staff control enhances personal control, modulates the experience of pain and increases the parturient's sense of personal satisfaction in her childbirth. These findings indicate that midwives should do everything possible to bring about a positive perception of their role in helping the woman to cope with her labour. Factors which may be associated with this positive perception include attendance at antenatal classes, effective analgesic relief and the parturient's use of coping strategies.

The amount of social support the midwife gives during labour is also likely to affect the parturient's experience and her perceptions of the care she receives. Research studies carried out in America have shown that the continuous presence of an experienced, supportive woman in labour is associated with a more efficient labour, with lower rates of assisted delivery and with a healthier baby. These studies involved the use of a *doula* – a lay woman who gave constant emotional and physical support throughout active labour and delivery. However midwives in this country are well placed to give similar psychological support, information, encouragement, physical comforting and monitoring.

Some aspects of the *doula's* role could also be performed by the parturient's partner or other chosen birth companion, though he or she would need to have sufficient experience and knowledge of childbirth if the giving of information was to be effective. Perhaps this aspect of psychological care is best left to midwifery staff, with the birth companion providing the continuous presence, the support and encouragement, and the physical comforting.

The father of the baby and partner of the parturient is the person who is nowadays most likely to act as a companion for the woman in childbirth. However, some men refuse to perform this role and some women prefer to cope with childbirth by themselves or with the assistance of a female companion. It is important that maternity staff recognize that the presence of the partner during labour is not always helpful for the parturient, or for her partner who typically finds the experience anxiety-provoking and distressing as well as exciting and rewarding. It is best if parturients and their partners are allowed to decide for themselves about the presence and identity of the birth companion and if staff do not automatically assume that fathers should be there and consequently drag them into the labour ward with the same alacrity with which formerly they threw them out.

Women who are unaccompanied in labour should receive extra psychological support from the attendant staff. Those who are accompanied by a partner who is there in body but not in spirit probably need the same degree of staff involvement. The father's apparent uninterest may however reflect his confusion, his feelings of inadequacy, his anxieties about the well-being of his partner and their baby, and his distress at witnessing her pain. Antenatal or intranatal education of fathers might reduce some of these anxieties and allow him to act as a more effective birth companion. Supporting the father may help him to support the mother and since he knows and loves her so well (usually) he is potentially the best supporter she can have.

Some births are likely to be especially stressful for the mother and father if the mother and/or baby are at risk, or if the previous perinatal experience has been bad. In these cases, maternity staff need to give maximal psychological care to both parents. It is, I think, unethical in such circumstances to depend upon the father's supportive abilities. He is unlikely to be able to perform the supportive role adequately since he will be highly anxious and upset. The mother will need the very best of psychological as well as physical care to enable her to deliver safely and efficiently. She should not be dependent on her partner for such care; it places too large a responsibility upon him which could devastate both of them if things go wrong. The father in this case needs psychological care for himself, not just in order to facilitate his supportive qualities. Midwifery staff should therefore include the father in their care-giving during every childbirth, but especially in those which are associated with risk or loss.

Some births, particularly those which take place at home, will be attended by other family members, or by friends. As in all births, the midwife's aim should be to maximize the care that is given to the mother in childbirth. Friends and relatives who are acting as birth companions need to be encouraged and educated towards providing her with optimal psychological care. Children who are present at the birth need to be cared for, so that any anxiety and distress they might experience does not affect the parturient. The principles of professional care are the same, though the circumstances of the birth and the constituents of the family to be cared for may vary. Everything should be done to increase the amount of support that can be given to the woman in childbirth from the midwife and from any other people who are present at the birth and are capable of giving support. The midwife should also assume responsibility for supporting the woman's family if they are present during the birth in order to improve their experience and to prevent them exacerbating her stress, pain and anxiety.

Further reading

Beck N., Geden E. A., Brouder G. T. (1979). Preparation for labour: a historical perspective. *Psychosom. Med.*, **41**, 243–58.

Lewis C. (1986). *Becoming a Father.* Milton Keynes: Open University Press.

Melzack R. (1984). The myth of painless childbirth. *Pain,*19, 321–37.

Niven C. (1991). Coping with labour pain: the midwives' role. In *Midwives, Research and Childbirth. Volume 3* (Robinson, S., Thomson A., eds). London: Chapman and Hall.

Oakley A. (1979). *Becoming a Mother.* Oxford: Robertson.

References

Ascher B.H. (1978). Maternal anxiety in pregnancy and foetal homeo-stasis. *Obstet. Gynaecol. Nursing*, May/June, 18–21.

Astbury J. (1980). Labour pain: the role of childbirth education, information and education. In *Problems in Pain* (Peck C., Wallace M., eds). London: Pergamon.

Beail N., McGuire J. (1982). *Fathers: Psychological Perspectives.* London: Junction Books.

Beck N., Geden E. A., Brouder G. T. (1979). Preparation for labour: a historical perspective. *Psychosom. Med.*, **41**, 243–58.

Bonica J. J. (1984). Labour pain. In *Textbook of Pain* (Wall P. D., Melzack R., eds). Edinburgh: Churchill Livingstone.

Bonnel A. M., Boureau F.(1985). Labour pain assessment: validity of a behavioral index. *Pain*, **22**, 81–90.

Brant H. A.(1962). Childbirth with preparation and support in labour: an assessment. *N. Z. Med. J.*, **61**, 211.

Brazelton T. B. (1961). Effect of maternal medication on the neonate and his behaviour. *J. Paediatr.*, **58**, 513–18.

Brewin C., Bradley C. (1982). Perceived control and the experience of childbirth. *Br. J. Clin. Psychol.*, **21**, 263–9.

Brown A. (1982). Fathers in the labour ward: medical and lay accounts. In *The Father Figure: Some Current Orientations and Historical Perspectives* (McKee L., O'Brien M., eds). London: Tavistock.

Burns J. K. (1976). Relation between blood levels of cortisol and duration of human labour. *J. Physiol.*, **254**, 12–13.

Byrne-Lynch A. (1990). Self-efficacy and childbirth. *J. Reprod. Infant Psychol.*, **8**, 300.

Cartwright A. (1979). *The Dignity of Labour: A study of childbearing and induction*. London: Tavistock.

Currer C. (1986). Health concepts and illness behaviour: the care of Pathan mothers in Britain. Unpublished PhD thesis. University of Warwick.

Dick-Read G. (1942) *Revelation of Childbirth*. London: William Heinemann.

Drescher V. M., Gantt W. H., Whitehead W. E. (1980). Heart rate response to touch. *Psychosom. Med.*, **42**, 559–65.

Eysenck S. B. G. (1961). Personality and pain assessment in childbirth in married and unmarried mothers. *J. Mental Sci.*, **123**, 123–9.

Fox C. A. (1979). The effects of catecholamines and drug treatment on the foetus and newborn. *Birth Family J.*, **5**, 157–65.

Garcia J. (1982). Women's views of antenatal care. In *Effectiveness and Satisfaction in Antenatal Care* (Erkin M., Chalmers I., eds). London: Heinemann Medical.

Henneborn W., Cogan R. (1975). The effect of husband participation on reported pain and probability of medication during labour and birth. *J. Psychosom. Res.*, **19**, 215–22.

Hiller C. A., Slade P. (1989). The impact of antenatal classes on knowledge, anxiety and confidence in primiparous women. *J. Reprod. Infant Psychol.*, **7**, 3–15.

Homans H. (1982). Pregnancy and birth as rites of passage for two groups of women in Britain. In *Ethnography of Fertility and Birth* (MacCormack C., ed.). London: Academic Press.

Janis I. L. (1958). *Psychological Stress*. New York: Wiley.

Johnson J., Rice V., Fuller S., Endress M. (1978). Sensory information, instructions to a coping strategy and recovery from surgery. *Res. Nursing Health*, **1**, 4–17.

Johnston M., Carpenter L. (1980). Relationship between pre-operative anxiety and post-operative state. *Psychol. Med.*, **10**, 361–7.

Jones A. D., Dougherty C. (1984). Attendance at antenatal classes and clinics, medical intervention during birth and implications for 'natural childbirth'. *J. Reprod. Infant Psychol.*, **2**, 49–60.

Kennel J. H., Klaus M. J., McGrath S. et al. (1988). Medical intervention: the effect of social support in labor. *J. Pediatr. Res.*, **5**, 28–31.

Kirkham M. (1989). Midwives and information giving during labour. In *Midwives, Research and Childbirth, Volume 1* (Robinson S., Thomson A. M. eds). London: Chapman and Hall.

Kitzinger S. (1989). Perceptions of pain in home and hospital deliveries. In *The Free Woman: Women's Health in the 1990s* (van Hall E. V., Everaerd W., eds). Lancashire: Parthenon.

Klaus M. H., Kennel J. H., Robertson S. S., Sosa R. (1986). Effects of social support during parturition on maternal and infant morbidity. *Br. Med. J.*, **293**, 585–7.

Klaus M., Klaus P. *Mothering the Mother*. In press.

Kondas O., Scetnicka B. (1972). Systematic desensitisation as a method of preparation for childbirth. *J. Behav. Ther. Exp. Psychiatry*, **3**, 51–4.

Lederman R. P., Lederman E., Work B. A., McCann B. S. (1978). The relationship of maternal anxiety, plasma catecholamines and plasma cortisol to progress in labor. *Am. J. Obstet. Gynecol.*, **132**, 495–500.

Lewis C. (1986). *Becoming a Father*. Milton Keynes: Open University Press.

Ley P. (1982). Giving information to patients. In *Social Psychology and Behavioral Medicine* (Eiser J. R., ed.). Chichester: Wiley.

Lumley J., Astbury J. (1980). *Birth Rites: Birth Rights*. Melbourne: Sphere Books.

McCorkle R. (1974). Effects of touch on seriously ill patients. *Nursing Res.*, **23**, 125–32.

McIntosh J. (1989). Models of childbirth and social class: a study of 80 working class primigravidae. In *Midwives, Research and Childbirth, Volume 1* (Robinson S., Thomson A. M., eds). London: Chapman and Hall.

Melzack R. (1984). The myth of painless childbirth. *Pain*, **19**, 321–37.

Melzack R., Schaffelberg D. (1987). Low back pain during labor. *Am. J. Obstet. Gynecol.*, **156**, 901–5.

Melzack R., Wall P. D. (1988). *The Challenge of Pain*. 2nd edn. London: Penguin.

Michie S., Marteau T. M., Kidd J. (1990). Antenatal classes: knowingly undersold? *J. Reprod. Infant Psychol.*, **8**, 248.

Morgan B., Bulpitt C. J., Clifton P., Lewis, P. J. (1982). Analgesia and satisfaction in childbirth. *Lancet*, **2**, 808–10.

Nettlebladt P., Fagerstrom C-F., Ugddenberg N. (1976). The significance of reported childbirth pain. *J. Psychosom. Res.*, **20**, 215–21.

Niven C. (1985). How helpful is the presence of the husband at childbirth? *J. Reprod. Infant Psychol.*, **3**, 45–53.

Niven C. (1986). Factors affecting labour pain. Unpublished doctoral thesis. University of Stirling.

Niven C. (1987). The assessment of pain in childbirth. Paper presented at the Annual Conference of the International Society for Psychophysics. University of Stirling, Scotland.

Niven C. (1988). Labour pain: long term recall and consequences. *J. Reprod. Infant Psychol.*, **6**, 83–7.

Niven C. Coping with labour pain: the midwives' role. In *Midwives, Research and Childbirth. Volume 3* (Robinson S., Thomson A., eds). London: Chapman and Hall. In press.

Niven C., Garden I. (1986). Coping with dysmenorrhoea. Report to Scottish Health Education Group, Edinburgh.

Niven C., Gijsbers K. (1984). Obstetric and non-obstetric factors related to labour pain. *J. Reprod. Infant Psychol.*, **2**, 61–78.

Niven C., Gijsbers K. Coping with labour pain. In press. Oakley A. (1979). *Becoming a Mother.* Oxford: Robertson. In press.

Oakley A., MacFarlane A., Chalmers I. (1982). Social class, stress and reproduction. In *Disease and the Environment* (Rees R. A., Purcell H., eds). Chichester: Wiley.

O'Driscoll K., Stonge J. M., Minogue M. (1973). Active management of labour. *Br. Med. J.*, **3**, 135–7.

Phares E. J. (1976). *Locus of Control in Personality.* Morristown, New Jersey: General Learning Fairway Press.

Ray C., Fitzgibbon G. (1981). Stress arousal and coping with surgery. *Psychol. Med.*, **11**, 741–6.

Reading A. E., Cox D. N. (1985). Psychosocial predictors of labour pain. *Pain*, **22**, 309–15.

Richman J., Goldthorp W. O. (1978). Fatherhood: the social construction of pregnancy and birth. In *The Place of Birth* (Kitzinger S., Davies J., eds). Oxford: Oxford University Press.

Scott-Palmer J., Skevington S. M. (1981). Pain during childbirth and menstruation: a study of locus of control. *J. Psychosom. Res.*, **25**, 151–5.

Skelton I. (1984). Acupuncture in labour. In: *Research and the Midwife* (Robinson S., Thomson A., eds). Conference Proceedings.

Slade P., McPherson S., Hune A., Maresh M. (1990). Expectations and experience of labour. *J. Reprod. Infant Psychol.*, **8**, 256.

Stewart D. (1982). Psychiatric symptoms following attempted natural childbirth. *Can. Med. Assoc. J.*, **127**, 713–16.

Tan S-Y. (1982). Cognitive and cognitive behavioural methods for pain control: a selective review. *Pain*, **12**, 201–28.

Watson E. (1984). Health of infants and use of health services by mothers of different ethnic groups in East London. *Commun. Med.*, **6**, 127–35.

White D., Woolet A. (1987). The father's role in the neonatal period. In *Parent Infant Relationships* (Harvey D., ed.). London: Wiley.

Williams S., Dickson D., Forbes J. et al. (1989). An evaluation of community antenatal care. *Midwifery*, **5**, 63–8.

Wolkind S., Zajicek E. (1981). *Pregnancy: A Psychological and Social Study.* London: Academic Press.

Woolet A., Dosanjh-Matwala N. (1990). Asian women's experiences of childbirth in East London: the support of fathers and female relatives. *J. Reprod. Infant Psychol.*, **8**, 11–23.

Woolet A., Lyon L., White D. (1983). The reactions of East London women to medical intervention in childbirth. *J. Reprod. Infant Psychol.*, **1**, 37–46.

Worthington E. L. Jr. (1982). Labor room and laboratory: clinical validation of the cold pressor test as a means of testing preparation for childbirth strategies. *J. Psychosom. Res.*, **26**, 223–30.

Wuitchik M., Bakal D., Lipshitz J. (1989). The clinical significance of pain and cognitive activity in latent labor. *Obstet. Gynecol.*, **73**, 35–41.

3 Immediate postnatal period

- The mother's experience
- The baby's abilities
- Mother–infant interaction
- The father
- Overview and summary
- Further reading
- References

This period covers the first week of the baby's life and the beginning of at least 16 years of parenting for the father and mother.

Following a hospital birth, the mother and baby may spend the first postnatal week in hospital. Increasingly however early discharge is becoming the norm so that many healthy mothers and babies will spend most of that time at home with the father and any of the baby's siblings. Psychologically this can be advantageous in that it allows the family to become familiar with its new member and to enact their new roles as soon as possible, avoiding the disruption of these processes imposed by separation. However it means that no matter how supportive the community services provided, the full responsibility for the baby, 24 hours a day, is shifted from the hospital staff with all their experience and expertise to often inexperienced, inexpert and exhausted parents.

The mother's experience

The first hours following the birth are characterized by physical exhaustion – labour is indeed hard work – and a range of intense emotional reactions which are determined primarily by the nature of the birth experience and the condition of the baby. When the birth has gone well, mothers are often 'high as a kite'; excited, elated and in an exalted frame of mind. However mothers whose birth experiences have been more negative are likely to feel very unhappy (Thune-Larson and Moller-Pedersen, 1988). Under normal circumstances these feelings moderate until the onset of the 'fourth-day blues'. These in fact can be third, fourth or fifth day blues and are not best described as 'blues' – a mild form of depression or feeling down – but as emotional lability. British mothers most commonly report feeling tearful, tired, anxious, over-emotional, up and down in mood, low-spirited and muddled in thinking (Kennerley and Gath, 1986). Feelings of depression were apparent in a smaller group of women who participated in this study. An Australian study (Hapgood et al., 1988) where subjects rated their mood state daily for 2 weeks following childbirth also found that lability of mood was the most significant emotional feature at this time.

This study found an association between lability of mood in the puerperium and the presence of psychiatric symptoms up to 14 months later. Particularly marked and prolonged blues have also been associated with the subsequent occurrence of postnatal depression (Cox, 1986; Sandler et al., 1990). This is not to say that all women who have the blues will go on to suffer from postnatal depression or some other form of postnatal mental illness (see Chapter 6). However it suggests that some women may progress from mild emotional disturbance in the first few postpartum weeks to more serious mental illness later.

For the mother the first postnatal week is therefore a time of fluctuating emotions, the intensity and nature of which are somewhat unpredictable. This can make her feel somewhat uncertain about her reactions to events, and this uncertainty can increase the strain of caring for a new baby and adjusting to motherhood. Fortunately the existence of the blues is well recognized and most mothers will be prepared for a weepy phase somewhere in the first week. However the nature of the emotional lability may be understood less well, especially by non-professional carers looking after the mother at home. Midwives all know how tiresome postnatal women can be, always bursting into tears or resenting the slightest wrong word. (Of course they usually deal with this with professional kindness and understanding.) Now that postnatal women are cared for at home, fathers and other non-professional carers need to be prepared for the appearance of the blues by the community midwife and to be supported by her/him in coping with its manifestations.

Although postnatal women can appear to act irrationally or become upset unnecessarily, much of their behaviour is understandable if the experience of the new mother is looked at more closely.

New mothers would be likely to have problems in sleeping even if they didn't have to care for their baby during the night. Excitement, anxiety and change are all likely to affect sleeping patterns – and new mothers have plenty to be excited and anxious about! Mothers who are caring for their baby at home will necessarily have their sleep disrupted by the need to feed the baby during the night. (Even if the father feeds the baby at night, and less than 20% of British fathers share this task equally with their wives (Beail, 1985), few mothers would sleep through night feeds in the immediate postnatal period.)

If the mother is in hospital she may be relieved of this task, but sleeping in a strange environment with lights and strange noises is always difficult, so she still may have problems in sleeping soundly. If the hospital operates a 24-hour rooming-in policy, her sleep will be disrupted not only by her own baby's cries and feeding needs but by those of all the other babies in the ward.

Woolet and Dosanjh-Matwala (1990) found that 44% of a sample of London Asian women complained of having insufficient rest while in hospital. The authors attributed this in part to the emphasis Asian cultures place on the need for rest and recuperation after child-birth – an emphasis which is not apparent in current British obstetric practice. However Ball (1989), using a substantial sample of ethnic majority British women, found that 41% recorded low satisfaction with their rest in hospital, the main cause of which was their lack of sleep at night. This was more marked in the units where 24-hour rooming-in was practised. Therefore cultural differences are not apparent here. Lack of deep sleep contributes to feelings of depression and lethargy (Weinmann, 1981) so this factor is likely to cause emotional upset in many new mothers. Ball found that it was significantly related to a lack of emotional well-being and to low self-esteem in her subjects.

These findings would suggest that enabling mothers to have suffi-cient sleep is a simple but important way of giving them psychological support. While mothers are in hospital, midwives could consider whether they might benefit more from a couple of nights of undisturbed sleep before going home to face an extended series of broken nights, than from the opportunity to be with their baby 24 hours a day. Of course some mothers will not wish to be separated from their baby at any time but other mothers, perhaps especially multiparous ones, would welcome a couple of nights of undisturbed rest. Breast-feeding mothers will need to feed their babies during the night if they are to stimulate their milk production adequately, but their babies could be cared for by the staff for the rest of the night along with the babies of bottle-feeding mothers. Mothers who stay in hospital for a prolonged period of time following childbirth should be offered the opportunity to stay in a single room so that they can become familiar with their own baby's night-time routines but not be disturbed by the wakening of other babies. All postnatal women should be encouraged to sleep whenever possible, during the day as well as at night, so they can recuperate from the exertions of childbirth and acquire as much rest as possible while their baby is night-waking.

Many units promote 24-hour rooming-in in order to facilitate mother–infant bonding. Even the strongest advocates of the importance of early and extended contact to the formation of the mother–infant bond, Klaus and Kennel, recommend that babies should be kept by their mothers during the day but be brought to them for feeding during the night, rather than have them permanently by their bedside (Klaus and Kennel, 1982). So a need to promote bonding need not entail sleepless nights for new mothers. Anyway, the importance of early, extended contact may have been overstated (see below). I suspect that 24-hour rooming-in may also be promoted because it provides an efficient (i.e. cheaper) way of managing postnatal wards with fewer staff – but then I'm just an old cynic.

The unfortunate reality of staff shortages may involve postnatal mothers in engaging in more self-help than is strictly desirable, especially when they have experienced complications such as Caesarian section.

After having such a big operation [Caesarian] I was in need of rest, I was left to look after my child. Doctors say you mustn't go home, you need rest. But I would have got more rest at home (subject of Woolet and Dosanjh-Matwala, 1990).

In a study concerned with indications and outcomes of Caesarian section carried out in a Glasgow hospital (see Chapter 4), Hillan (1989) noted that only 56% of subjects who had a section felt that they had enough rest in the postnatal wards. Her control group, who had vaginal deliveries, were more satisfied with the amount of rest that they had, except for one woman who said that 'she didn't get enough rest because she had to help the women who had been delivered by Caesarian section too much' (Hillan, 1989, p. 164).

It seems therefore that maternity hospitals are not providing many of their postnatal mothers with sufficient opportunities to rest after the birth of their babies. (Edith Hillan and Jean Ball, cited above, are both midwives so this is not a case of 'outsiders' being critical of midwifery practice.) Though some mothers may be fit and ready for anything the moment they have delivered, most mothers require some period of recuperation before taking on round-the-clock care, and assuming total responsibility for an infant – responsibilities and care which will last for many, many years. There is a well known myth that women in 'primitive' societies give birth by the side of the fields and immediately restart their interrupted tasks. In fact most societies proscribe normal activity for mothers for a considerable time after the birth and allow them to take up their mothering role gradually. In 'primitive' societies they may be separated from the rest of the tribe and cared for by female members of the family; they may have special foods to eat, be required to rest; and their families and the new infant may be taken care of by other relatives (Paige and Paige, 1981). Underlining these practices is often the idea that women who have given birth are 'unclean' – as menstruating women are – a belief that many of us might wish to challenge (Dobson, 1988). However, the practices themselves ensure that the new mother and her baby are given a lot of care and attention – a situation that many modern mothers giving birth in more 'civilized' societies might envy.

Sleep deprivation and insufficient rest are likely to remain a problem for most mothers for many weeks after they bring the baby home (see Chapter 5). Feeding problems can continue for some time as well but many mothers find that their initial anxieties over feeding are only temporary (Ball, 1989). However as Moss et al. (1987) have reported, first-time mothers are more concerned about infant feeding than about any other aspect of postnatal adjustment or care. Almost 70% of their London subjects said that the early feeds had been anxiety-provoking or problematic in some way and some of these mothers were unhappy about the help they received with these problems from hospital staff, especially at night. This unfortunate finding has been echoed by Ball who showed that problems with feeding were related to an inability to obtain enough rest in hospital and to the provision of conflicting advice about how, when and what to feed.

Thomson (1989) found that mothers in a Scottish hospital were subject to a:

hospital breast feeding policy which took no account of the physiology of lactation. They [the mothers] were only allowed to feed every four hours and only for restricted times at each feed. They were also required to give a complementary feed after each breast feed. They were therefore not giving adequate stimulation to the breast to produce enough milk to meet the babies' needs (Thomson, 1989, p. 268).

These mothers were also subjected to conflicting advice: 'When we were given the fourth set of advice from the fourth person in four days, we [the mother and the baby] were both totally confused (subject of Thomson, 1989, p. 233). It was therefore hardly surprising that a third of the sample had abandoned breast-feeding by 6 weeks after the birth.

Hopefully few hospitals now implement such rigid feeding regimens, so that mothers who intend to breast-feed can receive better support. However, breast-feeding mothers are then faced with the giving of more frequent feeds and/or more prolonged feeds, and the necessity for night feeding. So even although most breast-feeding mothers will take pride in providing their baby with 'the best' – the breast – establishing successful breast-feeding can have some drawbacks.

One of these is nipple pain. Drewett and colleagues (1987) found that over 60% of their sample of breast-feeding mothers drawn from a north of England district general hospital experienced nipple pain on the second postpartum day, a third of whom characterized it as 'distressing', 'horrible' or 'excruciating' at worst. Although the incidence of nipple pain declined gradually, 20–25% of subjects still had pain on the 15th and 30th days. Uterine cramps associated with feeding were also most prevalent on the second postpartum day, and along with perineal or episiotomy pain (Reading, 1982) combine to make the postnatal woman's experience of feeding far from comfortable. Illingworth and Stone (1952) have shown that nipple pain is more prevalent when rigid feeding regimens are practised, as in the hospital where Thomson's research was undertaken (see above). Thomson (1989) found that nipple pain was given as the second most common reason for abandoning breast-feeding by her subjects, so the occurrence of intense discomfort during feeding can have lasting consequences which may affect the baby as well as the mother.

Research involving ethnic minority women who follow traditional Pathan Muslim practices as far as possible shows that many did not have female relatives in this country who were available to provide the traditional forms of female support which should be given to the woman in the postnatal period (Currer, 1986). In hospital these women regarded the midwives as surrogate sisters who replaced their own sisters in teaching them important child care tasks like bathing the baby. This standing in for absent kin places female staff in a special position with regard to the care of these women. It allows them to provide much needed support which can substitute for family provision in an unusually effective way so that the care and attention given to the woman and her baby (especially physical attention paid to the baby) are greatly appreciated. It is also likely to maximize the impact of the education and advice given.

However Currer (1986) records some instances where the surrogate sisters did not seem to provide adequate care. Some of her subjects felt that they had been ignored by staff or that the staff were hostile towards them. Sometimes their customs were denied in ways which seemed unnecessary. For instance, the requirements of purdah that women should not be seen in bed by the male visitors of other mothers could be satisfied by the pulling of the curtains round the bed during visiting time. But apparently this angered some of the staff and was prevented. Specially butchered meat is required by Muslim women but is generally not provided by maternity hospitals. In the past, extra amounts of food which could be eaten was normally provided to compensate for the lack of halal meat. However, new catering practices make this difficult, so mothers are given normal-sized portions of food, some of which is prohibited. Thus Currer found that her subjects were faced with the choice of breaking their religious practices or going hungry – which is clearly not in the interest of mother or baby. Many mothers solved this dilemma by getting food brought in from home – a strategy which seems to be utilized by increasing numbers of ethnic majority hospitalized mothers as well but which goes against the ideal of the provision of proper care.

It is therefore obvious that mothers who are in their first postnatal week have a number of sensible reasons for feeling weepy, crotchety or 'not my usual self'. They will also, like all of us who have just come through some major life event, feel a bit deflated – remember how you felt after your finals! Add to this the effects of wildly fluctuating hormone levels and you have the perfect prescription for the blues. Studies carried out in other cultures, for example Morbach's (1983) study of Japanese mothers, show that though the incidence of the blues is similar to that in the UK, the nature of its symptoms varies. In Japan, where motherhood is very highly valued and copious postnatal support is provided by the family, the blues are less blue. Emotional lability is characterized more by positive feelings than by negative ones, presumably reflecting the culture's view of motherhood and the care and consideration given to its new mothers.

Midwives cannot unaided change our society's view of motherhood but they can ensure that new mothers receive as much practical and emotional support as possible. In hospital and in the community this involves recognizing the concerns of postnatal mothers and addressing them in ways which are likely to ameliorate them, not exacerbate them. For instance, staff collaboration over the provision of advice is vital so that conflicting opinions are not pressed on anxious and confused mothers. Women who are suffering severe pain, whether nipple pain, uterine pain, episiotomy pain or incision pain, should be offered analgesics which will not affect breast milk and/or be coached in the use of pain-coping strategies – one of my labour pain subjects for example used the breathing techniques taught at antenatal classes to cope with severe nipple pain, and found them very effective (see Chapter 2; Coping with childbirth). Nipple pain may also be prevented, or at least made less likely, if mothers are guided by staff into implementing helpful practices such as avoiding incorrect placement of the baby at the breast and the use of rigid feeding regimens (Illingworth and Stone, 1952). Since nipple pain and uterine cramps peak at 2 days postpartum, when many women return home, hospital and community staff should ensure that this problem does not 'slip through the net' and fail to be treated by either party.

Community staff are especially well placed to encourage husbands and families to provide emotional support as well as practical support to the new mother in their care. Time spent teaching the father about his partner's needs is likely to be time well spent. He is better placed to meet them than an overworked community midwife. His own needs are considered below (see The father) but meanwhile I want to consider the issue of bonding.

The first postnatal week is the time for getting to know the baby. This is when, according to some theorists, the mother becomes quickly and fully attached or bonded to her baby. Other theorists would consider that maternal attachment has already been initiated during pregnancy, and still others would look at attachment as a long-term process. Bonding theorists, the most prominent of whom are the American paediatricians Klaus and Kennel, originally suggested that close intimate physical contact between mother and baby must occur immediately after birth and recur frequently throughout the first few postnatal days in order for the mother to become adequately bonded to her baby. This theory was based on the results of a number of studies in which groups of mothers were given extra contact with their babies over the first few postnatal days. The behaviour of these mothers in interacting with their babies was subsequently compared with that of mothers who only had routine contact with their babies, which at that time in American hospitals consisted mainly of contact for feeding – rooming-in was not the norm. Klaus and Kennel found differences in maternal behaviour which apparently lasted for up to 2 years (Klaus and Kennel, 1976). These behaviours – more eye contact, more fondling, more attentiveness during medical examination of the baby, different speech patterns – were taken as evidence of increased maternal attachment to the baby.

Klaus and Kennel's findings were widely publicized and were influential in changing hospital practice, enabling mothers to have extra contact with their babies on a routine basis. However, they also raised anxieties about bonding in mothers who had to be separated from their babies at birth or during the first postnatal days because of maternal illness, premature delivery or other neonatal problems. Some academics and practitioners interpreted the findings of these studies as showing that these mothers would inevitably have problems in forming normal bonds with their offspring.

Put as simply as this, bonding doctrine (as the hard-line version of bonding theory became known) should make you all pause for thought. Surely you've known mothers who have been separated from their babies at birth, but who subsequently doted on them? And what about adoptive parents – don't they love and care for their children; children with whom they had no early postnatal contact? It gave many researchers pause for thought as well, so numerous studies have been carried out to test Klaus and Kennel's findings. A number of these, e.g. Carlsson et al. (1978), De Chateau and Wiberg (1977), Hales et al. (1977), found that extra contact was associated with an apparent increase in maternal attachment behaviours in the short term, i.e. during the first few postnatal days. However, Carlsson et al. (1979) found no difference between extended-contact and routine-contact mothers at 6 weeks and Svejda et al. (1980), using a double-blind experimental design and random assignment of mothers to extra-contact and routine-contact groups, found no differences at all in maternal behaviour between the two groups.

It therefore seems sensible to conclude that close, intimate physical contact immediately after birth and in the first few postnatal days is not essential for adequate bonding. Or as Klaus and Kennel themselves put it:

At present there are no definitive studies to either confirm or refute the existence of a sensitive period [for bonding] or to assess the length of time required in the first hours and days after birth to produce such an effect (Klaus and Kennel, 1983, p. 575).

They go on to say:

Obviously, in spite of a lack of early contact experience by mother in [American] hospital births in the past 20 to 30 years, almost all these parents became bonded to their babies. The human is highly adaptable, and there are many fail safe routes to attachment. Sadly, some parents who miss the bonding experience (during extended contact in the first postnatal days) have felt that all was lost for their future relationship. This was and is completely incorrect (Klaus and Kennel, 1983, p. 576).

Staff shortages in maternity hospitals and the trend towards early postpartum community care are as likely to ensure that babies are cared for from birth onwards by mothers rather than by midwives as any theoretical concerns. It is important however that staff realize that the period after birth and during the first few postnatal days is no longer seen as critical for the development of bonding. Therefore a mother who doesn't want to cuddle or suckle her baby immediately after birth is not at risk of failure to bond. Neither is the mother who feels too exhausted or too sore to show much interest in her baby. Robson and Kumar (1980) have shown that such feelings are quite common immediately following delivery, but normally dissipate within the first few postnatal days. Furthermore Woolet and Dosanjh-Matwala (1990) have shown that women who come from cultural groups where the baby is regarded as the property of the extended family and is cared for by them rather than by the individual mother do not regard mother–infant bonding as a significant cause for concern. So staff should not be alarmed if these women appear to be less anxious about bonding to their babies than ethnic majority women who have 'read all about it' in our culture's literature on parenthood.

The amount and type of contact a mother has with her baby in the first few postnatal days can therefore be determined by the mother's needs and feelings, not by a necessity to bond her to her offspring. 'Attachment' and 'bonding' are just scientific euphemisms for 'love' and we all know that love is sometimes at first sight, sometimes a more gradual process and that sometimes we initially loathed the person we have come to love now we know them better. If you ask mothers about how they come to love their babies you get much the same answers, e.g. 'I fell in love with him the moment I set eyes on him and it's never changed since'; 'At first I found her boring. I'm getting closer now but I still need more time. But I know I'll get closer, very close; it was just the same with my first child'. 'Feelings grow and change, they don't remain static. The more feelings you have the more you get out of the relationship' (mothers discussing their feelings of attachment to their babies; Wiszniewski, 1988, pp. 17, 18).

So far we have looked at the immediate postnatal period from the mother's point of view only. We can't examine it from the baby's point of view as we can't ask her/him if s/he has one – if only babies could talk! We can however examine their abilities which they demonstrate in a number of non-verbal ways. Some of these are laid out in the following section.

The baby's abilities

Psychologists, like parents, have long puzzled over neonate abilities. What can s/he do; what can s/he see or hear? We used to think, precious little. The neonate's mind was held to be a blank slate. The world s/he existed in was a 'booming buzzing confusion' (James, 1890). In recent years much painstaking research has revealed that young babies have a host of abilities, many of which make it easier for adults to interact with them satisfactorily and care for them efficiently.

For instance, newborn babies 'prefer' – will look longer at – face-like stimuli – light-coloured, oval shapes with dark areas corresponding to the placement of eyes, nose and mouth – to stimuli of similar size, shape, and light and dark distribution (Fantz, 1963). They also prefer moving stimuli to stationary ones (Carpenter, 1974), solid objects to two-dimensional ones (Fantz, 1966) and shapes with strong contours (Salapatek, 1975). Although this doesn't necessarily mean that they prefer real faces over Mr Men stickers or Cabbage Patch dolls, it does mean that they will spend a lot of their waking moments looking at any available face rather than at other interesting but non-human patterns, such as the wallpaper. Newborn babies don't seem able to discriminate between one face and another, partly because they concentrate their attention on the outer contours of a face, rather than its inner features (Salapatek, 1975; perhaps this is why a new hairdo can upset babies). Babies of 3 months, however, scan the internal as well as the external features of a shape and can discriminate between their mother's face and that of a stranger; between two strangers' faces, and even between facial expressions such as smiles and frowns (Barrera and Maurer, 1981).

Newborn babies are also especially sensitive (physiologically) to sounds which have the structural qualities of human speech in frequency, range and tonal shape (Hutt et al., 1968) and to the patterns of human speech such as its phonemic structure (Morse, 1972). Again this ensures that their perceptual abilities are directed towards humans and human interactions.

Adult human beings increase these perceptual effects by presenting their face to the baby's face, eyes to eyes, at a distance that is within the baby's focus, and by talking to babies so that speech sounds are always available (Schaffer, 1984). This may be instinctive behaviour, or it may be the result of imitation or trial-and-error learning, with the infant reinforcing the adult through her/his attention. These are matters which psychologists hotly debate. The most important point for you perhaps is to realize that these behaviours are produced without any need to train or encourage the adult accordingly.

Thus babies exist in a world of faces and voices with which they are well equipped to deal both physiologically and psychologically. And adults, in interacting facially and vocally with their babies (see Mother–infant interaction, below), are rewarded by the baby's attention. (If you don't think this is important, try interacting with someone who stares at the television rather than at you and listens to their portable cassette player rather than to the sound of your voice. Babies can be a lot more satisfying to interact with than teenagers, just because they pay you some attention.)

Babies are very good at learning. They learn through the mechanisms of classical and operant conditioning. In classical conditioning two stimuli are paired together (occur at the same time) and eventually the response which occurred to the first stimulus now occurs to the second. The famous example, no doubt quoted in your psychology lectures, was of Pavlov's dog, where the presentation of meat powder (stimulus) was paired with the sound of a bell. Eventually through the process of classical conditioning, the dog salivated (response) to the sound of the bell.

Babies learn by this conditioning process. For instance, in the laboratory they can be easily and quickly conditioned to a time pattern (Lipsitt, 1982), so an association between an event such as feeding or playing or bathing and a particular time or time interval can be easily learned by babies. They can also quickly learn to associate stimuli which are regularly paired with feeding with the feeding act itself, so that preparatory feeding actions (e.g. the mother loosening her blouse) produce rooting and suckling. These anticipatory behaviours can be observed in babies by the fourth feed (Call, 1964). (Later of course these can be clearly observed when babies scream the place down at the sound of the liquidizer or the sight of a bottle being heated.)

In operant conditioning (Skinner (1971) being the name you have most probably come across in this context) a behaviour which is followed by a positive reinforcement – a reward – is more likely to occur again. So student midwives who are praised for being kind and considerate to mothers are more likely to behave this way in the future than if their behaviour is ignored or disapproved of – 'you should be working, not wasting your time talking to mothers!' In the psychological laboratory, babies have demonstrated very rapid operant conditioning. For instance, they will learn to turn their head to the left or to the right if the desired direction of head-turning is reinforced by the provision of milk or a sweet solution. Obviously this works in real life as well, as babies are reinforced for head-turning and rooting by the provision of breast milk. Of course head-turning and rooting are innate responses to contact with the breast, but these innate reflexes are shaped by learning so that they become more efficient (quicker and more likely to lead to rapid attachment to the nipple), more flexible (they can operate from a variety of starting points) and more finely tuned to the actions and make-up of the feeder, so that the baby's behaviour during feeding will be disrupted by the unfamiliar actions of a substitute feeder (Call, 1964).

There is also some evidence to suggest that babies can learn by imitation from very early in life (Meltzoff and Moore, 1984). Experimental results, which apparently show babies a few hours old imitating adult gestures such as the sticking out of their tongue, are contentious since other researchers have failed to replicate them (find the same results when repeating the same experiment). Even if babies don't learn by imitation until they are somewhat older, the learning ability of the neonate is still remarkable.

Neonates display many abilities that I have not discussed here and interested readers are directed towards any textbook in developmental psychology to learn more about their visual and auditory capabilities, their olfactory and tactile capacities and their cognitive abilities. All the abilities I have discussed are related in some way to interaction. Babies look, listen and learn. The person they look at, listen to and learn from most frequently is their primary caretaker – typically, but not necessarily, their mother. Looking and listening are essential components of mother–infant interaction, and learning, as we will see, is often its result.

Mother–infant interaction

Interaction is a two-way process, so mothers look and listen as well as babies. As the baby grows older, mother–infant interactions become more complex and increasingly sophisticated (see Chapter 5). But simple interactions are apparent from the very beginning when they involve feeding and the establishment of regular and predictable sleep/wake cycles. These tasks involve both the mother and the baby attending to one another, adapting to one another and learning from one another. This is not a one-way process, with the mother training a helpless, passive infant either well or badly. Anyone who has ever tried to teach or train anyone or anything knows that it's not that simple. The recipient of the training has to be actively involved and the trainer has to adapt to his, her or its abilities, level of knowledge etc. It is just the same with babies, as you will see when we look at feeding and sleeping interactions in more detail.

Feeding, whether by breast or bottle, obviously involves two people whose actions need to be co-ordinated smoothly together so that the baby ingests the optimum amount of milk while expending the minimum amount of energy (otherwise more calories will have to be ingested to compensate for the increased requirements incurred by energy expenditure). As we have already discussed (see The baby's abilities, above) babies are innately programmed to root and suckle, and quickly learn to adapt and improve these abilities so that they attach and feed more efficiently. Their sucking behaviour can, and does, occur in the absence of milk (non-nutritive sucking) when the sucking rate is generally two sucks per second and is organized in a burst–pause fashion: suck, suck, suck, suck, suck, suck — pause — suck, suck, suck, suck, suck, suck, and so on. When milk or some other liquid is available, the rate of sucking is slower and the pauses are shorter. Indeed at the beginning of the feed there are continuous bursts of sucking (Wolff, 1968).

Mothers generally act to reinforce their baby's naturally occurring feeding behaviour. They hold the baby in such a way as to utilize the rooting response to direct the baby to the nipple, and they don't allow clothing to touch the baby's cheeks during attachment or feeding since this will misdirect head-turning and rooting. They generally avoid stimulating the baby during sucking bursts since this tends to interrupt them, but interact with the baby during the pauses (Kaye, 1977). Thus the baby in these instances is 'training' the mother whose task is to observe the baby's behaviours closely so she can adapt to them. Although most mothers are not conscious of doing so, it is evident that they do learn from the baby's behaviour, since the mothers of babies who do not display the normal regularities in feeding behaviour (such as premature babies) act differently during feeding sessions, for instance interacting more during bursts than during pauses (see Schaffer, 1984).

New, inexperienced mothers take time to adapt to their baby's feeding behaviour. At first they are relatively inefficient feeders when compared with experienced mothers or midwives. However, by the end of the first postnatal week, they are as efficient as the experienced multiparous mother, and both groups of mothers are more efficient than midwives. What changes most over this time is the mother's sensitivity to her own baby's behaviour during feeding. At first the inexperienced mothers tend to interrupt the baby more, attempting (unsuccessfully) to direct his/her behaviour; so they would try to make him feed when he was pausing and pause when he was feeding, whereas more experienced feeders would take their cues from the baby. However, frequent, repeated experience of feeding their own baby soon teaches them to act more like the experienced feeders. The midwives who participated in this study were also guided by the baby's feeding behaviour to some extent but, since they fed lots of babies, they didn't have the chance to study one particular baby's behaviour in detail or to adapt their feeding style to the needs of that one individual. Therefore with time, the mothers (or regular feeders) became more skilled than the most experienced staff (Thoman et al., 1970, 1971, 1972; see Schaffer, 1984).

This research into the basic interactions involved in feeding demonstrates some of the important aspects of mother–infant interaction which are involved in many different interactive situations (see Chapter 5). Some regularity of behaviour is necessary. In feeding it is provided by the baby's innate ability to root and suckle and by the pattern of feeding; the suck/pause routines, the prolonged bursts of sucking at the beginning of feeds and the more extended pauses which signal approaching satiation. Although the mother may not be consciously aware of these regularities or necessarily able to articulate them in the way that researchers do, she is quick to note any changes in the pattern, e.g. 'he's off his food today', and to comment on the meaning of the baby's behaviour. For example, mothers whose babies are at the prolonged pause stage of a feed often remark that 'she's had enough', 'he's sleepy', 'I'll just try and squeeze a bit more in', so they have obviously noted this regularly occurring behaviour and will usually respond to it. This observation of the baby's behaviour is important. If the mother fails to notice the baby's behaviour, perhaps because she is depressed or ill or is just too busy looking after a large family or coping with impossible circumstances, then she can't react to it and will fail to adjust her responses accordingly (see Chapter 5). For instance, trying to 'squeeze a bit more in' when the baby is signalling that the end of a feed is approaching is a strategy that many mothers attempt. It usually fails, so most mothers abandon it. But if the mother doesn't notice that the baby gets upset when she attempts to continue feeding him, or that he vomits up the extra milk half an hour later, then she might continue to use an unsuccessful feeding strategy instead of being guided by the feedback that the baby is providing.

Regularity in behaviour is provided by the mother or regular feeder as well. The way she picks up the baby, places him/her in the feeding position, interacts with him/her during feeding (sings, talks, strokes or snuggles) quickly assumes the regularity of a ritual. So her behaviour becomes predictable to the baby – s/he knows what's coming next and can react accordingly, as the research on anticipatory feeding behaviour shows (see The baby's abilities, above). Thus the baby reacts to what the mother usually does, and the mother reacts to what the baby usually does. Even although the onus is on the mother to adapt to the baby at this early stage in infant development, feeding interactions are not one-way affairs but are true interactions, with two partners participating. The speed with which a particular mother–infant pair build up this knowledge of one another's 'little ways' is apparent from the disruption of feeding which 1-week-old babies show if their regular feeder is changed (see Call, 1964, above).

Getting the baby to feed efficiently is probably the most important task of the neonatal period, since it is central to survival. However, the task which most mothers regard as equally important (and difficult) is that of getting the baby to sleep properly. Sleeping properly, in our culture, involves sleeping at night. Of course few mothers would expect a newborn baby to sleep the night through, but most have this as a clear aim in view which should be accomplished as soon as possible. Therefore any progression towards night-sleeping and day-waking is welcomed.

In other cultures, this emphasis is not so apparent. For instance, during the first 8 months or so of a baby's life, Kukwat mothers sleep with them in skin-to-skin contact, ready to suckle the moment they wake. (The fathers sleep elsewhere.) The babies sleep for short periods only and show no move towards sleeping more at night than during the day (Super and Harkness, 1982). British sleeping arrangements make this kind of approach unlikely to be popular with most mothers and fathers (though the provision of frequent breast-feeds night and day may optimally stimulate milk production).

All newborn babies tend to sleep for short periods of time and to be awake for even shorter periods which are randomly interspersed throughout the day and night. This pattern continues for the first few postnatal days with high levels of crying and restlessness. The mother spends a good deal of time trying to soothe the baby and get her/him off to sleep, but these interventions are generally unsuccessful. However by the end of the first postnatal week, her interventions appear to be more successful, and babies raised in western cultures already demonstrate a tendency to sleep longer at night and to be more wakeful and active during the day (Sander et al., 1979). These desirable developments were not so evident when the baby was cared for in a hospital nursery and was fed to a fixed schedule. When the baby roomed-in with the mother and demand feeding was practised, the mother could observe the baby's sleep/wake patterns more closely and gradually shape them so that they accorded more closely to a routine which she considered desirable. The results of this study make it obvious that the 'entrainment of states', as Schaffer (1984) calls the development of day-waking/night-sleeping, is a matter of 'shaping', i.e. of moving the baby slowly but progressively closer to a desired routine, rather that of imposing a strict time schedule.

Regular cyclic activity can be observed in utero (see Schaffer, 1984). This may be disrupted by the birth process and the need for the baby to adapt to an environment which is much more stimulating and diverse than the uterine one. Thus the irregular patterns of activity which are seen in the immediate postnatal period may be largely unrelated to the caretaker's behaviour – whatever she does, the baby will be restless and crying. As the baby recovers from birth and matures, so her/his own activity cycles will re-emerge. However, these temporal patterns can obviously be influenced by the caretaker. Otherwise all babies in all cultures would show the same patterns of day-waking and night-sleeping as ours do. Some cultures adapt more to night-waking and feeding than do others. The Kukwat might be regarded as being at one extreme – they adapt their lifestyle to allow the baby to feed and wake at night – and we might be at the other – we expect the baby to adapt, so Mummy can sleep with Daddy, Daddy can go to work, and Mummy can be wakeful during the day. No one culture's approach to the problems and demands of raising its young is right or wrong or best. But it's important to realize that these cultural differences do exist. We may be asking rather a lot of our babies in expecting them to adapt so quickly to our adult sleep/wake patterns. This doesn't mean we should abandon the attempt or put Daddy in the spare room. It merely suggests that mothers and their advisers shouldn't feel that they have failed if their babies don't sleep the night through.

Mothers and other infant caretakers influence the baby's sleep/wake cycle by reinforcing some behaviours and not others (see The baby's abilities, above). Day-waking is reinforced by feeding, attention, play, physical contact and stimulation. Night-waking is also reinforced by feeding and physical contact. However, most caretakers avoid utilizing the other reinforcers, so that gradually day-waking becomes more prevalent as it is subject to greater reinforcement. The time intervals between feeds are also manipulated so that the baby has the opportunity to learn that feeds normally occur at, say, 3-hourly intervals, not at hourly ones (as occurs in other cultures). Conditioning a baby to a temporal pattern is relatively easy, as was discussed in this chapter's section on The baby's abilities (see above). So babies can quickly learn to associate a particular time of day, or time interval, with a particular activity, provided this conditioning takes into account the basic needs of the baby for food and sleep which are affected by developmental maturity (a young or light baby needs more frequent feeding than a more mature baby). In fact babies learn these associations so well that caretakers disrupt temporal routines at their peril. Wake or feed a baby earlier than normal because you are going out, or off duty, and either s/he won't feed properly, or will feed fine and then be sick. Either way, the feeder will end up frustrated and the baby will be crying for more within a couple of hours.

Startlingly different approaches to infant care are apparent within as well as across cultures. Since Britain is a multicultural society, mothers of different ethnic origins may be influenced by traditional feeding or rearing practices, or may be more affected by the dominant British culture's normal or recommended practice. Mothers from the dominant culture may also vary in their views and in their treatment of infants. Fashions in infant care have veered from the strict (à la Truby King, 1913) to the permissive, yet babies have thrived on each of these regimens, in every culture, in the families who conform to the latest fashion and in those who do as Granny says. That fact pays tribute to the ability of babies to learn and adapt. It also, I suspect, pays tribute to the ability of mothers to ignore even the best of advice and to attend to what the baby is telling them. Current research in infant development (see, for example, Schaffer, 1984) would suggest that this – attending to the baby's regularities and peculiarities and responding to his/her cues and signals – is the best approach for mothers and for babies.

Midwives or health visitors who are giving advice to mothers about neonatal feeding or sleeping problems should take note of this research. The mother's views about rearing practices, and sometimes the wider family's views as well, need to be taken into consideration along with the health service's view of what is currently regarded as correct practice. The research findings which are presented in this chapter on infant abilities and mother–infant interaction are generally well established and are thus unlikely to be overturned tomorrow. They can be used as a basis for understanding the principles which underlie 'good' infant rearing practice, but not as a rigid prescription for precise action. Taken together with the findings laid out in the first section of this chapter (on The mother's experience) they would suggest that flexible feeding schedules are better than rigid ones since they stimulate breast milk production, help to prevent nipple problems and facilitate the entrainment of states (more night-sleeping and day-waking), so enabling mothers to sleep more in the long run. In the short term, however, a more regular feeding schedule may promote a more 'regular' baby, that is, a baby whose temporal conditioning has led him/her to wake and feed at regular intervals. Provided the time schedule is suited to the baby's nutritional status and requirements, this regimen is perfectly satisfactory, especially when the baby is bottle-fed. If, however, the baby is too immature or hungry to tolerate the fixed schedule, so s/he is waking early and crying frequently, this will increase her/his nutritional requirements, leading to the development of a vicious circle of unsatisfied needs and more upset for both mother and baby. Thus if the basic rule is adhered to – pay attention to the feedback you get from the baby – it will be obvious that the fixed feeding schedule should be altered.

The research presented on entrainment of states and the promotion of mother–infant interaction would also suggest that rooming-in is facilitative. However, the needs of the mother for rest and recuperation in the first few postnatal days may sometimes be better met by separating the mother and baby at night except for feeding if, and only if, the mother so wishes. After all, mothers will have many years to observe and adapt to their child, so missing out the night-time hours of the first 1 or 2 postnatal days may be no great loss. An extended-family approach to childrearing, which is practised by some ethnic groups within the UK rather than one based on mothering as an independent activity, de-emphasizes the need for exclusive mother–infant interaction. So the promotion of exclusive mother–infant interactions may sometimes be inappropriate. It may also discourage the development of an early, close relationship between the father and his baby.

I have already made the point that the adult involved in mother–infant interaction is the primary caretaker: the person who spends most time caring for the baby. This is usually the biological mother but it could be the adoptive mother, a nanny or a father. It is not usually a paediatric nurse or a midwife because shifts and days off necessitate shared rather than exclusive care. However when babies stay in hospital for a long time, such as very premature babies or ill babies, some degree of mutual, satisfying interaction between a baby and one or two 'special' midwives or nurses can occur. The difficulties this can cause are discussed in Chapter 6. What is important to note here is firstly that this kind of mutually satisfying interaction is an essential component of attachment, and secondly that it is not the exclusive prerogative of the biological mother.

The father

The majority of British fathers who participated in an early study of the effects of paternal contact with their offspring during or immediately after the birth reported that they had felt extreme elation; that they were strongly attached to the child; that they were delighted with the child's gender and felt that s/he was perfect; and that their child was distinctly different from any other newborn. These responses were recorded when they were interviewed a few days after the birth. This emotional involvement with the baby was termed by the researchers, Greenberg and Morris (1974), as 'engrossement' and was regarded as the male equivalent of maternal bonding, a concept which was receiving a great deal of attention at the time (see The mother's experience, above). However, subsequent British studies, which have observed the father's behaviour during hospital birth, have found that only about 50% appeared to be highly involved with their baby at this time (see Woolet et al., 1982). In-depth interviews of fathers also reveal that while many feel 'that something magical happens at delivery' (Lewis, 1986, p. 114), they also often feel oddly detached and left out.

Lewis suggests that feelings of being out of place in the delivery room once the birth is over and worries about holding a newborn baby make it difficult for fathers to interact with their offspring immediately after birth. However, Woolet et al. (1982) found that paternal involvement after birth was not affected by whether or not fathers held their baby (most fathers in their study did hold their newborn) or by what was going on around them (e.g. suturing), or by the state of the baby (crying, quiet or active). Fathers did appear to be more involved with sons than with daughters, but what was most evident was the tremendous variability in responses of fathers in the delivery room, with some fathers appearing to be totally engrossed in their baby but others seeming detached, disinterested, nervous or embarrassed. It is likely that these differences in part reflect the feelings of the individual father, but they are probably also affected by the ways in which attendant staff facilitate or inhibit the father's interaction with his newborn baby.

Influenced by theories of bonding and engrossement, a general expectation has arisen that parents will have strong positive emotional experiences after birth and that these will facilitate the development of enduring ties between the parents and their baby (see, for example Woolet et al., 1982 or Sluckin et al., 1983). Fathers, despite their presence at the birth, do not always experience such positive emotions (see above). Furthermore, their involvement with the baby at birth has not always been found to be strongly related to subsequent positive paternal behaviour (Woolet et al., 1982).

The behaviour of new fathers over the time when their partner is in hospital was studied by Lewis (1986) (the behaviour of fathers at, and after, home birth has not unfortunately been investigated empirically). He found that the new father's time was spent announcing the arrival of the baby to friends and relatives; making last-minute preparations for the homecoming such as finishing the decoration of the child's bedroom; and organizing their visits to the hospital. Although such activities keep fathers busy, they are unrelated to the concrete realities of caring for a newborn baby. These realities are experienced by the mother who has the opportunity to learn about her baby in detail and to develop the basis of her skills in infant care and interaction (see Mother–infant interaction, above). Many hospitals have open visiting for fathers and some encourage them to learn how to feed or bathe their baby, though Moss and colleagues in a London-based study 'The hospital inpatient stay: the experience of first-time parents' still found that husbands were 'merely visitors in the postnatal wards' (Moss et al., 1987, p. 165).

No matter how much time fathers spend in postnatal wards, they are likely to be relatively unskilled in neonatal care if compared to mothers. Thus when the baby comes home, the mother will be more proficient at feeding, bathing, changing and comforting the baby than the father. This difference in skill may set the scene for parental specialization, with mothers doing most of the basic child care.

The father's separation from his partner and his exclusion from the central task of getting to know the baby and learning to care for him/her may contribute to feelings of paternal depression which have been found in several studies to be relatively common in the early postnatal period (Atkinson, 1979; Zaslow et al., 1981; see Lewis, 1986). They might be alleviated if the birth took place in the parental home, and may indeed have become less common since prolonged maternal hospitalization has become rare. However these feelings may not be a consequence of separation and exclusion but may instead correspond more closely to a male version of the blues, reflecting the contrast between the emotional 'highs' of birth and the 'coming down to earth' of the immediate postnatal period.

The majority of British fathers now take time off work when the baby comes home (Daniel, 1980; Lewis, 1986). This compares with figures of around 30% in the 1960s (Newson and Newson, 1963). This paternity leave usually has to be taken from holiday entitlement as it is not funded by the government. (A Private Member's Bill brought to Parliament in 1979 which attempted to establish 7 days' funded paternity leave was described on the floor of the house as 'grotesque' and 'an incitement to a population explosion'; Equal Opportunities Commission, 1982). Though female relatives often help at this time if they can, Lewis found that the father was the only person available to help his partner during the postnatal period in 50% of the families he studied.

Although fathers are therefore often available to share infant care during the first days of the baby's stay at home, few apparently do so. For instance Graham and McKee (1979) found that at 1 month postpartum, 45% of British fathers had never changed a nappy, and 34% of bottle-fed babies had never been fed by their father at night. Oakley (1979) found that at 5 weeks, 52% of British fathers were doing little or no child care. More recent studies, by for example Beail (1985) who interviewed working- and middle-class London fathers between 8 and 12 weeks postpartum, have found similar results. Only 5% of fathers were sharing child care equally with their wives during the time that they were at home. Fifty-two per cent of the sample did little or nothing. The tasks which fathers were most likely to perform were playing, walking the baby round when crying, and feeding the baby during the day. The most unpopular tasks were changing dirty nappies, feeding at night and bathing the baby.

These studies all looked at the father's participation in child care (or lack of it) over a period of time which included the immediate postnatal period but was not exclusive to it. The majority of fathers would have returned to work during the time studied, and this may have influenced the way in which child care was shared by the couple (although Beail's study did ask about child care arrangements during the time the father was home). Lewis (1986) focused particularly on the immediate postnatal period when the father was off work and at home with his wife and baby. The majority of his subjects reported that the father took over responsibility for running the house at this time and left most of the infant care to the mother. Although Lewis unfortunately didn't ask parents why fathers did so little child care at this time, he reports that 'the impression gained in most households was that the "natural" division of labour was for fathers to take major responsibility for the housework while their wives mainly looked after the baby' (Lewis, 1986, p. 81). A number of fathers also commented that they were afraid to handle such a small baby and that they felt emotionally and practically unprepared for coping with the demands of parenthood.

Most of the fathers who participated in Lewis's study helped the mother to care for the baby at times, though usually only when asked. When they did so, or when circumstances forced them to take over infant care because the mother was ill (as happened in two cases), they frequently surprised themselves and their partners by demonstrating considerable competence. As we will discuss further in Chapter 5, mothers do not always welcome these demonstrations of male proficiency in child care, but they do suggest that 'fathers are competent too' (see Russell, 1983) and that fathers, if they and their partners so wished, could share infant care more equally with mothers.

After return from hospital, many mothers receive practical and emotional support from female friends and relatives as well as from the community midwife and health visitor. Although Lewis reports that the majority of the couples he studied commented very positively on the usefulness of this support, it appeared to have the effect of limiting the father's practical role. Female friends and relatives tended to take over from the father. Professional help and advice were directed towards the mother and baby, not to the father. Lewis quotes a highly involved father's comments on the midwife's visit: 'I opened the door and she didn't say anything except "where's baby and Mother?"' (Lewis, 1986, p. 86). Kerr and McKee (1981) have similarly reported that midwives tend to direct all their attention to the mother, ignoring the father because he is (or will be) out at work, or doing chores, or is regarded as uninvolved in child care.

Research (see above) would suggest that these assumptions are generally correct. But fathers who want to be more involved may be dissuaded from becoming so by the promulgation of such attitudes. They may also lack the basic knowledge of infant care they require if they are to be more involved and may need support and encouragement which they are not receiving. Female friends and relatives could provide this information and support for fathers but it seems that they do not do so (Lewis, 1986). It therefore falls to the professional carers to fill this gap.

It is not the job of the midwife or other health care professional to force her/his views about paternal participation in infant care on unwilling parents. However there is some evidence that children benefit from high levels of paternal involvement. Although these effects will probably not be apparent in the immediate postnatal period, the pattern of child care which evolves at this time may set the scene for later levels of involvement. Thus encouraging fathers to care for their babies when they come home from hospital may facilitate higher levels of paternal involvement later. Sharing infant care can also relieve the mother of some of the anxiety generated by the responsibility for the baby's health and welfare. Thus midwives and other professionals caring for the family around the time of birth should offer strong support and encouragement to fathers and mothers who go against cultural norms and attempt to share infant care more equally.

Some attempts have been made to tutor fathers in skills such as infant bathing, changing and feeding. These have had mixed results. For instance, an early Swedish study found that this sort of tutoring carried out in the immediate postnatal period was effective in that fathers were more involved in infant caretaking 6 weeks later (Johannesson, 1969). In contrast, Parke et al. (1980) found that fathers who watched a film of fathers engaging in such tasks were no more likely to change and feed their daughters 3 months later. They were however more likely to feed and change their sons.

Current research would suggest that British fathers coming from the dominant culture play an increasing part in events surrounding birth and the early postnatal period. Although they do not normally share infant care equally with the mother, they usually attend the birth and take time off work to be with their partners once the baby comes home, even if this means losing holidays or incurring some financial hardship. (For example, Lewis (1986) instances two subjects who asked to be made redundant following their child's birth because this was the only way they could be free to be with their wife and child at this time.) The part the father plays at this time probably reflects a changing societal view of appropriate male and female roles. It also reflects the fact that fewer female friends and relatives are able to be on hand to help the woman who has recently given birth, since more women work outside the home and families are more widely distributed geographically than in the past. However, many British women will be cared for by female friends and relatives as well as by their husbands during the postnatal period and the importance of this practical and emotional support must continue to be recognized. In particular it seems that female relatives are prominent in providing practical care and advice, while fathers excel in giving emotional support (Beail, 1985; Lewis, 1986).

Fathers who come from some of the minority British cultures, such as the Asian cultures, do not normally become involved with the care of either the mother or the child in the immediate postnatal period. For instance, Punjabi women are traditionally cared for by female relatives during the 40-day postpartum period known as the *Chalia* or *sawa maheena*, during which they recover from the 'pollution' of childbirth. Tradition also dictates whether it is the mother's relatives or the father's who should look after the mother and baby at this time (Dobson, 1988). Although not all Asian women living in this country follow traditional practice in detail, it is unusual for them to be attended postnatally by male rather than by female relatives (Woolet and Dosanjh-Matwala, 1990). While most postpartum Asian women are well cared for by their female relatives, obviously some will have no female relatives available in this country to provide the appropriate care (or occasionally they will not be well regarded by their affinial family i.e. their husband's family and so will not receive the customary care). Asian women who are living within a nuclear family in the UK, rather than in an extended family, can sometimes receive very little postnatal support (Dobson, 1988; Woolet and Dosanjh-Matwala, 1990). Midwives and health visitors need to be aware of this and should not assume that all their postpartum Asian mothers will be well cared

Asian fathers who go against their traditional practices and care for their wife and baby themselves will require a lot of support from community midwifery staff.

Overview and summary

The first few postnatal days encompass a period of immense change for baby and mother alike. The baby has to adjust to a totally different environment from the warm, wet, cushioned, stable world of the womb which s/he has inhabited for 9 months. The baby is however well equipped to accomplish the necessary adaptation. The neonate is able to learn through the processes of conditioning and thus, after some initial disruption brought about by the experience of birth and the transition from one environment to another, can gradually acquire desirable behaviours such as feeding efficiently and sleeping more at night than during the day. The baby's perceptual abilities are especially sensitive to visual and auditory stimuli which emanate from human beings, e.g. to face-like stimuli and the wavelengths of the human voice. This ensures that much of his/her waking moments will be spent attending to the primary carer, and since the primary caretaker is equally prone to attend to the baby, the stage is set for interaction between them.

The interaction which develops between a newborn baby and the primary caretaker is usually termed 'mother–infant interaction'. However although the primary caretaker is most often the biological mother, another woman or a man may equally well fulfil this role. The important features of mother–infant interaction are apparent from the very beginning of the baby's life, with the mother closely observing the baby's regularities of behaviour – his/her 'little ways'; adapting her interventions so that they fit into these regularities rather than disrupt them; and monitoring the effect of these interventions on the baby and adjusting them accordingly. Thus although the mother gradually shapes the baby's behaviour to accord more closely to her culture's norms of desirable behaviour, for example with regard to feeding frequency, she is at the same time influenced by the feedback which she receives from the baby which in turn shapes her behaviour. So mother–infant interaction is a two-way affair; a true *inter*action.

The immediate postnatal period is therefore a time during which the primary caretaker learns about the baby's regularities of behaviour. A time when everything the baby does is closely observed, and when the caretaker is constantly changing her behaviour so that it is maximally effective. Close and frequent contact between the baby and the caretaker is thus conducive to this dynamic, learning process. However research evidence would not now suggest that this kind of contact *must* take place if the mother is to become normally attached or bonded to her baby. Mothers who have to be separated from their babies because of maternal or neonate illness need not suffer a failure to bond. Primary caretakers who are not the biological mother and who have not had the opportunity to have close, intimate, physical contact immediately after birth can still learn to love their babies. Mothers who are exhausted after the birth and/or who feel an initial indifference to their baby need not be regarded as automatically at risk of bonding failure. But most primary caretakers want a lot of contact with their baby in the early postnatal period and this fact alone, rather than an overenthusiastic, over-rigid misinterpretation of bonding theory, should determine that such contact is facilitated.

When the primary caretaker is the biological mother, the immediate postnatal period is additionally a time to recuperate from the birth and adjust to the realities and responsibilities of being a mother. For the woman who has given birth for the first time, the postnatal period is also a period of fundamental role adjustment. Until recently, the mother would be cared for during the first postnatal week in hospital where she would be surrounded by expert maternity staff who were available 24 hours a day. Now, although hospital birth is still much more common than home birth, many mothers go home after a short period of hospitalization where their minute-to-minute care and support are provided by female relatives and male partners who may be as inexperienced, anxious and unskilled as the women themselves. If postnatal women are to receive the best of care at a time when they are engaged in crucial tasks, the community midwife must seek to educate and support her informal carers. The new father who can't understand the fourth-day weepiness; the grandmother who advises a rigid feeding schedule; the friend who regards the postnatal period as a time for visitors rather than for rest – all need sensitive supervision if the mother is to benefit from their care rather than suffer from its consequences. The new father in particular needs to be included in the midwife's concern for the mother and baby since in many cases he will be her sole source of support at this time and since his involvement may help to alleviate feelings of paternal incompetence and exclusion.

Maternal distress in the immediate postnatal period usually takes the form of the blues, which are so common as to be regarded as normal (though the rare condition of postnatal psychosis can develop at this time; see Chapter 6). The blues are typically self-limiting, but recent research suggests that women who have particularly marked or long-lasting blues may be more prone to a subsequent postnatal depression. Thus when the care of the postnatal woman is transferred from midwifery to health visiting staff, the occurrence of severe or long-lasting blues should be noted so that those who will be caring for the family throughout the forthcoming postnatal months are warned of the possibility that the woman may develop a subsequent, serious depression. Maternity staff should therefore not dismiss third-, fourth- or fifth-day distress as 'just your hormones' but seek to alleviate it if possible.

Research suggests that some of the maternal distress associated with the early postnatal period is due to a lack of adequate rest. Mothers cared for in hospital wards might get more sleep if babies were not roomed-in for 24 hours a day. There is no evidence that a couple of nights' separation, except for feeding, disrupts bonding, and though it may delay the entrainment of the baby's states, sleep/wake cycles are anyway disrupted by the birth process itself. However mothers who are separated from their babies may not sleep because they miss them or are worried about them, so maternity staff might facilitate rest more effectively if they offered the mother a number of opportunities for peaceful sleep both at night and during the day, and left her to choose how to utilize them. The use of single rather than shared rooms would enable mothers to have their baby beside them, but not to be disturbed by the crying of other babies. However, while some mothers enjoy the privacy and quiet that a single room offers, others dislike the isolation. Again the best solution seems to be to offer mothers the choice. Mothers cared for at home should be encouraged by their formal and informal carers to sleep when the baby sleeps and let the housework and the visitors 'go to pot'. They have more important things to do than dust the furniture and cater to the needs of doting relatives!

Feeding difficulties, which can cause considerable distress, often resolve themselves as mother and baby become more expert, but contradictory advice can exacerbate any problems which exist and undermine the mother's confidence. It should be easier for the community- rather than hospital-based midwife to ensure that the postnatal woman receives consistent advice and support for the feeding method of her choice, although the advice of grannies, other mothers and occasionally also fathers cannot be overlooked.

Caring for postnatal women at home ensures that they can make choices about when and how they wish to feed their baby; when, where and with whom they wish to sleep; by whom they are attended; and by whom they are visited, for how long and how frequently. In hospital, many of these choices are heavily influenced by the staff who have such a degree of power that only one 'choice' – that which the staff support – can seem to be available. On her own home territory, the mother can ignore the advice of the midwife, as every community midwife is all too aware. This is because the mother at home is naturally more powerful than the health care professional. In hospital, health care professionals must empower the mother, if they wish her to be able to make her own decisions and feel confident in her own judgements. Like the community midwife, they should seek to provide the best advice, information, education, physical and psychological care for the new mother, but they need to acknowledge her right to go against their advice, ignore their information and reject their care. This is what empowering involves and its consequences can be hard for a caring, knowledgeable midwife to accept. Such acceptance however may not only be good for the morale of the new mother, but will also relieve the midwife from the necessity of always knowing what is best and the crushing responsibility of trying to ensure that what's best is implemented.

Further reading

Schaffer H. R. (1984). *The Child's Entry into a Social World*. London: Academic Press.
Sluckin W., Herbert M., Sluckin A. (1983). *Maternal Bonding*. Oxford: Blackwell.
See also recommended reading for Chapter 5 which encompasses the wider postnatal period.

References

Atkinson A. K. (1979) Postpartum depression in primaparous parents: caretaking demands and prepartum expectations. Unpublished PhD thesis. Wayne State University.
Ball J. (1989). Postnatal care and adjustment to motherhood. In

Midwives, Research and Childbirth. Volume I (Robinson S., Thomson A. M., eds). London: Chapman and Hall.

Barrera M., Maurer D. (1981). Discrimination of strangers by the three-month old. *Child Dev.*, **52**, 558–63.

Beail N. (1985). Fathers and infant caretaking. *J. Reprod. Infant Psychol.*, **3**, 54–64.

Call J. D. (1964). Newborn approach behaviour and early ego development. *Int J. Psychoanal.*, **45**, 286–94.

Carlsson S. G., Fagenberg H., Horneman G. et al. (1978). Effects of amount of contact between mother and child on the mother's nursing behavior. *Dev. Psychobiol.*, **11**, 143–50.

Carlsson S. G.,, Fagenberg H., Horneman G. et al (1979). Effects of various amounts of contact between mother and child on the mother's behavior: a follow up study. *Infant Behav. Dev.*, **2**, 209–14.

Carpenter G. C. (1974). Visual regard of moving and stationary faces in early infancy. *Merril-Palmer Q.*, **20**, 181–94.

Cox J. L. (1986). *Postnatal Depression: a Guide for Health Professionals.* Edinburgh: Churchill Livingstone.

Currer C. (1986). Health concepts and illness behaviour: the care of Pathan mothers in Britain. Unpublished PhD thesis. University of Warwick.

Daniel W. W. (1980). *Maternity Rights: The Experience of Women.* London: Policy Studies Institute, no. 588.

De Chateau P., Wiberg B. (1977). Long term effects on mother–infant behaviour of extended contact during the first hours postpartum. *Acta Paediatr. Scand.*, **66**, 145–51.

Dobson S. M. (1988). Transcultural health visiting: caring in a multi-cultural society. *Rec. Adv. Nursing*, **20**, 61–80.

Drewett R., Kahn H., Parkhurst S., Whiltey S. (1987). Pain during breastfeeding: the first three months postpartum. *J. Reprod. Infant Psychol.*, **5**, 183–7.

Equal Opportunities Commission (1982). *Parenthood in the Balance.* Manchester: Equal Opportunities Commission.

Fantz R. L. (1963). Pattern vision in newborn infants. *Science*, **140**, 296–7.

Fantz R. L. (1966). Pattern discrimination and selective attention as determinants of perceptual development since birth. In *Perceptual Development in Children* (Kidd A. H., Rivoire J. L., eds). New York: International Universities Press.

Graham H., McKee L. (1979). *The First Months of Motherhood.* London: Health Education Council.

Greenberg M., Morris N. (1974). Engrossement: the newborn's impact upon the father. *Am. J. Orthopsychiatry*, **44**, 520–31.

Hales D., Lozoff B., Sosa R., Kennel J. H. (1977). Defining the limits of the maternal sensitive period. *Dev. Med. Child Neurol.*, **19**, 454–61.

Hapgood C. C., Elkind G. S., Wright J. J. (1988). Maternity blues: phenomena and relationship to later postpartum depression. *Aust. N. Z. J. Psychiatry*, **22**, 229–306.

Hillan E. M. (1989). Caesarian section: indications and outcomes. Unpublished PhD Thesis. University of Glasgow.

Hutt S. J., Hutt C., Lenard H. G. et al. (1968). Auditory responsivity in the human neonate. *Nature*, **218**, 888–90.

Illingworth R. S., Stone D. G. H. (1952). Self-demand feeding in a maternity unit. *Lancet*, **1**, 682.

James W. (1890). *The Principles of Psychology*. New York: Dover.

Johannesson P. (1969). Instruction in child care for fathers. Unpublished doctoral dissertation. University of Stockholm.

Kaye K. (1977). Towards the origin of dialogue. In *Studies in Mother–Infant Interaction* (Schaffer H. R. ed.). London: Academic Press.

Kennerley H., Gath D. (1986). Maternity blues reassessed. *Psychiatric Dev.*, **4**, 1–17.

King F. T. (1913). *Feeding and Baby Care*. London: MacMillan Press.

Kerr M., McKee L. (1981). The father's role in child health care: is Dad an expert too? *Health Visitor*, **54**, 47–52.

Klaus M. H., Kennel J. H. (1976). *Maternal–Infant Bonding*. St Louis: C. V. Mosby.

Klaus M. H., Kennel J. H. (1982). *Parent–Infant Bonding*. St Louis: C. V. Mosby.

Klaus M. H., Kennel J. H. (1983). Parent to infant bonding: setting the record straight. *J. Pediatr.*, **102**, 575–6.

Lewis C. (1986). *Becoming a Father*. Milton Keynes: Open University Press.

Lipsitt L. P. (1982). Infancy and life span development. *Human Dev.*, **25**, 41–8.

Meltzoff A. N., Moore M. K. (1984). Newborn infants imitate adult facial gestures. *Child Dev.*, **54**, 702–9.

Morbach G. (1983). The occurrence of maternity blues in Scottish and Japanese mothers. *J. Reprod. Infant Psychol.*, **1**, 29–35.

Morse P. A. (1972). The discrimination of speech and non-speech stimuli in early infancy. *J. Exp. Child Psychol.*, **14**, 477–92.

Moss P., Bolland G., Foxman R., Owen C. (1987). The hospital inpatient stay: the experience of first time parents. *Child Care, Health*

Dev., **13**, 153–67.

Newson J., Newson E. (1963). *Infant Care in an Urban Community.* London: Allen and Unwin.

Oakley A. (1979). *Becoming a Mother.* Oxford: Robertson.

Paige K., Paige M. (1981). *The Politics of Reproductive Ritual.* Berkeley: University of California Press.

Parke R. D., Hymel S., Power T. G., Tinsley B. R. (1980). Fathers and risk: a hospital based model of intervention. In *Psychosocial Risks in Infant–Environment Transactions* (Sawin D. B., ed.). New York: Bruner/Masel.

Reading A. E. (1982). How women view post episiotomy pain. *Br. Med. J.*, **284**, 28.

Robson K., Kumar R. (1980). Delayed onset of maternal affection after childbirth. *Br. J. Psychiatry*, **136**, 347–53.

Russell G. (1983). *The Changing Role of Fathers.* Milton Keynes: Open University Press.

Salapatek P. (1975). Pattern perception in early infancy. In *Infant Perception: From Sensation to Cognition, Volume 1* (Cohen L. B., Salapatek P., eds). New York: Academic Press.

Sander L., Stechler G., Burns P., Lee A. (1979). Changes in infant and caregiver variables over the first two months of life. In *Origins of the Infant's Social Responsiveness* (Thoman E. B., ed.). Hillsdale, New Jersey: Laurence Erlbaum.

Sandler M., Glover V., Hannah P. (1990). Postnatal depression, predisposition and prediction. *Journal of Obstetrics and Gynaecology*, **10**, 229–41.

Schaffer H. R. (1984). *The Child's Entry into a Social World.* London: Academic Press.

Schaffer H. R. (1984). *The Child's Entry into a Social World.* London: Academic Press.

Skinner B. F. (1971). *Beyond Freedom and Dignity.* New York: Knopf.

Sluckin W., Herbert M., Sluckin A. (1983). *Maternal Bonding.* Oxford: Blackwell.

Super C., Harkness S. (1982). The infant's niche in rural Kenya and metropolitan America. In *Cross Cultural Research at Issue* (Adler L. K., ed.). New York: Academic Press.

Svejda M., Campo J., Emde R. (1980). Mother–infant 'bonding': failure to generalise. *Child Dev.*, **51**, 775–9.

Thoman E. B., Barnett C. R., Leiderman P. H., Turner A. (1970). Neonate–mother interaction: effects of parity on feeding behavior. *Child Dev.*, **41**, 1103–11.

Thoman E. B., Barnett C. R., Leiderman P. H. (1971) Feeding behaviors of newborn infants as a function of parity of the mother. *Child Dev.*, **42**, 1471–83.

Thoman E. B., Olsen J. P. (1972). Neonate–mother interaction during breast-feeding. *Developmental Psychology*, **6**, 110–18.

Thomson A. M. (1989). Why don't women breast feed? In *Midwives, Research and Childbirth. Volume I* (Robinson S., Thomson A. M., eds). London: Chapman and Hall.

Thune-Larsen K-B., Moller-Pedersen K. (1988). Childbirth experience and postpartum emotional disturbance. *J. Reprod. Infant Psychol.*, **6**, 229–40.

Weinmann J. (1981). *An Outline of Psychology as Applied to Medicine.* Bristol: John Wright.

Wiszniewski C. (1988). The process of attachment in mothers of preterm babies. Psychology honours projects, Glasgow Polytechnic.

Wolff P. H. (1968). The serial organisation of sucking in the young infant. *Pediatrics*, **42**, 943–56.

Woolet A., Dosanjh-Matwala N. (1990). Postnatal care: the attitudes and experiences of Asian women in East London. *Midwifery*, **6**, 178–84.

Woolet A., White D., Lyon L. (1982). Observations of fathers at birth. In *Fathers: Psychological Perspectives* (Beail N., McGuire J., eds). London: Junction Books.

Zaslow M., Pedersen P., Kramer E., Suwalsky J., Fivel M. (1981). Depressed mood in new fathers: interview and behavioural correlates. Paper presented to the society for Research in Child Development, Boston.

4 When things go wrong

This chapter will consider Caesarian birth, traumatic birth, miscarriage, stillbirth and neonatal death, premature birth and the birth of a handicapped child. It therefore encompasses a considerable range of 'things that go wrong' within maternity care which necessitate the provision of extra help. Of course the birth of a premature or handicapped baby need not be perceived negatively. Nor is a Caesarian birth 'wrong'. But I want in this chapter to focus on the mother's and father's experience, and they typically describe these experiences in terms of 'something going wrong'.

Some parts of this chapter may not be easy to read; they were not easy to write! I would urge you to study them however. The psychological distress and damage that can be caused to traumatized and bereaved mothers and fathers by staff insensitivity is considerable. But kindness and understanding are remembered with gratitude and though they can't make things better they do help people to cope in tragic circumstances (see below).

Caesarian birth

Delivery by Caesarian section is becoming increasingly common in this country. Although it carries more risk than vaginal delivery (Hillan,

1989), some readers might consider its place in this chapter to be unwarranted. However most women expect to deliver vaginally, or 'normally' as it may be described, and there have been a number of reports of negative feelings such as fear, disappointment, anger and low self-esteem being associated with delivery by section (e.g. Affonso, 1977; Lipson and Tilden, 1980).

A major study of the short- and longer-term consequences of Caesarian section carried out in Glasgow (Hillan, 1989) found that only 12% of a group of 50 primiparous mothers who had emergency sections had anticipated anything other than a 'normal' delivery. Forty-eight per cent of the subjects had welcomed the news that they were to have a section since it meant that an unexpectedly long and painful labour would soon be ended. However 26% had been terrified at the prospect of surgery, fears about their own survival and about that of the baby being compounded by anxiety about the unknown. And the remaining subjects reported that either they were so exhausted that they didn't care what happened to them or that, though they were unhappy about the prospect of surgery, they accepted it for the sake of the baby. So the prospect of Caesarian delivery created anxiety in many subjects.

The majority of Hillan's (1989) subjects had attended antenatal classes where elective Caesarian sections were briefly discussed. However, as in many classes, the positive aspects of birth were emphasized and deviations from the course of normal labour were not considered in sufficient detail to prepare the parturients who went on to have Caesarians for that experience. As we have discussed previously (see Chapter 2) antenatal preparation might be more effective if it focused on realistic preparation rather than on reassurance. Caesarian section is after all a form of surgery, so the provision of accurate preparatory information, which has been shown to reduce postoperative distress and improve recovery from surgery, is likely to help many of the parturients who experience it cope with it better and recover more quickly (see Chapter 2). Information about the procedural and experiential aspects of sectioning could be given to all parturients who attend antenatal classes but would probably be more effective if restricted to Caesarian subjects and given around the time of surgery. For women who are undergoing elective sectioning, all the psychological preparation which is given to 'cold' surgical cases would be appropriate. Although the woman requiring an emergency section may be too anxious, too drugged or too exhausted to take in long detailed explanations of procedure, simple sensory information could be given immediately before the operation.

Research has shown that women generally experience more satisfaction with the delivery experience if their partner is with them in the operating theatre during the Caesarian section surgery (e.g. Hillan, 1989) but little is known of the man's view of the experience. He is likely to find it stressful and anxiety-provoking. So if the woman's partner is to be present, he will need to be informed and reassured by staff as well.

Information about the reasons for Caesarian section surgery and about the prospects of it being required in future deliveries should also be carefully given. Hillan found that 48% of her subjects wanted more information of this kind before they left hospital and that 3 months later 16% of her subjects still did not know or understand why they had required a section. This made planning a future pregnancy difficult.

Hillan compared subjects who had experienced emergency Caesarian sections with a matched control group of primiparous mothers who had delivered vaginally. The Caesarian subjects suffered more physical discomforts and ill health following childbirth. During their hospital stay 82% of the Caesarian group suffered pain from their abdominal wound. Though 88% of the vaginally delivered mothers were suffering perineal pain at this time, the Caesarian mothers suffered more intense pain for longer and 68% reported that it made it difficult for them to care for the baby, compared with only 24% of the control mothers. The Caesarian group also suffered more backache, headache, wind, constipation and pain at the site of their intravenous infusion than the control group, though few of these problems were noted in the midwifery Kardex or in other reports. These findings support the Caesarian mother's feelings that the staff on the postnatal wards were often apparently unaware of the physical and psychological difficulties they were experiencing, with some 30% of this group commenting unfavourably on this aspect of staff support.

> I felt they expected you to do far too much in the postnatal wards. Although it was busy they just left you most of the time. There was lots I wanted to ask and I ended up weeping most of the time (Hillan, 1989, p. 192).

As I have already commented in Chapter 3, Hillan also found that only 56% of subjects who had a section felt that they had enough rest in the postnatal wards.

Oakley (1980) has commented on the way that Caesarian sectioning is conceptualized as distinct from other forms of abdominal surgery. This may affect staff perceptions so that women who have just been sectioned are seen as fundamentally well, as are vaginally delivered mothers, and so are considered fit to participate in normal activities and baby care. If they were viewed as postoperative patients, staff care might be directed more towards recovery from major surgery and the opportunities for rest and recuperation could be increased. (One of my students mentioned today that she had given birth by section in the hospital studied by Hillan 5 years ago and then again last year, that is, *after* Hillan's study. She said that the care she was given recently was excellent. It was dramatically better than the care she had received previously. Thus it seems that the results of Hillan's study had been acted upon and that care improved as a result.)

Once they went home, more of the Caesarian mothers felt unwell than did the control mothers. Forty-nine per cent felt that they had not yet returned to 'their normal selves' by 3 months postpartum whereas only 30% of the control mothers felt this way. Forty per cent felt less healthy since delivery compared with 28% of the control mothers. However there were no differences between the groups in overall ratings of happiness or unhappiness, nor in positive or negative changes within the marital relationship. Caesarian mothers resumed normal sexual relationships sooner than vaginally delivered women and fewer reported sexual problems following delivery. In the main this was due to the incidence of dyspareunia related to perineal pain within the vaginally delivered group (22%). So there are apparently some advantages to Caesarian section delivery! However the memory of a distressing and unexpectedly painful delivery made more Caesarian mothers reluctant to contemplate a future delivery.

Some studies have found that women who have been delivered by Caesarian section surgery are more negative about their baby or have difficulty in interacting with him or her (e.g. Wenderlein and Wilhelm, 1979). A study carried out in Sweden, however, found no differences in parenting behaviour between Caesarian mothers and vaginally delivered mothers (Hwang, 1987). Hillan found differences between her Caesarian and control groups, with only 36% of the Caesarian mothers feeling close to their baby at birth compared to 56% of the vaginally delivered mothers, and 40% of the Caesarian mothers still not feeling close at 2 months postpartum compared to 18% of the controls. Thus her subjects were more like Wenderlein and Wilhelm's subjects in this respect. The explanations that Hwang offers to explain why his findings do not replicate the other findings many of which emanated from America may suggest why both the American and the British mothers adjust less well than the Swedish mothers.

They may have to do with differences between Caesarian birth in Sweden and in the USA . . . the hospital stay in USA is relatively brief. Because medical services in Sweden are state supported, Swedish mothers receive hospital care for a longer period of time. Data that indicate that the Caesarian mothers were more positive toward the hospital stay suggest that these mothers benefit from a longer post-delivery recovery (average, 7.2 days) and as a consequence may be more rested and able to cope when they return home (Hwang, 1987, p. 13).

Medical services in the UK are also state-supported but Hillan's study makes it clear that few Caesarian mothers in this country are likely to go home feeling 'more rested and able to cope'. Another benefit of being a Swedish mother rather than a British or American mother is that up to 9 months' paid paternity leave is available in Sweden, so fathers can be easily available to give practical and emotional support to their partners during their recovery from surgery. Hwang's study found that the fathers of Caesarian-delivered infants did participate in a greater amount of care-giving over the first few postnatal months than the fathers of vaginally delivered infants. It seems therefore that both their partners and their offspring benefited as a result of these enlightened policies.

Childbirth as a traumatic experience

Some women experience childbirth as traumatic. In these women childbirth gives rise to nightmares and constant and repeated recall which is associated with considerable negative affect. Some of these women try not to think about their childbirth experiences but find that they constantly spring to mind, often accompanied by vivid and distressing flashbacks of 'the worst bits'. Others go over and over the events in their mind. In these ways such women resemble the victims of post-traumatic stress disorder, whose sufferings following on from the traumatic experience of war or disaster have received much publicity of late.

Unsurprisingly, women who suffer from this type of childbirth-related post-traumatic stress are generally reluctant to contemplate a future pregnancy. Their sexual and marital relationships may also suffer (Stewart, 1982).

Until recently, the existence of a childbirth-related post-traumatic stress disorder has only been apparent to clinicians who are involved either in treating its symptoms (nightmares and acute anxiety) or in marital or sexual therapy.

I had the opportunity to follow up some of the subjects who had participated in my research on 'Factors affecting labour pain' (Niven, 1986) 3–4 years later. I found that most of these subjects recalled their childbirth accurately and with equanimity but that 5 out of 33 respondents reported that their recall caused them anxiety and distress. Four of these five subjects were reluctant to give birth again; three had experienced nightmares, or as one of them put it 'daymares: waking ones as well as sleeping ones'; and one spontaneously reported postnatal problems in sexual adjustment. These results would suggest that there are a considerable number of women who suffer from a mild form of post-traumatic stress disorder associated with childbirth. The total number of women who participated in the original study was 100. Some 30 or so follow-up postal questionnaires were returned with 'not known at this address', so the maximum number of potential respondents was around 70, and probably less. Therefore even if traumatized subjects were more likely to respond than untraumatized ones, the incidence of this negative reaction to childbirth is at least 7%. The distress this causes to new mothers, the difficulties it may cause for their postnatal adjustment and for any future pregnancy and birth, is therefore potentially significant and needs to be further researched.

The numbers I dealt with were too small to make statistical analysis of possible causes feasible. Stewart (1982), a clinician who has written about women who reported similar symptoms following childbirth, has suggested that this traumatized reaction is a consequence of the unrealistic expectations built up through attempts at natural childbirth. However her subject group – Canadian women consulting a psychiatrist – may not reflect the experience of ordinary British mothers. Thune-Larsen and Moller-Pedersen (1988), working in Norway, suggest that traumatic births which were related to subsequent emotional disturbance, involved intense pain and anxiety, loss of control, dissatisfaction with childbirth experience, with coping and with support from medical and midwifery staff. However, the conclusion that a birth was traumatic was drawn by the authors, not by the subjects, and the assessment of emotional disturbance was made at 5 days postpartum. It therefore corresponds more closely with the blues than with long-term post-traumatic stress. However, the factors they isolated could potentially be related to longer-term post-traumatic stress.

In my study I found that two out of the five traumatized subjects had reported very high pain levels at the time of birth and three had assessed their birth as highly stressful. Two had forceps deliveries. Three had large babies (over 8 lb 14 oz). Three were perhaps overconfident primiparous mothers and one other subject had given birth using solely natural childbirth methods without any analgesia. One might therefore suggest that their births had been particularly traumatic and that their reactions were perfectly understandable. However no one subject had experienced all of these potentially negative factors and every negative factor had been experienced as severely or more severely by a subject who was not traumatized – who reported normal long-term adjustment and recall of birth experiences (Niven, 1988). There was therefore nothing in my data obtained at the time of birth (see Chapter 2 for details) or at the time of follow-up which could point to a clear source of the trauma or to why some women go through very difficult childbirths but emerge feeling confident in their ability to cope with that and other difficult or painful experiences (Niven, 1988), while others suffer the birth and then continue to suffer every time it is recalled. The four 'traumatized' subjects who had received analgesia during the birth were all dissatisfied with its effects and also felt that they had not received adequate support from the staff. Given the importance of staff support in childbirth and its intimate relationship to analgesic satisfaction (see Chapter 2) it may be that these variables are significant. However further research will be needed to elucidate this hypothesis.

Until this research is carried out it behoves midwives and other maternity staff to be aware of the existence of these problems, and to do everything possible to alleviate distress in mothers who react negatively to their childbirth experience. Discussion with the midwife who was attendant upon the birth may help clear up confusion over the cause of events and the likelihood of them happening again. Merely allowing the mother to express her feelings instead of putting them down to the fourth-day blues may also help. Women who have suffered this kind of reaction and who have wittingly or unwittingly become pregnant again may need special care (see Chapter 1). However in order really to help these women we need to know more about their experience and come to understand it by seeing it through their eyes, not ours.

Green et al. (1988) found that the well-being of women at the end of the puerperium was not related to the number or kind of interventions that they had experienced during childbirth but rather to their belief that the 'right thing happened'. This belief was in turn related to the amount of information they had received about the reasons for the interventions. Although Green's research deals with emotional reactions in the short term, rather than in the long term, it suggests, as my research has done, that staff–parturient communication is extremely important.

Miscarriage, stillbirth and neonatal death

All these tragic events involve loss. They differ from each other in their timing, in the degree to which the fetus or baby was developed and in the certainty which the parents would have that they would be delivered of a live healthy baby. Some potential fathers or mothers might welcome the early miscarriage of an unwanted pregnancy, but the majority experience this as the loss of their baby, with all the hopes and dreams they had about this baby, and thus share many of the feelings of parents who lose a baby at birth or in the early postnatal period.

These mothers and fathers will suffer grief and bereavement going through the lengthy, painful process of attempting to adjust to their loss. There are many models of the grieving process. Perhaps the most useful one is still that presented by Parkes (1972). His original work was based on grieving following the death of a spouse but the thoughts, feelings and behaviours of the bereaved that he describes can be helpfully related to parents mourning the loss of their baby. The bereavement process with specific regard to perinatal death has been described by Sahu (1981).

Perinatally bereaved parents will probably experience times when they feel completely numb and unable to accept or believe the reality of what has happened. The mothers may still feel the baby inside them, the fathers hear the baby cry. Hallucinations in those close to someone who has just died are quite common and are normal – that is, they are not a sign that the person is going mad (Parkes, 1972). This phase of numbness and disbelief typically gives way to a phase characterized by extreme restlessness, the searching phase, as Parkes has denoted it. Periods of searching may involve a search for the baby's physical presence which leads the parents to want to see the baby, hold him or her, or to be beside the grave if there is one. The search for a reason as to 'why did this happen', 'why did it happen to us?' may involve the parents in reviewing every detail of the pregnancy and birth in an effort to understand what caused the fetus to be aborted, the baby to die; then re-reviewing it and re-re-reviewing it over and over again, trying to make sense of something in which there may be little sense.

The eventual acceptance that the baby is lost often terminates the search and leads to feelings of intense sadness and depression which last for some considerable time. Eventually the parents may be able to recover from the loss, rebuilding their lives and adjusting their hopes. This recovery does not mean they have got over it. They have not forgotten the baby, nor replaced it with another one, a puppy, a new house or any of the things that people say help you to forget. These things help you to cope with some aspects of the loss, they keep you busy, give you something to cuddle and may give your life some new meaning and happiness. But the new life incorporates the loss within it. It is always there. Furthermore the feelings of loss can be reactivated by an anniversary (of the baby's birth or what would have been the baby's birth, for instance), a subsequent pregnancy (see Chapter 1), or the opportunity to see, hear, feel, or smell someone else's baby.

I have emphasized in the above section that parents 'may feel', 'could possibly experience' the various phases of the bereavement process outlined above. Research into bereavement has necessarily been restricted to a small number of studies, involving probably a rather atypical range of subjects – those willing to participate in such studies. It is therefore inappropriate to apply the findings of such research in too rigid a manner. The studies that have been carried out are however invaluable in giving us insight into some of the thoughts and feelings experienced by some of the bereaved. These insights are needed since fortunately bereavement is not a ubiquitous experience, at least for the relatively young amongst us. Such research has allowed us to understand that the bereaved feel angry – 'why did this happen to us?', 'why couldn't the doctors/midwives do more to save the baby?', guilty – 'why did I smoke that cigarette?', 'why didn't I make her take more rest?' and restless – in their search for the baby, as well as sad. They suggest that typically bereavement is a lengthy process, lasting at least a couple of years, and that it varies in its nature from time to time; it is not a gradual attenuation of the same kind of sad feelings.

Although we may seek to understand and empathize with the feelings of the bereaved, it is very difficult, if not impossible, to know just how they feel. This is where self-help groups can be most useful. The members of the Stillbirth and Neonatal Death Society or the Miscarriage Association really do understand what it is like to have experienced perinatal loss, because they too have experienced it. Bereaved families may feel more comfortable talking to the members of such groups than to professional carers. They may not wish to talk to them at the time of their loss but may find such discussion invaluable at a later phase of the bereavement process. Other families may find early contact with 'someone who knows what it's like' tremendously consoling. The professional's aim should be to make available information about relevant self-help groups, so that the family can have access to them if they wish and when they wish.

Research into the effects of being bereaved has shown that the death of a close family member is associated with higher than normal rates of physical and mental illness which are evident for a considerable period following the death (Parkes, 1972). Miscarriage and perinatal death are similarly associated with high rates of psychological distress and psychiatric disorder. A study by Friedman and Gath in Oxford, for instance, found that of 67 women interviewed 4 weeks after spontaneous miscarriage, 32 could be rated as psychiatric cases suffering from 'a depressive type illness' (Friedman and Gath, 1989, p. 811). This rate of 'caseness' is four times the rate found in the general population of women. A Swedish study found that 19 out of 56 women who had suffered a stillbirth reported a variety of symptoms including anxiety attacks, phobias, obsessions, depression and psychotic reactions in the 2 years following the death of their baby (Cullberg, 1971). These studies show that the degree of psychological distress following the loss of a baby in pregnancy or around birth is often so intense that it is rated as psychiatric illness of the depressive kind. The kind of symptoms that reflect this rating are sadness, irritability, tiredness, crying, self-blame and loss of sexual interest (Friedman and Gath, 1989). These symptoms are the normal consequences of bereavement and it is only their intensity or duration which distinguishes those women who could be classified as mentally ill from those who are deeply distressed but who would not be rated as psychiatric cases. This distinction is less important than is the understanding of these women's feelings. Friedman and Gath's subjects typically reported a few days of emotional numbness followed by a period of deep distress. At this stage, two women took overdoses and one attempted to cut her wrists. Feelings of guilt were common, with many of the women fearing that they might have caused the miscarriage by doing something they shouldn't or not doing something they should. Twenty-four of the women felt that they were still pregnant, reporting comforting thoughts such as that there had been a misdiagnosis of spontaneous abortion, or that they had been carrying twins and had only lost one of them. They constantly had to remind themselves that this was not so.

Studies of stillbirth, e.g. Savage (1988), describe women suffering very similar feelings, with the most intense distress lasting many months. Guilt and inadequacy are expressed by many mothers who have had a stillbirth. They feel that they have let down their partners, their families and their baby. They talk of failing as a woman and as a mother (Cullberg, 1971). Oglethorpe (1989), in a review of parenting after perinatal bereavement, discusses the multiple losses that these women suffer. They lose a loved baby, the person that baby would have become, and the opportunity of being a parent. The baby is mourned as a baby but also as a child who would have grown up, had birthdays, Christmases and gone to school.

It is invidious to compare the results of studies on the consequence of reproductive loss (involving miscarriage, stillbirth or neonatal death) with those of loss of a close adult family member. Each loss is unique. A general comparison does suggest that some aspects of reproductive loss may interfere with the bereavement process making it more difficult for parents eventually to come to terms with their loss. The circumstances of the loss may be associated with traumatic birth experiences and may thus give rise to the kind of post-traumatic stress disorder described above. Tylden (1990) has described the extreme effects of this in a small number of women referred to a psychiatric service. Symptoms of anxiety and depression were present with disturbed sleep and horrifying nightmares. Rumination about the traumatic events was present in all the sufferers, and acute anxiety attacks could be triggered by mention of the name of the hospital, the doctors and midwives involved and the clinical condition experienced. Many of these women could not stay at home alone and could not return to work. Their partners had to give up their jobs to look after them, sometimes for years. Their children suffered from the effects of maternal depression and emotional lability. Thus the particular circumstances surrounding a perinatal death may make the grieving process more akin to that surrounding a traumatic loss by war, accident or disaster.

The 'normal' bereavement process (remembering the full range of normality may not be known) can be interrupted at various points and may never be completed. For example, people can remain at the stage of non-acceptance of the loss, feeling that it has not really happened. Clinical work involving bereavement counselling suggests that this sense of unreality is more likely to persist in cases where the physical evidence of death is unavailable, for instance following a disaster such as Lockerbie or Piper Alpha where bodies cannot be recovered. Parents who lose a baby at birth have little physical evidence of the baby's life, still less of his or her death, so they could find it similarly difficult to accept that their baby is dead. However it is now common practice for parents who have lost their babies to be able to see and hold the baby and to have photos of the baby to keep. This provision facilitates their search for the lost baby and should help them to accept the reality of the loss and eventually recover from it. One British study has found that a majority of parents did not want to see their baby after stillbirth, especially if the baby was abnormal (Cooper, 1980), but the majority of such studies indicate that most parents want time with their dead baby and the opportunity to see, hold, name and say goodbye to him or her (see, for example, Murray and Callen, 1988).

Parents who lose their babies during pregnancy often have nothing to grieve over. There may have been a glimpse of a fetus, or a photo of a scan, but there is nothing to correspond to their image of the baby as a baby, and this is largely what they wish to grieve for. They may therefore be in a position equivalent to that of the relatives of the disaster victims, never quite believing that it has happened and therefore unable to come to terms with the fact that it has. This sense of unreality can be magnified if the pregnancy had been unannounced so that the pregnancy, never mind its loss, was not apparent to the world at large.

Miscarriage, stillbirth and neonatal death all involve the loss of a baby with whom the parents had little real relationship. They didn't have time to get to know him or her (with a miscarriage they may not even know whether it was a him or a her) and this too can make it difficult to grieve. Parents who lose a baby during the neonatal period at least have some memories of the baby as a person; a person with a personality; someone that however briefly they could relate to, interact with, nurture, comfort or care for. These memories and experiences may aid their eventual recovery as they show better longer-term adjustment than parents who have lost their baby at birth (Oglethorpe, 1989).

People in our safe, sanitized society have little experience of death, still less of infant death – it mostly takes place behind hospital doors. Our mourning rituals are private and attenuated, and perinatal death and miscarraige are not subject to any required, formal societal procedures such as the registration of the death or the holding of a funeral. All these factors discourage public acknowledgement of the loss of a baby in pregnancy or around birth and consequential public expression of mourning. Colleagues and acquaintances, even friends and family, don't want to talk about it because they don't know what to say. The bereaved are avoided at first and then expected to be back to normal within a short time. However, research has indicated that the process of bereavement is facilitated by an acceptance of grieving, so that the bereft are free to express their grief publicly if they so wish. For instance, Cullberg (1971) found that those of his subjects who suppressed their feelings had severe psychological symptoms for longer following stillbirth than those who expressed their feelings. It seems that this grieving process must be gone through if the bereft are ever to recover from their loss, but the attitudes of many in our culture make it more difficult for them to do so. This inhibitory effect is likely to be particularly powerful when it concerns the loss of a pregnancy which can be dismissed as 'not a real loss', or the loss of a baby which people find it difficult to empathize with because, thankfully, it is nowadays a very uncommon experience.

I have discussed so far the feelings of the mother and father as if they were equivalent. This is in order to emphasize that fathers suffer just as mothers do; a fact which goes largely unrecognized. The woman is likely to get cards, flowers and sympathy from at least some of her friends and family for some short time. The man is asked: 'How is your wife?' He is expected to play the supportive role that he would have played had the pregnancy and birth had its anticipated happy outcome, or the self-sacrificing role of the partner of a sick person. He is expected to be strong, as men are supposed to be. Yet although he has not had the physical experience of pregnancy or birth as his partner has, he may be as upset or more upset by the loss of his baby (see Chapters 1–3 for the father's reaction to pregnancy, birth and fatherhood). Reactions to loss are individual. They have to do with the love that the individual had for the person who is lost and with the meaning of the relationship between them. They cannot therefore be predicted, but everything we know about fathers suggests that they will suffer, grieve and mourn if they lose a baby and that their needs and feelings should be considered as well as those of the mother. There is some evidence which suggests that men react differently to reproductive loss and may recover from it more quickly than women (Forrest et al., 1982) but it is difficult to determine whether these findings accurately reflect gender differences or merely social attitudes which go against men showing or discussing their feelings.

The provision of support, understanding and comfort from the woman's partner seems (as we note constantly in this book) to be important. Single women are found to be more likely to be diagnosed as psychiatrically disturbed following miscarriage than women who are married or in a stable relationship, the majority of whom receive a great amount of support from their partner (Friedman and Gath,

1989). Women with a poor marital relationship are more likely to be psychiatrically disturbed following perinatal death than those with a good marital relationship (Forrest et al., 1982). Prolonged grief reactions following a perinatal bereavement are more common in women who have a poor relationship with their husband and who do not have a (perhaps compensatory) supportive social network (Forrest et al., 1982).

Mutual support and grieving can bring couples closer together. Friedman and Gath found that 50% of their married subjects reported that their relationship had improved since the miscarriage. However perinatal bereavement can place an unbearable strain on a couple's coping resources and the incidence of marital breakdown following infant death is increased. This may be because each partner grieves in a different way and so is unavailable to help the other in coming to terms with their loss. As men are generally regarded as more stoic, they may wish to deny their distress and 'not talk about it because it's upsetting'. This strategy will be unhelpful to the woman if she wishes to grieve more openly and to be comforted, and in turn her overt distress may interfere with her partner's attempts at denial (Oglethorpe, 1989). Of course, the situation may be reversed, with the man grieving more openly than the woman, or perhaps more commonly the man may concentrate on comforting his partner in the period following the miscarriage or death and only become aware of his own need to grieve once she has apparently recovered. A study of paternal grief following cot death (Mandell et al., 1983) found that fathers did commonly adopt the role of manager of events like the funeral and comforter, rather than of mourner. They note, however, that health care staff unwittingly reinforced this behaviour and may have made it more difficult for fathers to express their own grief. Since the repression or denial of grief has been associated with the development of abnormal grief reactions, the concern is that this behaviour may be unhealthy in the long term.

Other members of the family suffer too. Grandparents are often very wrapped up in the birth of a new family member and will suffer considerable loss if that baby dies. There is some research which indicates that older people cope with bereavement differently (one hesitates to use the word 'better' in this context), perhaps because bereavement is more familiar or because they have come to terms with their own mortality (Parkes, 1972). However, old people are more frequently bereaved and the loss of a grandchild may be superimposed on the loss of a spouse and so be particularly painful. Their reaction to the loss of a grandchild may involve feelings of anger and frustration, and just like everyone else they will search their minds for a possible cause for the event. Unfortunately this can sometimes lead them, particularly the paternal grandparents, to blame the mother or to push for another pregnancy to make up for their loss (Woodward et al., 1985). The parents may also wish to have a baby again and this wish can be taken as a sign of recovery from their loss. However a rapid subsequent pregnancy is usually inadvisable as it is associated with greater psychiatric morbidity and with problematic adjustment to the pregnancy, birth and upbringing of the subsequent child who may seem like the ghost of the one who died rather than an individual in his or her own right (Oglethorpe, 1989).

The reaction of siblings will depend very much on their age. Developmental studies show that the young child's understanding of death is very different from an adult's. Children under 5 lack the biological concept of death as the cessation of life and of normal human activity. For instance, they think that people who are dead still eat and drink as they did before, but that they do these things in another place (e.g. in the grave or in heaven) where they are inaccessible. It is this inaccessibility which distresses young children. They can't see or talk to the person who has died, they can't play with them.

The other thing that upsets children is that Mummy and Daddy are upset. Sometimes the parents are so upset that the child is left virtually parentless for a time. In other cases the parents become extremely anxious about their surviving child/ren, infantilizing them and overprotecting them. Many parents strive to act normally but most cannot achieve this aim. Children are very sensitive to their parents' behaviour. Even the youngest child will note disturbed parental behaviour or interaction (see Chapter 5) so they will know that something is wrong. However, since young children don't understand death as adults do, and since all children can be quickly distracted from distressing events, they have no basis for empathizing with their parents' feelings, especially months or years after their sibling's death. So they know *something* is wrong, but not *what* is wrong. They may attribute Mummy's tears or Daddy's temper to something they (the child) have done; to them being bad; or to being unloved or unlovable.

It is obvious that this is not helpful for the child and could lead to them exhibiting behaviour problems of some sort such as withdrawal or school refusal. Encouraging the parents and child/ren to talk to each other about the death of the baby may help. The cause of the parents' odd behaviour will become more clear to the child, and the parents can stop bottling up their grief and pretending to be fine when they're not.

This approach can be especially helpful when older children are involved. Although teenagers experience emotions much as adults do, and so have some basis for empathizing with their parents' feelings, they are likely to have no experience of bereavement, and to feel at a total loss as to what to do or say. So if their parents don't talk about it, then they won't either, thus bottling up their own grief and making it more difficult for everyone to express their feelings.

It can be helpful for the parents to talk too. A number of studies have shown that bereavement counselling can shorten the duration of the bereavement process (Forrest et al., 1982; Woodward, 1985). Talking about the loss is one of the central aspects of such counselling. The listener however has to be sensitive. The insensitivity of friends, family and hospital staff has been shown adversely to affect parental grieving (Benfield et al., 1978). And Murray and Callen (1988) found that the single greatest predictor of serious depression in mothers who have lost a baby around the time of birth is dissatisfaction with support and comfort from professionals during and after the hospital stay.

It is not easy to be sensitive to parents who have just lost a baby. Most of us are unused to dealing with such situations and feel incompetent, embarrassed, upset and helpless. Mander (1991a), in a study of midwives' attitudes towards bereaved mothers, reports that many midwives find it particularly difficult to adjust from working with mothers who have a successful birth to those who have lost a baby or who are relinquishing the baby for adoption – a situation which involves similar feelings of grief and bereavement. They also feel very uncertain about their role during the birth as well as afterwards, being unsure about when it is appropriate to stay with the parents offering comfort and when it is best to leave them in privacy (Mander, 1991a). Perhaps asking the parents what they would prefer would be the best course here. This is probably also the best course to take with regard to other aspects of care such as the choice of room or the duration of the hospital stay. However, recent research suggests that midwives feel that it is inappropriate to burden the mother with such mundane decisions (Mander, 1991b).

Some behaviours, which probably reflect the sense of awkwardness and uncertainty which staff feel, can instead communicate insensitivity. For instance, pretending that the loss hasn't happened and talking about the weather doesn't help. Neither does saying, 'never mind, you can have another one', or 'it might have been worse, you could have lost it later', or 'I had a terrible time when I lost my first baby', or 'it didn't bother me a bit'. All these things have been said to me, and I can vouchsafe that they were the opposite of helpful. I feel personally that putting women who have lost a baby or a pregnancy in hospital wards beside pregnant women, or women with babies, is so grossly insensitive it amounts to cruelty, although I recognize that it is done with the best of intentions directed towards the best physical care. However, Lewis and Bourne (1989) have drawn attention to the disadvantages of putting a bereaved mother in a side room by herself. They point out that the mothers can more easily be isolated from staff and others when they are in a side room and that this may reinforce the irrational feelings of shame and the sense of ostracism that are so common after a perinatal loss.

Giving the parents the opportunity to grieve in private, as and how, and for as long as they wish, is helpful. So is the expression of genuine sympathy and understanding. Flexibility in the provision of care is important: choice of rooms; allowing husbands to visit and stay with their partners when they want to rather than when hospital routines decree; allowing women to go home when they choose; putting physical care in second place to psychological care (but not forgetting it). The best help I received was from a very junior student midwife who accompanied me on my return from theatre. She just held my hand while I howled and cried. And from a senior midwifery sister, who a little later came and bathed me in a quiet, semi-darkened room very gently, as if I was a child myself. At that point I was totally vulnerable and having her as a substitute mother was incredibly comforting.

Sensitivity can be improved by training in bereavement counselling. However parents who have lost a baby in pregnancy or around birth are most likely to encounter midwives, junior doctors, general practitioners, health visitors, auxiliaries and porters – none of whom routinely receive such training. These staff can increase their sensitivity by reading about the experiences of men and women who have been bereaved – articles such as those by Forrest et al. (1982), Woodward et al. (1985), Savage (1988), Oglethorpe (1989) and Lewis and Bourne (1989) are listed in the reference section. They can try to imagine how they would feel if it happened to them, although this is sometimes too painful and is anyway very difficult. They can pester the 'powers that be' for some basic training which ideally involves all the staff who will come into contact with the parents, from the porter down to the consultant. But perhaps the most important thing for all of these people to do is to concentrate on listening to the mothers and fathers rather than agonizing over what to say. A genuine 'how are you?' and the creation of time and privacy for parents to respond is a million times more helpful than the expression of ghastly clichés.

I think it is helpful if people acknowledge the loss formally when they meet the bereaved for the first time. 'I was very sorry to hear that . . . ' is fine, or a touch, or a cuddle if you can't manage the words. It needn't be long-winded. It's the recognition of the reality of the loss which is important, bringing it into the public domain. Cards, flowers, visits, the provision of mementoes of the baby (such as name tags), help to arrange registration of the baby's birth where possible (the forename of a stillborn baby can now be registered; see Oglethorpe, 1989) or a funeral or memorial service if wanted by the parents – the provision of all these serves to mark the loss formally and is usually of some comfort to the parents (Oglethorpe, 1989). Maintaining contact with the parents is also important. They will usually want information about 'what went wrong' and perhaps at some stage about what to do in the future. Friedman and Gath found that their miscarriage subjects' greatest dissatisfaction was with the information and advice they received on discharge from hospital. Sixty-nine per cent of these women consulted their general practitioner in the 4 weeks following discharge, most of them hoping to obtain some explanation for their miscarriage and expecting that there would be an explanatory note from the hospital. They were disappointed. As Friedman comments:

> Nowadays it tends to be assumed that modern medicine treats most problems; mothers often find it difficult to accept that medical management has little to offer. In the case of miscarriage this may explain some of the dissatisfaction women have with their medical management, but it accentuates the need for explanation (Friedman, 1989, p. 45).

Rowe et al. (1978) have shown that bereaved mothers who had contact with a physician after they had left hospital had a better understanding of the causes of their baby's death and that this understanding was directly related to greater satisfaction with medical care and the absence of protracted and problematic grief reactions. This type of contact can be provided by doctors, midwives or health visitors in the community or through hospital follow-up. It allows proper physical care to be given to women who have all the usual postnatal sequelae but who may not be provided with the normal postnatal services such as 6-week postnatal checks and health visitor visits. It also allows proper psychological care to be given and maintains a point of contact which may not be useful to the parents at the time of the death but can be taken up at some point in the future, when and if they wish to utilize it.

Many mothers who have lost a baby at birth or in the neonatal period are given the opportunity to talk or are provided with some form of bereavement counselling. However, the provision is uneven and fathers, and couples who have lost a baby in pregnancy rather than perinatally, rarely receive adequate support (Friedman and Gath, 1989; Oglethorpe, 1989). Provision of some form of counselling which could be carried out by specially trained staff or form a central part of routine midwifery and medical care for families following any sort of reproductive loss could therefore be useful.

However it is very important to realize that there are times when the bereaved just cannot talk about it; it's too painful and they don't have the words to express their feelings accurately. There are also times when they feel all right and times when even though they don't feel all right, they'd rather just pretend that they do. As research into coping with stressful events such as bereavement progresses, it becomes abundantly obvious that there is a lot still to learn about the complexity and subtlety of the human coping response. Everyone copes differently. There are no simple prescriptions available for the bereaved. Talking about it often helps, but sometimes it doesn't and if the person you are talking to is insensitive, it can make it worse. So the bereaved should never be forced into talking about how they feel, just as they should never be forced to see or hold their dead baby. What is important is that the opportunities to do so are made available by staff and that they continue to be available for as long as possible: a picture of the baby held on file can comfort a mother who after the funeral wants to see the baby she didn't want to hold at the time of his death; locating the grave of a baby who died 14 years ago can comfort a mother expecting her eighth subsequent baby (Mary Cronk, personal communication); the chance to talk about his feelings may be resisted by a father for months but may be vital when he eventually comes to accept the reality of his loss.

This brings me to the staff. It's obvious from what has been discussed that the staff caring for a family who have lost a baby can do a lot to help. They can make it possible for the parents to see and hold the baby. They can allow them to talk about their feelings of loss. They can provide information about the pregnancy and birth which may help the parents to come to terms with what has happened. All of these things are likely to involve the staff in distressing circumstances.

Whisking a fetus or dead baby away and avoiding any discussion of what has happened is much easier on the staff. We don't do that any more, which makes things better for the parents in the long run but much worse for the staff in the short run. They are forced to confront the parents' grief and often the anger which goes along with it which may, fairly or unfairly, be directed at them or at colleagues. Being with parents who are cradling their dead baby or expressing their feelings of anguish and misery brings home to the staff their own losses. These may be associated with personal bereavement, for example with loss of parents or of a pregnancy (miscarriage is after all fairly common), or they may involve the loss of this particular baby, or of other mothers or babies. Medical, midwifery and nursing staff care about those they care for. Midwifery is an area in which staff get particularly close to the mothers and mothers-to-be they care for, and where a positive outcome is the norm. Midwifery staff are therefore quite likely to suffer from bereavement-type reactions when they lose a baby and when they share the distress of the parents. They can therefore expect to experience some of the feelings associated with the bereavement process. Feelings of disbelief (especially if the death was unexpected), guilt, sadness, unfocused anger are, I'm sure you'll agree, quite common following the loss of a baby in your care. I think it is important to acknowledge these feelings in yourself and in colleagues, and not look on them as a sign that you're 'not coping', or 'being silly'. Just as it's generally helpful to allow the bereaved to express their feelings and to talk about what has happened, it's helpful for the staff to do so as well – they are after all bereaved too.

When I discuss this with midwives, health visitors and nurses they often ask whether or not I think they should show their feelings in front of the grieving family. I never have a clear-cut reply to these kinds of questions, since I firmly believe that health care staff are best able to decide the answer for themselves, provided they have been presented with all the relevant information on which to base their decision. However, wearing my consumer hat for a brief moment, I think I would always find a genuinely upset midwife, health visitor, nurse or doctor much more comforting than one who is efficient but detached. And being upset doesn't preclude efficiency!

So far spontaneous abortion has been discussed (perhaps overmuch, sorry!) but not clinical abortion, nor recurrent miscarriage. A thera-peutic abortion which has to be carried out because of genetic defects in the baby is likely to produce similar reactions to miscarriage, with the additional stress of the parents being required to take the conscious decision about ending the pregnancy. Iles (1989) found that 39% of women who had a termination of pregnancy because of fetal abnormality were rated as being psychiatric cases at 1 month after the termination. Their levels of depression, anxiety and the intensity of their grief were more severe when the abnormality was non-life-threatening, for example when the baby had spina bifida and thus might have survived, rather than being anencephalic. Second-trimester abortions were also associated with increased psychiatric morbidity, as were a history of psychiatric illness and poor social support. In discussing the management of termination for fetal abnormality, Iles recommends that the parents should not be rushed into making their decision. (The section below, which considers the breaking of bad news to the parents of a handicapped child is of considerable relevance.) During the termination, the timing of which should be left to the parents to decide if at all possible, the mother should never be left alone. It is important that the staff make it clear to the parents that they recognize that this is the termination of a wanted baby and not of an unwanted pregnancy. Iles also advises that staff should ensure that analgesia is adequate – advice that one hopes would be unnecessary since it is self-evident. But perhaps not! The decision of whether or not to see the baby should be left up to the parents but Iles recommends that they be encouraged to hold the baby (wrapped up if they prefer) and that photographs be taken and retained for parents who did not want to see the baby at the time but may wish to do so later.

Abortions undertaken on social grounds may apparently be welcomed by the potential mother and father. However, the decision to have an abortion is usually a very vexed one and the treatment these couples, or more often single women, receive is frequently less than maximally supportive. Furthermore, research on desirability of pregnancy (see Chapter 1) demonstrates clearly that wanting or not wanting the baby you are expecting is not a black-and-white affair; the desirability of a pregnancy often changes over time. These factors make it likely that many women choosing to have an abortion will experience bereavement reactions. This process of bereavement in these women (and in the fathers) may in fact be more distressing and protracted because of the guilt they feel and because of the lack of social support available to them. Research indicates that a mid-trimester abortion involving an induced labour is especially traumatic. However, women who present late requesting termination are often very young, have denied the pregnancy or have been ambivalent about whether or not to continue it, and/or have poor social support. Such factors in themselves are often related to poor psychiatric outcome. It is therefore difficult to determine whether it is these factors or the undoubtedly more traumatic aspects of a mid-trimester compared to first-trimester termination which result in increased psychological distress in this group (see Iles, 1989). The increased psychiatric morbidity associated with late termination for fetal abnormality (see above) would suggest that the timing and method of delivery do exacerbate distress.

When the psychological consequences of social termination are considered, they must be set alongside the consequences of being refused an abortion. Brody et al. (1971) found that women who had been refused an abortion were psychiatrically disturbed for longer than a comparable group who had been granted one, and Pare and Raven (1970) noted that a third of women who were refused abortion reported resenting their babies 1–3 years later. However, McCance et al (1973) found no greater levels of depression amongst a group of women refused abortion than among a group who had been granted it. As abortion laws change and social attitudes alter, more recent research is clearly needed to increase our understanding of the psychological processes involved.

Recurrent miscarriage is obviously deeply distressing as the couple will have been bereaved repeatedly, each miscarriage bringing back the grief associated with the previous ones (Gannon, in submission). Many of these couples will also be childless and will therefore feel that each lost pregnancy makes it less likely that they will ever become parents (though the validity of this belief is a subject of considerable current debate; see Gannon, in submission). In Friedman and Gath's study of the psychiatric consequences of miscarriage (1989), they found that women who had miscarried before are more likely to be clinically depressed, as are women who are childless. This depression may last for a considerable period of time and may affect the women's adjustment to any subsequent pregnancy (see Chapter 1). Pregnancy is also likely to be a highly stressful experience for these couples with acute anxiety about any sign which might indicate that the pregnancy will not survive. This stress in itself may affect the viability of the pregnancy (see Chapter 1) and thus make it more likely to end in another miscarriage (Gannon, in submission). In order to break this vicious circle, counselling and psychological support are sometimes provided for women who have miscarried a number of times and in whom no obvious physical abnormalities are apparent. As the rate of spontaneous miscarriage in such women has not yet been clearly established, it is impossible to evaluate the success of these programmes. However

Gannon concludes that since such programmes have been shown to be helpful to women suffering from other disorders of pregnancy such as hyperemesis gravidarum, it is possible that they may act to relieve stress and prevent miscarriage.

It seems that there is little that physical medicine can do to prevent miscarriage, except advise bedrest in the knowledge that there is no good evidence of its benefit (Friedman, 1989). Therefore the provision of psychological support for such couples seems justified. (Incidentally there is no evidence that women who habitually miscarry have some personality defect. Gannon reviews the relevant studies and shows that the personality characteristics which have been associated with recurrent miscarriage could be the result of the traumatic, stressful experience of repeated miscarriage rather than its cause.)

The birth of a handicapped* child

This event also involves loss. The loss in this case is not associated with death but with life. Therefore the feelings of all involved are likely to be confused. The loss experienced when a handicapped baby is born is the loss of the perfect baby that the parents expected to have. All the hopes and plans which an apparently normal pregnancy bring concern a normal, healthy, perfect baby. Of course as we have noted in our discussion of anxiety during pregnancy, most parents-to-be worry that their baby might be handicapped. However these worries do not usually prepare the parents for the reality of having a handicapped child. Before the parents can come to terms with this reality they have to cope with their feelings of loss. These can be equated with the feelings which follow a death. Disbelief, guilt, grief, anger and depression – all the features of the bereavement process – are likely to be experienced by the parents of a handicapped child. These parents need to mourn for their lost, perfect baby. The acknowledgement of this need is difficult for any parent who has lost a baby (see above) but it is made more difficult for these parents since they actually have a baby. So their feelings of loss are confounded by their feelings about the baby and this is likely to exacerbate their confusion: is the sadness they feel associated

---

* I use the term 'handicapped' here rather than the correct term, 'impaired', because this is the term that most parents will use. It does not signify that the impairment is necessarily pathological, i.e. that it will in all cases result in negative outcomes for the child and the family.

with the baby who is alive or with the perfect baby who should be alive but isn't? They also feel guilty: they shouldn't be grieving for a fantasy baby when their real baby needs their love and care.

There is some evidence that parents of handicapped children may have problems in accepting the baby's handicap because they haven't come to terms with their loss. It is easy to see how these mothers and fathers may not be able to complete the bereavement process because they feel their grief is inappropriate and should therefore be ignored. They could therefore 'get stuck' in a denial of their loss and so fail ever to resolve their feelings about the baby they have lost, and consequently they may be unable to form a normal attachment to the handicapped baby. (Parents who lose one of a set of twins or triplets suffer similar feelings; Oglethorpe, 1989.) The feelings of loss are not confined to the postnatal period. They are likely to be reawakened at significant times, when, for example, the child should have started at the local primary school, or should have gone on to secondary school, or would have begun dating boy/girlfriends (Knussen, personal communication). These parents, like other parents who have lost babies, need to have their loss acknowledged by the staff who care for them and to be given the opportunity to express their feelings if they so wish. The parents of a handicapped child will continue to be in contact with health care professionals for a considerable time following the birth. There are therefore repeated opportunities for professionals to offer support and a listening ear.

Breaking the news to parents that their baby or child is handicapped is a very difficult and distressing task (some handicaps are not apparent at birth and so only become diagnosed later on in the child's life). Staff insensitivity or incompetence at this time is deeply resented by parents, just as it is when perinatal death occurs. Cunningham and colleagues (1984) in a study of 62 parents of Down's syndrome children born in Greater Manchester found that 58% were dissatisfied with the way they had been told that their baby had Down's syndrome. Forty-four per cent complained that they were told either too late or when the parents were not together. Thirty-eight per cent complained that they had been 'fobbed off' and not given straight and honest answers to questions.

It is possible that this dissatisfaction reflects parents' reactions to the news, not to the manner of its telling. (In ancient times the bearer of bad tidings was often put to the sword.) However a subsequent study showed that parents who were told 'well' remembered only feelings of shock and sadness and expressed their gratitude to staff for performing the task with sensitivity and kindness (Cunningham and Davis, 1984).

These parents were told about their baby's handicap by a consultant paediatrician accompanied by a specialist health visitor, both of whom saw the parents again approximately 24 hours later. This second discussion allowed the parents to have many of their questions answered frankly, competently and honestly at a time when they were more able to absorb information. At the time of the diagnosis, they were so shocked that little information could be understood and still less retained (see Chapter 2). The health visitor could be contacted at any time by the parents and maintained regular contact with the family at home.

The news was broken to the parents in a quiet, undisturbed private room, and they were able to stay there together for as long as they wished. The baby was not excluded since this had been found to accentuate feelings that the baby was unacceptable and was being ignored or rejected by staff. Many parents emphasized how important it was to them that the baby was held and touched and cuddled by the doctor or health visitor. The news was broken as soon as possible, except when the mother was ill. This was in accordance with the results of a number of studies which found that most parents wanted to know at once and found a prolonged period of 'being kept in the dark' insulting and also usually ineffective, in that many had already guessed that something was wrong – most often because of atypical staff behaviour (see Cunningham et al., 1984). However, as pointed out in earlier chapters, not all parents conform to one mould, and a small minority of parents may appreciate a few days of normality during which they can celebrate the birth of that child (Knussen, personal communication). Concern had been expressed by clinicians that parents who were told that their baby was handicapped before they had become attached or bonded might be more likely to reject him or her. However there is no evidence that this is the case (Cunningham and Sloper, 1977) and anyway theories of bonding do not now consider the period immediately following the birth as crucial (see Chapter 3).

All of the parents who had been told of their baby's handicap in this manner expressed their satisfaction, compared with 20% of a contemporary control group whose complaints closely accorded with those of an earlier study described above (Cunningham et al., 1984). Although the numbers involved were small, these results strongly suggest that breaking bad news, while always distressing, can be done satisfactorily. The staff involved will suffer distress as well as the parents and may share a sense of guilt and inadequacy. But at least they will know that they have done the best that can be done at this time for the family that they care for, and they will have set in train a process of sympathetic and realistic support that will do much to help them in the future (Cunningham and Davis, 1984).

When parents are told that their baby is handicapped, they are likely to feel shocked, distressed and grief-stricken. They may experience other intense and confusing feelings as well. For instance, many parents feel revulsion at the idea of abnormality (as do many non-parents and professionals) and feel a sense of shame and embarrassment about having an abnormal child. If the survival of the baby is in doubt, they may try to avoid becoming attached to the baby so as to lessen the pain they will experience if s/he dies (similar attempts are sometimes made by mothers of premature babies). At the same time they often feel very protective towards this particularly vulnerable baby and so feel guilty about their revulsion, and angry when friends and family react negatively towards the baby, or pressure them to put the baby into 'a home'. They are likely to be very fearful about the future and all its uncertainties and usually feel that they are, and will be, inadequate parents. They need help in coming to terms with these feelings and most writers conclude that skilled counselling needs to be made available to these parents on a long-term basis. Cunningham and Davis (1985) offer guidelines for such counselling and emphasize the importance of a known and trusted person providing support and information. These guidelines can be summarized as follows:

1 Avoid all unnecessary jargon.
2 Don't give a lecture, allow parents to ask questions. The emphasis should be on listening.
3 Allow pauses in the conversation and give the parents time to think.
4 Try to get the parents to talk about their feelings, hopes and beliefs. Giving (hypothetical) examples of 'how other parents feel' can make the expression of negative feelings more acceptable. Some parents may prefer to read about these feelings privately rather than talk about them with professionals.
5 Choose words carefully. Saying: 'Have you noticed something funny, or odd, about the baby?' can be very hurtful to a mother who thinks the baby is beautiful.
6 Be as objective as possible about the child, being neither overpositive nor overnegative.
7 Do not avoid being honest. If you don't know, say so but say you'll find out, and do so.

8 Show respect and liking for the parents and child. Avoid suggesting that the parents are inadequate or that you don't want to see or handle the child.

9 Don't give the impression that you don't have time to talk. Let them know if you have to go by a certain time so as to allow for the last-minute, often most important questions which invariably arise just as the discussion is ending. Allow yourself time for them (Cunningham and Davis, 1985).

I reproduce these guidelines here because they reinforce much of what I have been noting elsewhere in this chapter and throughout the book. The findings of Cunningham and Davis's study can be applied to a number of situations where distressing news has to be conveyed, for instance when diagnosis of fetal abnormality is made in pregnancy or when there is concern for a baby's survival at birth or in the neonatal period.

Knowledge of bereavement can help us to understand the slow process of parental adjustment to handicap. It involves grieving. It is likely to incoporate an initial period of disbelief or non-acceptance and it will take a variable amount of time for parents to come to terms with the realities of the situation they face as mothers and fathers of a handicapped child. For these parents, and of course for the child as s/he grows, the process of adjustment is life-long. The practical difficulties involved in parenting are immense, and the emotional consequences of being handicapped or of loving and caring for a handicapped person in a prejudiced and often uncaring society can be devastating.

However, the stress and distress associated with caring for a handicapped child vary considerably and depend on a large number of interrelated factors, including the parents' perceptions of the child, their hopes and ambitions for themselves, the handicapped child and the rest of the family; the resources, personal, financial, practical and social that they can call upon; and the care-giving demands and supervisory responsibilities involved. These factors can be more important than the type or objective severity of handicap (Knussen and Cunningham, 1988).

The father's reaction to the birth of a handicapped baby often differs from the mother's. Fathers often find it harder initially to adjust to having a handicapped child than mothers. Many mothers go through an initial period of depression, anger, anxiety or despair, but then experience a phase of euphoria in the first postnatal year when the baby acts and interacts (see Chapter 5) much like any other baby, with his or her handicap only becoming apparent again once attainments like walking and talking are obviously delayed (Cunningham and Sloper, 1977). However, as we have so often discussed in this book, support from fathers as well as from female relatives is crucial to maternal well-being (Byrne et al., 1988) and fathers of handicapped children have been found to be more involved with child care than is usual within our society (McConachie, 1982).

For both mothers and fathers, the birth of a baby who has some physical or mental impairment can result in long-term distress or disturbance. However, sometimes such disturbance is temporary, or intermittent, being associated with a particular stage of the parents' or offspring's life cycle. Many parents state that having a child with disabilities increases the quality of family life (Knussen and Cunningham, 1988):

> I remember my midwife saying to me at one time: 'It's the genes. A normal child has 24 genes, a mongol has 25.' She said, 'It's like a cake. You put the ingredients in for an ordinary cake but accidentally a little coconut falls in. It's still a nice cake, but it has that little extra.' Well I think that little extra in Melanie is love. She loves everybody and she is happy from morning to night time. She seems to spread happiness all around her – my children adore her' (extract from case history of Melanie, written by her mother: Cunningham and Sloper, 1977).

Premature birth, neonatal care and the separation of mother and baby

Mothers and babies may be separated after birth because of maternal illness or, more commonly, because of infant illness, handicap, prematurity or low birthweight. Long-term separation (of a number of days or weeks) is usually now avoided unless the baby's condition necessitates intensive care. In Chapter 3 we discussed the evidence which indicates that contact in the first few postnatal days is not essential for the formation of adequate mother–infant bonds but that close contact at this time and during the remainder of the early postnatal period does help the mother and father to form a strong attachment to their baby. Obviously babies whose condition requires that they remain in an incubator, perhaps being ventilated, monitored and fed intravenously, cannot have normal close contact with their parents. The parents cannot care for their baby as they would normally and the kind of mother–infant, father–infant interactions which usually occur during the early postnatal period cannot develop. Furthermore, the survival of such a baby is at risk. All of these factors will distress the baby's parents and may interfere with their feelings about the baby and their attachment to him or her. A study carried out in Glasgow, initially by one of my students, Cathy Wiszniewski (Niven et al., in press), found that virtually all of the mothers of preterm babies interviewed reported that they had found it difficult to feel close, attached or bonded to their babies at some time during their stay in the neonatal care unit. They also expressed feelings of shock, numbness and disbelief immediately after the birth; acute distress and anxiety about the possibility that the baby might not survive; guilt at deserting the baby, if they were discharged before their baby; and a sense that the baby wasn't really theirs, which was only completely dissipated once the baby came home (Niven et al., in press).

American researchers have viewed the birth of a premature baby as a time of acute emotional crisis for the parents, and have found that mothers who could not participate in the care of their babies while in hospital were not confident about their care-giving skills once the baby came home (e.g. Leifer et al., 1972). Research into child abuse has variously found that preterm babies (Elmer and Gregg, 1967), low birthweight babies (Starr et al., 1984) and babies who have been in neonatal care (Lynch and Roberts, 1982) are more likely to be abused later in life. These findings have been attributed to bonding difficulties experienced by the abusing parents caused by their separation from the baby after birth.

This evidence, which emanates from a variety of types of study, would appear to suggest that prolonged separation of mother and baby after birth does affect mother–infant relationships in some way and may interfere with attachment between mother and baby or father and baby. However 90% of the Scottish mothers we studied reported very high levels of attachment to their babies once they had come home (Niven et al., in press). This finding is supported by the writings of some clinicians concerning parental adaptation to prematurity (Sammons and Lewis, 1985) and is in agreement with the current position on maternal bonding which indicates that separation after birth will not inevitably lead to a failure to bond. Furthermore the link between prematurity and later abuse has not been replicated in a recent study of the aetiology of child abuse, though the association between low birthweight and abuse was still apparent (Starr, 1988).

Some writers consider that any link between illness in infancy and later child abuse may be due to factors which are not associated with separation of mother and baby. For instance, it may reflect the continued stress of caring for a sick child, since premature or low birthweight babies often have health problems for a number of years and abuse has been associated with illness and hospitalization in children who were full-term and of normal weight at birth (Starr, 1988). Or it may be that abuse is more likely when parents have a stressful lifestyle or live in a stressful environment. These stresses may also have been related to the development of obstetric problems which in turn had caused the prematurity or low birthweight (see Chapter 1).

It seems therefore unlikely that the majority of parents who are separated from their babies in the early postnatal period will have long-term problems in attachment. However a small proportion of parents of sick babies will undoubtedly experience such problems, just as a small proportion of parents who have not been separated from their babies will fail to bond with them or later abuse them. When bonding doctrine (the view that the mother's attachment to the baby was formed in the first few postnatal days) was current, much attention was paid to the mother's behaviour towards the baby in the early postnatal period, and any apparent lack of affection was held to be indicative of lasting attachment problems. Thus a mother who was too exhausted or ill to care much about her baby, or was temporarily uninterested in its charms or merely undemonstrative, was held to be at risk of bonding failure. Now that it is recognized that such reactions in mothers are quite common and normal (Robson and Kumar, 1980) and that attachment is a gradual process, there is less emphasis placed on parental behaviour in the immediate postnatal period. Instead studies seek to elucidate factors which are more generally associated with attachment problems in the long term.

Much of this research is focused on problems of child abuse and results indicate that sociodemographic factors in the parents such as young age, single status, financial and physical deprivation, marital disruption and lack of practical and social support are statistically associated with higher than average levels of child abuse (more children from poor, single-parent, deprived, unsupported families will be abused than from more advantaged or from two-parent families). However, it can be clearly demonstrated that the majority of children who come from such at-risk families will not be abused (Leventhal, 1988). Other complex factors such as the characteristics of the child (e.g. sickly or 'unfriendly'), the parents' perceptions of the child (e.g. as having a lot of power, while the parent has very little) and the development of faulty interactions between parent and child are likely to be involved (Browne, 1988). Readers who are especially interested in research on child abuse are directed to the book by Browne et al. (1988) listed under Further reading.

Such studies, while obviously crucially important in investigating child abuse, may not be the best way of exploring difficulties of attachment which are unrelated to abuse. After all, a mother or father may not feel very close to a certain child but would never dream of abusing him or her. In our study of attachment in mothers of preterm babies (Niven et al., in press) we found an association between lack of social support and reports of low attachment once the baby had returned home. We also found that mothers who had experienced previous reproductive problems involving infertility, miscarriage or stillbirth reported comparatively severe attachment problems during their baby's stay in hospital; one of these mothers, who had conceived through in vitro fertilization, reported continued problems after the baby had come home. Other studies have shown that reproductive problems can cause severe stress and can be unresolved for long periods of time (see Chapters 1 and 2) and studies of infertility investigation and treatment and specifically of in vitro fertilization have also found that it causes intense distress (Reading et al., 1989). It is therefore possible that the existence of previous reproductive problems could add to the anxiety, distress and guilt experienced by most mothers who are separated from their babies at birth, and could thus exacerbate the problems which they experience.

Poverty, deprivation, single parenthood and lack of social support have all been associated with both premature birth and with attach-ment problems (Leventhal, 1988). One subject we studied sadly characterized this all too clearly. She was young, single and unsup-ported, and came from a deprived part of Glasgow. Unlike all our other subjects, she reported that she felt less close and attached to her baby after he had come home: 'Its lonely at home', she said. 'There's no one to make a fuss of us or to help me look after him. It was different in the hospital and I felt like I loved him lots. But now he's home, it's hard and I don't feel the same. I still love him . . . but . . . it's all the responsibility, all the time . . . '.

The hospital involved does its very best to provide some continuing back-up for the families who have had a baby in neonatal care. They have a home-visiting service and return visits to the hospital's clinics are arranged. But they can't provide the kind of social and practical resources that this young mother needs. That's the job of society, not of its health service, though some voluntary or professional support provision such as that documented in Chapters 1 and 6 might be of some help.

Attachment problems are not the only difficulties experienced by the parents of babies cared for in neonatal units. Lack of confidence in care-giving used to be a dominant problem when parents were not involved in looking after their babies. However, a study by Leifer et al. (1972) demonstrated clearly that if parents were involved as soon as possible in feeding, washing and changing their babies, their confidence increased markedly. Parental involvement has therefore been encouraged in most neonatal units and is usually beneficial for parents and babies in allowing them to get to know each other and to begin to interact with one another more normally. Most mothers who participated in our study reported that caring for their babies was the first thing that made them begin to feel 'like a real mummy'. Until then they felt more like a visitor and that the baby was the staff's baby, rather than theirs. However, many felt awkward and incompetent in their attempts to handle, feed and change their tiny, frail babies in comparison to the staff who of course were skilled and well practised in the provision of infant care. One subject commented that she felt that her mothering skills were 'on trial' and that she had to 'pass a test' before her baby would be allowed home in her care. Such feelings were rare, but all parents are bound to be relatively unskilled in giving care to premature, sick or handicapped babies. It is up to staff to praise parents' efforts and to assure them that their initial difficulties are normal (and shared by staff when they first work in neonatal care) and will disappear with practice.

Feelings of intense fear and anxiety about the baby's survival are inevitable. They can be alleviated to a certain extent by giving the parents as much information as possible about the baby's condition, the medical equipment and procedures but it must be recognized that it is often impossible to tell the parents the one thing that would really relieve their anxiety – that their baby will be all right. Like feelings of guilt, of anger or of loss which these parents of 'imperfect' babies may experience, their feelings of anxiety can only be acknowledged and ventilated; they can't be wiped out by the wave of some magic wand.

It has also been demonstrated that because of the high levels of fear and anxiety suffered by mothers who have just given birth to a preterm baby, information which is given at that time is often not understood or is instantly forgotten. Even when information is given during the baby's stay in the neonatal intensive care unit rather than immediately following the birth, Calam et al. (1990) found that 24% of their 79 subjects could only recall sketchy details of what they had been told and 11% could remember nothing. Twenty-three per cent understood little of what they recalled. The medical prognosis for 50% of the babies implied a risk of cerebral palsy which had been communicated to the mothers. However, at 6 weeks after the birth, not one of the mothers seemed to have grasped the implications of this risk and had unrealistically high expectations of what the future held for these babies. This parental optimism is quite normal within the first year of life of a handicapped baby (see The birth of a handicapped child, this chapter) and may not be related to an inability to understand or remember information given. However, along with the other findings of this study, it should serve to caution staff about their belief in the power and efficacy of the information which they transmit.

The feelings of neonatal staff can also give rise to difficulty. Neonatal staff get very close to the little scraps of humanity whose lives they strive to save. When they succeed, they can resent handing over their charge to parents who may not be able to care for him or her as expertly as the staff. When the staff fail and the baby dies, their grief and sense of failure can be profound. These difficulties are reflected in the comparatively high rates of staff sickness, turnover and 'burn-out' associated with neonatal care (Duxbury and Thiessen, 1979). A study carried out in England which compared the experience of working in a neonatal unit with that of working in a children's orthopaedic ward confirmed that neonatal work was perceived by staff as more stressful. It also demonstrated that neonatal staff experienced higher work loads, less autonomy, less job satisfaction and poorer support from peers and supervisors than did orthopaedic staff (Spinks and Michaelson, 1989). These difficulties, added to those associated with the nursing of very sick babies in a 'high-tech' environment, are bound to lead to staff stress and distress. Once again, psychology can offer no magic solutions. (More staff, more pay, and more sensitive superiors would all probably help, but psychology can't provide them.) However the material presented elsewhere in this book should allow the reader to realize that the provision of mutual social support – people to talk to, shoulders to cry on – and an acknowledgement that the problem is a natural consequence of doing the job properly, not a sign of weakness or a symptom of inefficiency, should help. In some units clinical psychologists who are attached to the hospital have encouraged the formation of staff support groups. The psychologist sometimes leads these groups, or may act as their facilitator. S/he may additionally offer individual counselling or therapy for staff members. Psychologists who are attached to units in this way often act as counsellor or therapist for the parents as well as for the staff. Although the basic psychological support for the parents will always come from midwifery, nursing and medical staff, clinical psychologists can provide an important additional service. They can offer counselling to all parents who wish to avail themselves of this 'listening ear'. They can act as specialist therapists when parents are experiencing acute psychological difficulties; for example, they might offer therapy to parents who have previously suffered reproductive loss, or where one of a set of twins has died, or when the baby has to remain in hospital for a very long period of time. Even when the unit has no official contact with a clinical psychologist, informal links could be made between neonatal staff and local clinical psychology staff. This would ease the process of referral and would enable staff to have access to a possible source of psychological support.

An important recent study funded by the World Health Organization has looked at the provision of family and staff support for families with a very low birthweight baby. It was carried out in the seven largest neonatal intensive care units in Scotland and was unusual in that it included consideration of the role of grandparents as major support figures. Although they are sometimes mentioned in other research studies, their role is generally downplayed. However, McHaffie (1990) managed to record the views and experiences of 182 grandparents from 88 families. Both the grandparents and the parents felt that while the baby was in hospital, the grandparents' role should focus on emotional support rather than on advice and information, which would often be inappropriate. This was sometimes difficult for the grandparents who felt that they were closely involved in supporting their family but that their role was not given any recognition by the hospital staff – for instance, they were not allowed to phone to find out how their grandchild was but had to get this information from the parents who could find the constant reporting of 'no change' upsetting.

Listening was rated as the most important aspect of this grandparently support. The parents felt that this kind of emotional support should also be available from midwifery/nursing staff (rather than from medical staff whose role was seen as more focused upon information and instruction). However, although 90% of the parents rated the midwives and nurses as being 'as supportive as they could be', many were frustrated that the staff had so little time to listen to them.

A recent presentation has detailed the inclusion of grandparents in a prenatal meeting on the care and development of twins designed to increase the psychological support available for these families (Bendefy et al., 1990). This kind of approach might be usefully implemented postnatally as well as prenatally in families where extra support is necessary; this could be provided by grandparents working in conjunction with professional sources of support.

Until recently, concern for the psychological needs of those involved in neonatal care has centred on the staff and the parents. Concern for the baby was focused on his or her survival and optimum physical development. However, physical development and psychological development go hand in hand in infancy, and research into prematurity is now taking psychological factors into account.

The environment of the very premature baby is different from that of the fetus of the same age, who in utero is suspended from gravity, receives continuous gentle cutaneous stimulation from the amniotic fluid and is protected from overwhelming sensory experiences such as bright light or sudden loud sounds. The very premature or sick baby's environment also differs from that of the healthy full-term baby who can maintain respiratory, cardiovascular and temperature control unsupported. Full-term healthy babies have some degree of motor and muscular control and spend some of their time in an alert, awake state. This allows them to attend to sights and sounds within their environment and to learn from them and, most crucially, to begin to interact with the people who exist within it (see Chapter 3). Immature babies, in contrast, are floppy and tend to respond to disturbance with sudden jerky, frantic movements. They spend much of their time fluctuating between sleep and drowsiness. They are rarely alert and, if they are so, it is only momentarily and its timing cannot be predicted. They receive plenty of sensory stimulation from their environment – the incubator in a busy, noisy, brightly lit neonatal unit – and tactile stimulation from the staff, but this rarely corresponds to the kind of stimulation that they would have received if they were still in the uterus, or if they were a full-term healthy baby (Als, 1991). In fact the very premature baby whose existence is dependent on the equipment and skills of an intensive neonatal or special care baby unit is a unique 'species' of human being who occupies a unique environment. Neither the species nor the environment existed a decade ago (Wolke, 1987).

The intensive neonatal unit is typically brightly lit 24 hours a day. The intensity of light which reaches the infant with an immature visual system in an unshaded incubator has given rise to some concern, as has the lack of a normal diurnal pattern in light levels. The sounds which are most easily transmitted through the incubator are of low frequency. This means that speech sounds are masked, so babies in incubators do not have the opportunity to learn about speech sounds in the way that full-term babies can (see Chapter 3). However other sounds do penetrate. For instance, a study carried out in London found that sounds from squeaking door hinges, metal bowls being placed on the incubator, machinery banging into the incubator, radios playing and telephones ringing were predominant in recordings made from within the incubator. The sound patterns, like the light patterns, did not vary much between day and night (Wolke, 1987). Sudden loud sounds, such as the telephone ringing, or someone bumping into the incubator, produce sleep disturbance, motor arousal, acceleration of heart rate and respiration, decrease in transcutaneous oxygenation and increase in intracranial pressure in premature infants (Long et al., 1980). They are therefore potentially harmful to babies who have already existing cardiovascular and respiratory problems and inadequate cerebral blood flow. They also prevent the baby resting.

Handling by staff similarly disturbs the baby's rest. The sickest and most fragile infants are handled most by staff and least by parents and are often handled up to 234 times in a 24-hour period, with rest periods between handling of as little as 4.6 min (Murdoch and Darlow, 1984). Handling by staff is associated with monitoring, therapeutic and nursing procedures and is frequently aversive. Murdoch and Darlow found that 83% of all instances of hypoxaemia, 93% of all incidences of bradycardia and 38% of apnoea occurred during or immediately after routine handling of sick, premature infants. These babies were frequently observed to cry, often silently.

Parental handling is not usually aversive. Many parents are reluctant to touch or hold a very ill baby and instead spend a lot of time just watching him or her (Wolke, 1987; Niven et al., in press). In an effort to bond parents with their premature infant, some units encourage parents to hold the baby in their arms very soon after delivery. As we have pointed out elsewhere (see Chapter 3 and above) it is now recognized that this kind of early contact is not an essential prerequisite for adequate bonding. Holding the baby may be very rewarding for the parents but it may also be alarming and upsetting (Niven et al., in press). It will certainly be terrifying and deeply distressing for them if the baby 'goes off' while, or immediately after, being held. Looking at the baby or gently stroking him or her may be more appropriate for both the parents and their very sick or immature baby.

Gentle stroking can be used by staff or parents to soothe and comfort a baby who has been disturbed and distressed by some necessary but aversive procedure such as tube-changing. The balance of aversive/comforting handling should be considered by staff as well as the need to let the baby rest, particularly at night. Mann and colleagues (1986), in a well designed British study, showed that premature babies who were cared for in a unit where light and noise were reduced between 7 pm and 7 am slept longer, fed more efficiently and gained more weight after they returned home than babies who were nursed in perpetual light and noise.

As we discussed in Chapter 3, babies learn to adapt to the temporal and diurnal rhythms that they are regularly exposed to. In many cases this means that babies cared for in busy intensive neonatal units learn to be as awake during the night as during the day since the two are indistinguishable. This can cause many problems for the family once the baby goes home.

The premature baby may also suffer learning-related problems because of inadequate or inappropriate stimulation in neonatal care. The full-term healthy baby is given things to hold or feel or suck and is surrounded by attractive objects to look at and pleasant sounds to hear. All of these stimulate basic development and learning – about colour and form, texture and taste, pitch and tone. The very premature baby doesn't usually receive this kind of pleasant stimulation. They often have toys in the incubator beside them and the unit usually has bright mobiles and pictures. But the toys are typically placed above the baby's head where s/he can't see or feel them, and the mobiles are well out of visual range (20–40 cm in a neonate). Even very tiny babies try to hold on to something or to suck something. For instance, they try to hold on to the ventilator tube or to engage in non-nutritive sucking while being tube-fed (Wolke, 1987). Provision of something to grasp and explore – a dental roll, or a parental finger, and something to suck, may provide some important stimulation for these babies. Certainly a study of the provision of non-nutritive sucking opportunities found that this was associated with enhanced growth and maturation in premature babies (Bernbaum et al., 1983).

The very immature or sick baby may seldom be alert enough to benefit from pleasant visual, vestibular or vocal stimulation, though gentle stroking is practicable and can be helpful (see above). But as the baby progresses, such stimulation becomes feasible. The baby will be in the alert state for longer periods of time and so will be able to attend to her/his environment. The baby can be rocked, cuddled, sung to and provided with objects to explore. These provisions can be made by inanimate means: tapes, water beds, cuddly toys, but arguably the best providers are human. Progression in neonatal care usually involves a move to a post-intensive care unit. Here staff levels are lower and so staff may be unable to spend much time with the babies except for essential care-taking. Because they are so busy and are caring for so many babies, staff may also be unaware of the developing capacities of the individual baby. Tanke et al. (1984) have reported that while over time the abilities and capacities of incubated babies increase notably, the vocal and visual stimulation of these babies by the staff do not increase accordingly. This is where parents are vital. They have the time and motivation to attend to their infant's need for stimulation.

They need to be guided by the staff, though, to provide the right level of stimulation. Too much stimulation can be as bad as too little because it will cause the baby to 'turn off'. He or she will break eye contact, arch away, cry and may show physiological signs of distress such as changes in heart rate and respiration (see Wolke, 1987 and Chapter 5). The best way to judge whether or not the level of stimulation is right for the individual infant is to observe his or her behaviour. If the baby shows any of these signs of distress, stimulation should be reduced, and if the distress continues, it should be terminated. As I will discuss in more detail in the following chapter, sensitive interaction with babies depends on reading the babies' signals. Parents caring for their babies in neonatal units may not yet have developed this sensitivity (most will develop it eventually, as their baby teaches them to be more sensitive). They are also likely to feel awkward and unskilled (Niven et al., in press) and such feelings interfere with sensitivity – remember how difficult it was to interact with a patient when a clinical teacher or examiner was looking over your shoulder. So staff need to advise parents on how to be guided by their babies. And in order to do that, they need to develop their own sensitivity to the individual baby's signals. The cardinal rule that operates here is to observe the baby: not just skin colour, or heart rate, growth rate or weight gain, but the baby's behaviour – signs of distress, signals of interest, marks of pleasure.

If neonatal staff get into the habit of observing their patients' psychological signs as well as their physical ones, they will become more skilled at meeting their psychological needs. Current research suggests that meeting these needs is important and that more thought should go into providing an optimum psychological environment for the 'new species' of human – the very premature baby. Providing an environment that is not too noisy or too bright, that has a diurnal regularity and allows the baby to rest, and that makes available the right level of pleasant stimulation, within a neonatal unit dedicated to technology and intensive care, is difficult. It may be easier for staff to operate on a 24-hour-a-day basis, where night shift and day shift are largely indistinguishable; after all, premature babies aren't just born during the day, nor do they wait to have their crises till the day staff come on duty. It's more cheerful for the staff to have the radio playing; it's easier to have the phone at hand; and incubator tops provide nice flat surfaces to rest things on.

For years adult patients have been complaining that hospitals operate more for the benefit of the staff than for the patient. They've pointed out that we're noisy, that we don't let them rest – 'wake up and take your sleeping pill!' – and that it's hard to sleep when the lights are on and the ward's busy and the phone's ringing constantly. Some of these totally justified complaints have been recognized and some changes have been made. Premature babies can't complain. They often don't even have the energy to cry, but they suffer just the same. The same consideration needs to be given to them. Just because they're tiny and too ill to react doesn't mean that they're deaf or blind. They're another form of human being, not an entirely different species of animal. The needs of the normal baby are there in an attenuated form in even the earliest or sickest baby. And as your work succeeds and the baby grows and develops, s/he becomes more like the normal baby and requires more normal treatment. We would be quick to condemn parents who kept a 'normal' baby in a home with lights on and loud noise day and night; or who never cuddled the baby, or comforted her when she was hurt or upset; or who kept him shut away from normal stimulation and interaction. Yet much of that is the norm in intensive neonatal care. It may be unimportant for the very ill or very immature baby, though the evidence suggests that distress can affect survival. It may not have lasting effects on his or her development, though short-term effects are apparent. But I can't see that it's good midwifery, nursing or psychological care.

In seeking to change the situation, neonatal managers need to be aware of the stress that their staff are already experiencing, some of which may be relieved by having bright, cheerful surroundings in which to work. Other ways of alleviating staff stress must be sought, otherwise patient care will inevitably suffer. I noted earlier in this section that staff in neonatal units suffered from a lack of autonomy and reported relatively low levels of work satisfaction. Caring for their patients' psychological needs as well as their physical ones lies clearly within the remit of skilled midwifery and nursing care. It may therefore be more rewarding to nurse premature and sick babies in this way, and the consideration of their psychological and developmental needs could become an area of nursing, as opposed to medical, expertise.

Overview and summary

Although the majority of parturients experience childbirth as a demanding experience, few recall it as excessively traumatic. Those who do so suffer greatly, recall being associated with considerable distress, nightmares and reluctance to contemplate future pregnancy. Sexual and relationship problems have also been reported in clinical studies. The causes of this form of post-traumatic stress disorder are not yet clear but research into reactions to childbirth would suggest that the provision of sensitive care and careful explanation in the early postnatal period might ameliorate some of the negative effects of a birth which has been experienced as traumatic.

It seems that it is the woman's perception of the events surrounding birth which is important, rather than some objective assessment of the degree of pain, stress or intervention involved. Research into Caesarian section, for instance, has found that it has a number of negative consequences for the woman involved, but that there is no clear link between operative delivery and long-term traumatization. Most of the negative consequences of Caesarian delivery are physical rather than psychological. These might be ameliorated if women who have been sectioned had received more opportunity to rest and recuperate from their major surgery. However research indicates that these opportunities are often restricted by current hospital practice. The need for more information and explanation with regard to sectioning has been clearly established. Specific preparation for operative delivery might be usefully provided in the immediate antenatal period rather than at antenatal classes when the needs of women who will deliver vaginally predominate. Even when adequate preparation is achieved, women who require a Caesarian have a continued need for information about the reasons for sectioning, the course of their recovery and the implications for future childbirth.

When childbirth fails to conform to the parturients' view of normality or desirability, the woman may be left with a sense of loss or failure. In such cases, these feelings are usually (though not invariably) mild and transient. Women who miscarry, or whose baby dies around the time of birth, suffer extreme and long-lasting grief and bereavement. The grieving process can manifest itself in numerous ways, with feelings of anger, disbelief, restlessness and guilt occurring, as well as feelings of profound sadness, depression and despair. Nothing that midwives, health visitors or nurses can do will replace that loss or 'make it better'. However, thoughtless and insensitive treatment by staff can greatly exacerbate the mother's difficulties, whereas kindness and consideration are greatly appreciated and provide some consolation.

Our modern medicalized society has become somewhat detached from death and many people, health care practitioners included, find it difficult to deal with its consequences. We don't know what to say or do to help the person who has been bereaved and therefore find it easier to avoid them, or to avoid the topic of their loss. This may make it more difficult for the mother to go through the painful but necessary process of grieving and thus ultimately to come to terms with her loss. A listening ear and a comforting arm are often the most effective forms of communication and all health care professionals who are involved with the bereaved should strive to provide them on a long-term basis.

Fathers who are bereaved may show their distress in different ways to mothers. They may also recover from their loss more quickly. However, their need to grieve is even more often ignored, as staff, family and friends concentrate their attention on the mother. The father is experiencing his own loss and should be accorded the appropriate support and sympathy.

When a baby is born with a handicap, such as Down's syndrome, the parents are likely to react with initial disbelief, confusion and grief. They need to come to terms with the loss of the expected perfect baby, as well as with the presence and potential problems of having a handicapped baby. Some of these parents may feel a sense of revulsion or shame and it is important that staff show by holding, cuddling and admiring the baby that they find the baby as attractive and lovable as any non-handicapped baby.

Although communicating a diagnosis of perinatal death or handicap is formally a medical matter, many midwives and health visitors will be involved in breaking the news to shocked and distraught parents. The provision of clear, sensitive explanation to both parents, along with the ensuring of privacy, maintenance of contact and facilitation of discussion, ensures that this distressing task is accomplished in the best way possible. These principles of care can be applied to many other situations, for example those involved in the communication of test results in pregnancy.

Parents whose baby is born very prematurely, with a very low birthweight or with some other condition or handicap which requires intensive neonatal care, will experience many of the feelings that have already been associated with traumatic birth, loss and the birth of a less than perfect baby. Consequently staff need to ensure that the principles of support, explanation and communication outlined above are practised with the parents of these babies. The psychological needs of the babies themselves should be considered when nursing care plans are being developed.

The provision of skilled, 'high-tech', neonatal intensive care usually necessitates separation of mother and baby. This makes it difficult for mothers and fathers to feel close to their baby while she or he remains in hospital and requires the care of skilled staff. However it is now apparent that the lack of normal contact in the immediate postnatal period need not disrupt parent–infant bonding in the long term. Most parents who maintain contact with their baby while s/he is in hospital and become involved in his/her care will become normally attached to the baby in time. The stress associated with having a very early, light or ill baby is however extreme. It may temporarily interfere with bonding to the baby and will certainly cause the parents a great deal of distress. Recent research suggests that emotional support received from midwifery and nursing staff is greatly appreciated by such parents, although they feel that still more is required. The families themselves provide much of that support, and staff should do what they can to facilitate this family provision.

Further reading

Browne K. D., Davies C., Stratton P. (1988). *Early Prediction and Prevention of Child Abuse.* Chichester: Wiley.

Lewis E., Bourne S. (1989). Perinatal bereavement. In *Baillière's Clinical Obstetrics and Gynaecology. Volume. 3. Psychological Aspects of Obstetrics and Gynaecology* (Oates M., ed.). London: Baillière Tindall.

Oglethorpe R. (1989). Parenting after perinatal bereavement – a review of the literature. *J. Reprod. Infant Psychol.*, **7**, 227–44.

Parkes C. M. (1972). *Bereavement: A Study of Grief in Adult Life.* London: Tavistock.

Wolke D. (1987). Environmental and developmental neonatology. *J. Reprod. Infant Psychol.*, **5**, 17–42.

References

Affonso D. (1977). Missing pieces – a study of postpartum feelings. *Birth Family J.*, **4**, 159–64.

Als H. (1991). The neurobehavioural development of the premature infant and the environment of the neonatal intensive care unit. In *Manual of Neonatal Care* (Cloherty J. P., Stark A. R., eds). Boston: Little, Brown.

Bendefy I., Bryan E., Bielawske-Sowa A. (1990). Paper presented at the 10th Anniversary Conference of the Society for Reproductive and Infant Psychology. Cambridge, England.

Benfield D. G., Leib S. A., Vollman J. H. (1978). Grief responses of parents to neonatal death and patient participation in deciding care. *Pediatrics*, **62**, 171–7.

Bernbaum J. C., Pereira G. R., Watkins J. B., Peckham G. J. (1983). Non-nutritive sucking during gavage feeding enhances growth and maturation in premature infants. *Pediatrics*, **71**, 41–5.

Bicknell J., Hollins S. (eds) *Mental Handicap – A Multi-Disciplinary Approach*. London: Baillière Tindall.

Brody H., Meikle S., Gerritse R. (1971). Therapeutic abortion: a prospective study. *Am. J. Obstet. Gynecol.*, **109**, 347–53.

Browne K. (1988). Early child maltreatment: an interdisciplinary approach. Editorial. Early child mistreatment. *J. Reprod. Infant Psychol.*, **6**, 115–17.

Byrne E. A., Cunningham C. C., Sloper P. (1988). *Families and their Children with Down's Syndrome: One Feature in Common*. London: Croom Helm.

Calam R., Lambrenos K., Cox A. D., Weindling A. M. (1990). What is said and what is remembered: mother's recall of information about their preterm neonates. *J. Reprod. Infant Psychol.*, **8**, 291.

Cooper J. D. (1980). Parental reactions to stillbirth. *Br. J. Social Work*, **10**, 55–9.

Cullberg J. (1971). Mental reactions of women to perinatal death. In *Proceedings of the Third International Congress of Psychosomatic Medicine in Obstetrics and Gynaecology, Basel*. London: Karger.

Cunningham C. C. (1979). Parent counselling. In *Tredgold's Mental Retardation*, 12th edn (Craft M., ed.). London: Baillière Tindall.

Cunningham C. C., Davis H. (1985). Early parent counselling. In *Mental Handicap – A Multi-Disciplinary Approach* (Craft M., Bicknell J., Hollins S., eds). London: Baillière Tindall.

Cunningham C. C., Morgan P. A., McGucken R. B. (1984). Down's syndrome: is dissatisfaction with disclosure of diagnosis inevitable? *Dev. Med. Child Neurol.*, **26**, 33–9.

Cunningham C. C., Sloper T. (1977). Parents of Down's syndrome babies: their early needs. *Child Care, Health Dev.*, **3**, 325–47.

Duxbury M. L., Thiessen U. (1979). Staff turnover in neonatal intensive care units. *J. Adv. Nursing*, **4**, 591–602.

Elmer E., Gregg G. S. (1967). Developmental characteristics of abused children. *Pediatrics*, **40**, 596–602.

Forrest G. C., Standish E., Baum J. D. (1982). Support after perinatal death; a study of support and counselling after perinatal bereavement. *Br. Med. J.*, **285**, 1475–9.

Friedman T. (1989). Women's experience of general practitioner management of miscarriage. *J. R. Coll. Gen. Pract.*, **39**, 456–8.

Friedman T., Gath D. (1989). The psychiatric consequences of spontaneous abortion. *Br. J. Psychiatry*, **155**, 810–13.

Gannon K. Psychological factors in recurrent miscarriage: a review and critique. *J. Reprod. Infant Psychol.*, in submission.

Green J. M., Coupland V. A. Kitzinger J. V. (1988). *Great Expectations: A Prospective Study of Women's Expectations and Experiences of Childbirth.* Cambridge: Child Care and Development Group.

Hillan E. M. (1989). Caesarian section: indications and outcomes. Unpublished PhD thesis, University of Glasgow.

Hwang C. P. (1987). Cesarian childbirth in Sweden: effects on the mother–infant and father–infant relationship. *Infant Mental Health J.*, **8**, 22–30.

Iles S. (1989). The loss of early pregnancy. In *Baillière's Clinical Obstetrics and Gynaecology. Volume 3. Psychological Aspects of Obstetrics and Gynaecology* (Oates M., ed.). London: Baillière Tindall.

Knussen C., Cunningham C. C. (1988). Stress, disability and handicap. In *Handbook of Life Stress, Cognition and Health* (Fisher S., Reason J., eds). London: John Wiley.

Leifer A. D., Leiderman P. H., Barnett C. R., Williams J. A. (1972). Effect of mother–infant separation on maternal attachment behaviour. *Child Dev.*, **43**, 1203–18.

Leventhal J. M. (1988). Can child maltreatment be predicted during the perinatal period: evidence from longitudinal cohort studies? *J. Reprod. Infant Psychol.*, **6**, 139–61.

Lewis E., Bourne S. (1989). Perinatal bereavement. In *Baillière's Clinical Obstetrics and Gynaecology. Volume 3. Psychological Aspects of Obstetrics and Gynaecology* (Oates M., ed.). London: Baillière Tindall.

Lipson J. G., Tilden V. P. (1980). Psychological integration of the Cesarian birth experience. *Am. J. Orthopsychiatry*, **50**, 598.

Long G. J., Lucey J. F., Philip A. G. (1980). Noise and hypoxaemia in the intensive care nursery. *Pediatrics*, **65**, 143–5.

Lynch M. A., Roberts J. (1982). *Consequences of Child Abuse.* New York: Academic Press.

McCance C., Olley P. C., Edward V. (1973). Long term psychiatric follow-up. In *Experience with Abortion* (Horobin G., ed.). London: Cambridge University Press.

McConachie H. (1982). Fathers of mentally handicapped children. In *Fathers: Psychological Perspectives* (Beail N., McGuire J., eds). London: Junction Books.

McHaffie H. (1991). 'A study of support for families with very low birth weight babies'. Nursing Research Unit Report. Department of Nursing Studies, University of Edinburgh.

Mandell F., McNulty E., Carlson A. (1983). Unexpected death of an infant sibling. *Pediatrics*, **72**, 652–7.

Mander R. (1991a). Midwifery support of the mother relinquishing her baby for adoption: midwives' perceptions. *Midwives Chronical*, **104**, 275–84.

Mander R. (1991b). Midwifery care of the bereaved mother: how the decisions are made. *Midwifery*, **7**, 133–42.

Mann N. P., Haddow R., Stokes L. et al. (1986). Effects of night and day on preterm infants in a newborn nursery: randomised trial. *Br. Med. J.*, **293**, 1265–7.

Murdoch D. R., Darlow B. A. (1984). Handling during neonatal intensive care. *Arch. Dis. Child.*, **59**, 957–61.

Murray J., Callen C. J. (1988). Predicting adjustment to perinatal death. *Br. J. Med. Psychol.*, **61**, 237–44.

Niven C. (1986). Factors affecting labour pain. Unpublished doctoral thesis. University of Stirling.

Niven C. (1988). Labour pain: long term recall and consequences. *J. Reprod. Infant Psychol.*, **6**, 83–7.

Niven C., Wiszniewski C., AlRoomi L. Attachment in mother of preterm babies. *J. Reprod. Infant Psychol.*, in press.

Oakley A. (1980). *Women Confined.* Oxford: Martin Robertson.

Oglethorpe R. (1989). Parenting after perinatal bereavement – a review of the literature. *J. Reprod. Infant Psychol.*, **7**, 227–44.

Pare C. M., Raven H. (1970). Follow-up of patients referred for termination of pregnancy. *Lancet*, **i**, 635–8.

Parkes C. M. (1972). *Bereavement: a Study of Grief in Adult Life.* London: Tavistock.

Reading A., Cheng Li C., Kerin J. F. (1989). Psychological state and coping style across an IVF treatment cycle. *J. Reprod. Infant Psychol.*, **7**, 95–105.

Robson K., Kumar R. (1980). Delayed onset of maternal affection after childbirth. *Br. J. Psychiatry*, **136**, 347–53.

Rowe J., Clyman R., Green M. (1978). Follow up of families who experience a perinatal death. *Pediatrics*, **3**, 166–9.

Sahu S. (1981). Coping with perinatal death. *J. Reprod. Med.*, **26**, 129–32.

Sammons W., Lewis J. (1985). *Premature Babies: a different beginning.* St Louis: CV Mosby Co.

Savage W. (1988). The active management of perinatal death. In *Motherhood and Mental Illness 2* (Kumar R., Brockington I. F., eds). London: Wright.

Spinks P., Michaelson J. (1989). A comparison of the ward environment in a special care baby unit and a children's orthopaedic ward. *J. Reprod. Infant Psychol.*, **7**, 47–50.

Starr R. H. (1988). Pre and perinatal risk and physical abuse. *J. Reprod. Infant Psychol.*, **6**, 125–38.

Starr R. H., Dietrich K. N., Fishcoff J. et al. (1984). The contribution of handicapping conditions to child abuse. *Topics Early Child. Special Educ.*, **4**, 55–69.

Stewart D. E. (1982). Psychiatric symptoms following attempted natural childbirth. *Can. Med. Assoc. J.*, **127**, 713–17.

Tanke M. J., Hermanns J., Lechner M., Katz B. P. (1984). Social contacts with very low birth weight children. Presentation at 4th. International Conference on Infant Studies. New York.

Thune-Larsen K-B., Moller-Pedersen K. (1988). Childbirth experience and postpartum emotional disturbance. *J. Reprod. Infant Psychol.*, **6**, 229–40.

Tylden E. (1990). Post-traumatic stress disorder in obstetrics. Paper presented at the 5th International Conference of the Marce Society. University of York, England.

Wenderlein J., Wilhelm R. (1979). Sectio oder spontangeburt. Was wird belastender erlebt? *Z. Geburtshilfe Perinatol*, **183**, 453–60.

Wolke D. (1987). Environmental and developmental neonatology. *J. Reprod. Infant Psychol.*, **5**, 17–42.
Woodward S., Pope A., Robson W., Hagan O. (1985). Bereavement counselling after sudden infant death. *Br. Med. J.*, **290**, 363–5.

5 The early months

In this chapter I will consider the first few months of the baby's life, concentrating on the adjustments required within the family by the inclusion of a new and demanding member, and the manner in which the father, mother and siblings interact with the baby and care for him or her. This chapter deals with normal adjustment and normal interactions. Unusually problematic aspects of the family's experience of the early months are dealt with in Chapter 6.

The mother

In the previous chapter I discussed how childbirth could be a traumatic experience. But however demanding giving birth to a child might be, it pales into insignificance beside the task of the next 16, 18, 20 years – that of rearing the child. Once the mother comes home from hospital, the midwife stops calling daily, the cards stop arriving, the visitors tail off, Granny goes home and Daddy goes back to work, the magnitude of that task becomes apparent. The first reality for most mothers (biological or adoptive) is that the responsibility for the baby's care is for 24 hours a day, 7 days a week. As we'll see later in this chapter (The father), most fathers take relatively little responsibility for child care at this stage, and even if they do shoulder an unusually large share of the burden of baby care, as in the role reversal families studied by Russell in Australia where the mother went out to work and the father stayed home, the mother typically feels more responsible for guaranteeing the baby's overall well-being (Russell, 1983). This 24-hour-a-day responsibility has physical consequences – disrupted routines, sleepless nights (for example, the breast-feeding mother will only sleep for 3 or 4 hours at a stretch for up to 8 weeks), exhaustion; and psychological ones – a sense of being unequal to the task, a degree of inadequacy, worries about the baby's well-being (for instance, is he overfed, or starved; is he not sleeping enough or so sound asleep that I wonder if he's still alive?). So the new mother is likely to feel rather tired and irritable, unsure of herself, and somewhat anxious.

If the mother or other primary caretaker has given up work outside the home, she is likely to suffer some loss of independence, of income, of social contacts and of positive feedback about the meaningfulness of her job and her ability to perform it successfully. Very young babies, after all, show little positive appreciation of their mother's best efforts (they're about 6 weeks old before they smile properly and goo's and ga's come even later) yet demonstrate loudly their apparent displeasure, so the new mother gets no positive feedback from her baby to tell her that she is doing her job of mothering well. Our society shows little appreciation of the realities of motherhood although it ostensibly values it highly. As Margaret Oates, a psychiatrist with a special interest in childbearing, points out:

> mothers may be seen as less reliable employees, motherhood is used as an argument for women's non progression in the professions [I wonder which profession she is thinking of particularly?], children are not welcome in the work place, restaurants, hotels and shops, and sometimes not even at family gatherings such as weddings. Children are valued if they are quiet and untroublesome, soundly asleep and absent from evening entertainment with friends. Mothers are readily blamed for all the problems to do with children but are rarely praised if things are going well (Oates, 1989, pp. 794, 795).

All of these factors can lead to a sense of social isolation, of being undervalued, or being 'just a mother', and an element of grieving may be apparent in some mothers who are mourning their lost autonomy, financial independence and social life.

Such difficulties in adjustment are normal, both in the sense of being typical (i.e. statistically normal) and in being psychologically normal (Oates, 1989). They should not be equated with postnatal depression (see Chapter 6) but instead reflect the reality of caring for a young baby in a society which does not value child care highly – if it did it would pay child carers more money. This reality does not equate with the 'rosy glow' view of motherhood (the Princess Di, or designer baby version) put forward by much of the media, which ill prepares many women for the experience of motherhood and may raise false expectations which are then disappointingly dashed.

Despite these difficulties, most women cope with motherhood extremely well and feel positive about many of its aspects. Ball, for instance, in her study of postnatal adjustment in 279 English women broadly representative of the normal social class distribution, found that only 1.1% of her subjects were dissatisfied with motherhood 6 weeks after the birth (Ball, 1989). This is not because motherhood is easy, 'a piece of cake', but because most women are highly motivated towards caring for a tiny, helpless infant to the very best of their ability and find the provision of this care rewarding *despite* the tiredness, the loneliness, the boredom, the messiness involved, and because most women are wonderful copers!

Ball (1989), like many other researchers, found that mothers' own emotional well-being was less positive overall than their satisfaction with motherhood per se, and with their baby. She found that approximately 20% of her sample showed signs of emotional distress: only 10% were classified as 'very happy'. Postnatal distress will be dealt with in detail in the following chapter, but I want to make the point here that adjusting to motherhood and coping with a new baby puts strain on most women. This strain may affect their own well-being while leaving intact their positive feelings about their baby.

Some degree of anxiety about the total care of a small, helpless, vulnerable, dependent human being is inevitable. We discussed in Chapter 3 the abilities of neonates, some of which are quite remarkable. But these are not related to the ability to survive independently. Human babies will die if not cared for properly by another human being (Romulus, Remus and Tarzan excepted). The most vital aspect of that care concerns feeding, so it is no wonder that mothers worry about how best to feed their baby and about whether or not they are doing it successfully, and that questions and anxieties about feeding are likely to occupy much of a community midwife or health visitor's time.

Breast-feeding is recommended as 'best for baby' (Department of Health and Social Security, 1989) and I would have no argument with this recommendation, though as you will see below, it may not always be 'best for mother'. This is not the most appropriate place to debate the issue of breast versus bottle-feeding (see Further reading for some recent material on psychological aspects of this debate) but some material will be presented here which demonstrates the difficulties associated with breast-feeding. This may illuminate some of the reasons why mothers find it problematic.

Breast-feeding is the most common method of infant feeding used by women from many of the ethnic minority groups within the UK (Butler and Goldring, 1986). It is less common amongst the ethnic majority, and especially in young women from lower socioeconomic backgrounds (Thomson, 1989). Breast-feeding rates are increasing in England and Wales (Martin and Monk, 1982) but many studies show that a large proportion of women who breast-feed apparently successfully in hospital abandon breast-feeding in the subsequent weeks (Martin and Monk, 1982; McIntosh, 1985; Thomson, 1989; Wright, 1990). Some of these mothers may only have breast-fed in order to keep hospital staff happy. (Overenthusiastic breast-feeding propaganda can be hard to resist. I remember a young girl who didn't want to breast-feed being told by the 'breast-feeding sister': 'don't blame me if your baby dies of a stomach infection got from dirty bottles' – effective but hardly ethical!) Some may give up because breast-feeding is experienced as embarrass-ing in the 'outside world' whereas in hospital 'anything goes', while others may find that it interferes with their sexuality, their lifestyle or with their work patterns. Many of these mothers, like mothers who choose not to breast-feed, are likely to be quite happy with their switch to bottle-feeding and should receive the full support of their midwives and health visitors in optimizing their use of this method (Sanjack, 1988).

The woman's partner may object to her breast-feeding. Lewis, in his study of 100 Nottingham fathers, found that 32 claimed that breast-feeding was 'revolting, disgusting or embarrassing' (Lewis, 1986, p. 92). Their partners accounted for 32 out of the 52 women in this study who were not breast-feeding at 2 weeks after birth. So some mothers who give up breast-feeding may be doing so because it is embarrassing for their husbands, not for themselves, and because it interferes with their husband's sexuality, not their own (Thomson, 1989). Supportive fathers on the other hand were found to be important in encouraging continued breast-feeding, with 13 out of the 19 conti-

breast-feeding mothers in Lewis's sample remarking on their husband's help and support. Breast-feeding education and 'propaganda' might therefore be usefully directed at fathers-to-be as well as at mothers, and the support of the woman's partner for breast-feeding should also be enlisted in the postnatal period if at all possible. Women who feel that breast-feeding is best for their baby but whose partners are antagonistic towards this method of feeding are placed in a very difficult 'no-win' situation and need sensitive and understanding support from their professional carers.

Other mothers may suffer problems with nipples, abscesses and babies who are reluctant to suckle, some of which may be amenable to prevention or treatment (Thomson, 1989). But the most common reason given by women for abandoning breast-feeding is 'lack of milk' (Martin and Monk, 1982; McIntosh, 1985; Thomson, 1989; Wright, 1990) and many of these mothers are distressed and disappointed at their inability to continue breast-feeding or, as they see it, 'their failure' (McIntosh, 1985).

It seems unlikely that a high proportion of the reproductive population could be deficient in milk production, since the survival of the human species has been substantially dependent upon the ability of mothers to feed their young successfully. But once mothers are out of reach of the advice, encouragement and reassurance usually, but not invariably (see Chapter 3), provided by maternity hospital staff for breast-feeders, their confidence in this ability may wane. A recent study carried out in Salford found that women who had difficult pregnancies and deliveries and who had relatively high levels of depression and anxiety worried that their baby was not gaining enough weight and about colic, and as a result tended to give up breast-feeding early and introduce solids (Hellin, 1990). Breast-feeding mothers do not have the reassurance of being able to tell precisely how much milk their baby has received at each feed, nor how much was available. Thus any apparent upset or change in behaviour in the baby could be attributed to hunger and lack of milk rather than to a host of other possible causes. In contrast, the bottle-feeding mother has firm evidence that her baby has taken enough milk and so his/her crying, or frequent waking, or inability to settle, is attributed to other causes.

Bottle-fed babies can usually have as much milk as they want unless the milk packet's empty and someone's forgotten or couldn't afford to buy more. But since breast milk supply is dependent on the previous stimulation produced by suckling, sometimes there will not be as much milk available at that feed as the baby wants. Unless the mother understands that the baby will be compensated for this deficit at the following feed and will regulate her/his intake accordingly (Crow and Wright, 1976), she will judge quite accurately that she 'didn't have enough milk'. Comparison with the bottle-fed baby will accentuate this feeling of insufficiency, whereas comparison with other breast-feeding mothers and babies will show that such temporary shortfalls are normal. However some breast-feeding mothers may have bottle-feeding friends and will most likely have relatives and friends who have bottle-fed in the past when bottle-feeding was very common, so unhelpful comparisons are quite likely to be made.

Research has shown that breast-feeding mothers are not especially good at consciously estimating how much milk is demanded or available at a particular feed, being approximately correct only about 50% of the time on average (Wright, 1990). At 1 month postpartum, Wright found that 77% of mothers thought that there was a variation in hunger in their babies across the 24 hours where none actually existed (as measured by amount of milk taken at each feed); the mothers said that their babies were more hungry at certain feeds, but the babies took the same amount of milk at these feeds as at other 'not particularly hungry' feeds. Therefore breast-feeding mothers may perceive unrequited hunger in their babies where none exists.

The feeding pattern of babies alters as they mature. At 1 month of age, breast-fed babies take approximately equal amounts of milk at each feed across 24 hours. At some point between 5 and 7 weeks, the baby switches to taking a large meal between 4 and 8 a.m., with the remainder of the feeds becoming progressively smaller. This shift is likely to reflect the dropping of a night feed in girls and is accompanied by more frequent feeding in the late afternoon. Mothers interpret very frequent feeding as a sign of hunger in girl babies. They may therefore perceive this shift, not as a sign of a healthy, normal development, but as a sign of unrequited hunger and therefore of insufficient milk. Breast-fed male babies of this age tend still to feed in the early hours of the morning, so once again comparison with female babies, or with bottle-fed babies, may lead the harassed breast-feeding mother of a night-waking boy to conclude that she has insufficient milk to satisfy his needs (Wright, 1990). Wright points out that mothers are often unaware of these shifts and gender differences, as are many health professionals. Being forewarned about them may forearm mothers so that they do not lose confidence in their ability to feed their baby properly and consequently abandon breast-feeding for the reassurance of the transparent bottle.

All mothers have the opportunity to receive a postnatal check-up at 6 weeks postpartum. In a study of the psychosocial rather than medical effectiveness of such check-ups, Porter and McIntyre (1989) found that there 'seemed to be a preoccupation with form-filling and physical wellbeing to the exclusion of the woman's feelings about her body or her baby' (Porter and McIntyre, 1989, p. 91). Several women asked about breast-feeding problems at the postnatal clinics observed in this study, but the obstetricians or general practitioners who ran the clinics did not explore the women's problems or offer them any advice or reassurance.

Midwives or health visitors who are involved in such clinics are better placed to answer such queries and should endeavour to make their expertise available to the postpartum woman. They may also be better placed to provide psychological support, explanation and advice than medical staff. Although most postpartum woman will be attended by community midwives and health visitors, they may not always find them sympathetic or receptive to their problems. They can also be 'too close to home' so that some mothers may prefer to discuss their problems with a professional who knows them and their circumstances less intimately. Midwives who staff postnatal clinics and maternity day hospitals could thus provide a valuable source of expert advice and effective psychosocial care.

The father

In Chapter 3 we discussed the father's involvement with his baby at birth and the help and support he gave his partner in the period immediately after she came home from hospital. The vast majority of fathers return to work after 1 or 2 weeks and the amount of time and energy they have thereafter available for child care is substantially curtailed. Even in the time they are at home, however, fathers perform few baby care tasks regularly. Moss and colleagues (1987), in a study of primigravid women and their partners living in a relatively affluent suburb of London, found that 21% of fathers fed their child daily, 11% dressed them, 8% bathed them and 14% changed their nappies. These figures reflected the fathers' reports of their regular activities when their child was a year old. The mothers' reports of the fathers' child care activities were more conservative, except with regard to feeding. They reported that 5% of their partners dressed the baby; 7% bathed him/her, and 6% changed nappies. Overall, the amount of child care performed by fathers was found to increase slightly over the course of the first year, so the percentages quoted here are the best obtained, not the worst.

In the immediate postnatal period, Lewis reports that fathers did little child care but did housework instead (see The father, Chapter 3). Moss et al. (1987) found little evidence of this kind of indirect support continuing beyond the immediate postnatal period, with the mother at home resuming her role as the primary houseworker. Assessments of the father's contribution to child care relative to the amount of time he had available at home little affected the study's results. Moss et al. concluded, as have a substantial number of other British researchers (Graham and McKee, 1979; Oakley, 1980; Beail, 1985; Lewis, 1986), that though there is great variability in the amount of child care that fathers perform, it is rare for there to be any equal sharing of child care between the father and mother even within the time both are at home. In the majority of cases the father does little regular child care, feeding being the most common task performed and dirty nappy changing being one of the least common.

Recent research carried out in this and other countries, however, indicates that the situation may be slowly and gradually changing. Some few fathers are highly participant, sharing care almost (but not quite) equally with their wives (Russell, 1983; Lewis, 1986; Hwang, 1987). In these families, financial and work-related factors make it practicable or necessary for the father to be at home during the day for much of the time, and for the mother to work outside the home at these times. Shared child care is probably most common in Sweden. This is because of the enlightened policies there, which allow parental leave to be taken for approximately 6 months after the baby's birth by either the father or the mother, with remuneration at 90% of full salary. Further remunerated leave is available which can be taken at any time up till the child is age 7. These policies allow parents to share child care without suffering financial hardship as a result. However only a small proportion of Swedish fathers take parental leave during the first 6 months of the child's life (about 10% of fathers take small amounts of leave) while more fathers, about 28%, take advantage of the later leave arrangements, but again for short periods of time (Hwang, 1987). It seems that even in liberal, liberated Sweden, the myth of the 'new Mothercare man' the 'designer dad', is usually just that – a myth.

Australia is a country more commonly associated with the macho image. However, Russell in the early 1980s was able to find a sample of 71 Australian families where the father either shared, or had the major responsibility for, the day-to-day care of his children. Lewis, working in Nottingham in England around the same time, with a random sample of fathers selected from the local birth records (Lewis, 1986), found that 4 out of a sample of 100 men spent most of the day at home in order to look after their children. They all did so in order to allow their wives to work; so, as in Russell's study where 61 of the 71 families were better off financially after commencing shared caregiving, practical reasons for sharing child care seem to score over ideological ones.

Researchers who are currently investigating the role of the father in the family are generally agreed that there is not now one clear role model of the ideal father figure. Instead there are a number of father figure models, some traditional and some innovative. Russell describes well the range of father figures found in his study which, despite the cultural differences between Australia and here, are I think clearly recognizable.

There was the uninterested and unavailable father who was rarely at home and when he was, spent little time with his children.

There was the traditional father . . . a father who took little responsibility for the day-to-day care of his children but was available and played with them regularly.

There was the 'good father', described as such by his partner. They were more involved than traditional fathers, and it was more common for them to perform basic child-care tasks such as bathing, feeding and changing nappies. The good fathers were seen as good because they were willing to help mothers. They were not seen as having equal status with mothers.

Finally there was the highly participant, shared caregiver father. They carried out 46% of child care tasks per week. Nevertheless they were not as participant as their own spouses and many shared caregiving families agreed that mothers were still likely to take overall responsibility for the children, even though fathers contributed nearly as much to their day-to-day care (Russell, 1983, p. 199).

So the social institution of fatherhood is, as Beail (1985) noted, 'in a state of flux'. Which way it will go is unclear. Perhaps economic and demographic pressures will make more and more women work outside the home, as well as within it, and make shared parenting more of a necessity. Perhaps the current media obsession with fatherhood – all these adverts of fathers and babies – will persuade men that getting involved in child care is highly desirable. Perhaps on the other hand, the 'new age' image of the 1990s will persuade women that they want to retain their predominance in child care, and motherhood rather than fatherhood will suddenly become wildly fashionable.

Who knows? And maybe, who cares? Does it matter anyway? I think it does. Firstly it matters that midwives and health visitors dealing with families in the postnatal period do not assume that they will be dealing with one type of family: the traditional one perhaps where it makes some sense to concentrate efforts on the mother and largely ignore the father, or the one portrayed in the adverts, where the mother might seem less important than the involved and ever-competent dad. You need to assess each family as it comes, observing its dynamics and the way it distributes child care responsibilities. Don't rely totally on what the mother or father says they are doing – as we've seen in Moss's study, their reports don't always agree and other researchers have found that parental reports often imply an egalitarian distribution of child care when the realities are quite different (Lewis, 1989).

This gap between the ideal of equality within a relationship and the reality of an unequal distribution of child care and housework, with the woman typically doing most of it, has been noted by Lewis as the most consistent theme to emerge from his researches. It no doubt reflects the changing perceptions of male and female roles, and may be influenced by media hype which portrays the typical dad as far more involved than he actually is. Thus, even though the amount of help a modern mother gets from her husband far exceeds that received by her mother, her expectations are much greater. They are frequently unfulfilled, and this can lead to dissatisfaction and strain within the relationship (see, for example, Moss et al.'s study, detailed below). So the father who feels good about himself because he feeds the baby once a day and changes the occasional nappy finds his efforts are unappreciated. Yet he is probably doing as much as most fathers, and more than some.

Fathers who do attempt to share child care don't necessarily win either. Oates (1989) notes that many mothers feel very possessive about their babies in the early postnatal weeks and may resent anyone else handling them or appearing to usurp their mothering role. Lewis (1986) found that some mothers resented their partner's involvement, as illustrated by the following quotes from interviews with firstly a father, and then a mother.

> At the beginning I used to interfere . . . I think that's perhaps the right word . . . too much. You know, if she wanted to do something such a way I'd say 'I think this is a better way'. And I learned, through getting my fingers burnt, a little bit, that perhaps that wasn't the best way of going about

it . . . with regard to feeding. After the first couple of weeks I was back at work, you know . . . I hadn't got a say in it anyway 'cos I wasn't here'. (Interviewer to mother:Were you keen for Ron to give James his bottle?) 'No, I really wanted to do it myself this time, though I really felt he *ought* to. Just to show interest. I really contradicted myself a lot in my feelings over that. I didn't want anybody else to feed him but me, but I used to think he ought.' (Lewis, 1986, p. 248).

Fathers who actually participate in shared care-giving recognize the improvement in their relationship with their children as a clear benefit of this lifestyle (Russell, 1983). However if, as was usual in Russell's study, shared child care was brought about through a reduction in the father's commitment to work outside the home, with a corresponding increase in their partner's commitment to paid employment, several disadvantages were also apparent. Many of these fathers found it difficult to adapt to the caregiver's role, and found that they suffered a loss of the status that had been associated with their outside employment. The lack of adult company, the tiredness of their wife and the strain that was placed on the marital relationship also concerned a minority of the sample – mothers who give up work in order to have a family will recognize many of these feelings with a wry smile! The mothers in the shared care-giving families were bothered by feelings of guilt about leaving the children and the loss of contact they had with them, and by exhaustion – feelings which will be recognized by many 'working mothers'. Shared care-giving parents also argued about matters such as standards of housekeeping, or being soft with the kids, and consequently reported more quarrelling and irritability than did the comparable 'traditional' parents. So the shared care-giving ideal may not be so ideal after all, and the poor father, whatever he does, seems always to be in the wrong.

Mothers carry their babies for 9 months; they give birth to them, often painfully; they put a lot of time and effort during the early days and weeks into learning about them and how to care for them best. Our society, until very recently, has regarded child care as automatically women's work and has awarded mothers the role of child care expert, while making it difficult for their expertise and ability in other domains to be recognized. No wonder women are ambivalent about relinquishing this role, and are cautious about allowing their male partners to take over.

Yet sharing child care could have many advantages for women. It could allow their partners to relieve them of some of the physical burdens of child care and might perhaps lessen the mother's sense of overwhelming responsibility for the well-being of the baby. Thus sharing child care might reduce the amount of mental and physical exhaustion suffered by women in the postnatal period. However, this reduction will not occur if the burdens of work within the home are immediately replaced by equally onerous burdens of work outside the home. Sharing child care can help men to understand the realities of looking after children so that they become more sensitive to the difficulties experienced by mothers and others who care for children full-time, as Russell found. If it became more common or more entrenched within societal norms as it is in Sweden, it could gradually change attitudes towards fatherhood, where as Hwang notes:

> It is no longer very easy for fathers to avoid their share of responsibility. The knowledge that love develops through simple everyday actions – such as feeding, comforting, bathing, and playing with the children – is gradually seeping into most (Swedish) fathers' consciousness (Hwang, 1987, p. 136).

Such changes would surely be beneficial for fathers, and mothers, and children.

However we need to return to current British reality, where most fathers do relatively little child care in the first year of the baby's life. This is particularly so when the baby is young when many fathers feel incompetent compared to their partners who have had more practice at feeding, bathing and changing, and nervous of handling a small, fragile human being. (Mothers of course feel much the same at first but have no option but to get on with it.) Lewis, a man, perhaps explains their feelings best:

> While their wives are becoming more 'expert' in child care and, more particularly, in catering to the idiosyncratic needs of their own baby, fathers feel their role is diminished. So, when their participation conflicts with their work schedules, as it does most obviously in the case of getting up to feed the baby at night, they are often prone to abdicate responsibility (Lewis, 1986, p. 95).

If the baby is bottle-fed, then fathers tend to become involved in feeding soon after the first bottle is given. Even if they don't feed the baby themselves regularly, they often turn their attention to washing or preparing bottles (Lewis, 1986). If the baby is being breast-fed continuously, the father cannot be involved in feeding until the baby is weaned, so this again discourages involvement in the early weeks. This lack of practical involvement is perhaps one reason why some fathers feel quite detached from their offspring at this time and also report feeling left out of the close relationship which is developing between the mother and baby (Lewis, 1986). Since babies of under 2 months do not show obvious signs of being socially responsive, such as smiling or demonstrating greeting behaviour (see Adult–infant interaction, below), people who do not observe and interact with them closely will not perceive any sign that the baby responds to them. Thus fathers can quite easily feel that their existence is of no consequence to the baby; that they are dispensable, whereas the mother is indispensable.

As babies get older, however, fathers become emotionally closer to them. The baby is awake for longer when the father comes home. He or she is less fragile and less vulnerable, and is more responsive to the father's presence. The special relationship which develops between a father and his child starts to emerge in the first year, and in the majority of cases develops through play. This is the special role of the father – playing, rather than caring. Innumerable studies have found that fathers engage in more concentrated and active play than mothers (see Russell, 1983; Lewis, 1986; Lamb, 1987) and fathers spend much of the time they have with their babies in this kind of play. Playing with daddy becomes a regular evening ritual for many babies, and 70 out of the 100 fathers studied by Lewis had a special game that they looked forward to playing with their baby.

Playing, as we will see when we look at interaction patterns later on in this chapter, is very important for babies, and it is likely that it is an effective way for fathers to maximize the time that they have with their offspring, so that by around 18 months most babies will be closely attached to their fathers even though they have not been centrally involved in their care (Schaffer and Emerson, 1964; Lamb, 1981; Russell, 1983; Lewis, 1986; Hwang, 1987). This dominant aspect of father–infant interaction probably determines the nature of the relationship between the modern father and his young child, which has been characterized as 'mate' or 'super pal' rather than the stern, distant, disciplinary father figure of Victorian times.

So by the end of the first year many fathers will have become close to their baby and will have worked out ways of interacting with her or him which are mutually satisfying. However their relationship with their partner may have suffered from the strain which the demands of parenthood put on a marriage and the inequalities which are apparent in most families with regard to child care and housework. For instance,

Moss et al. (1987) found that at 7 weeks after birth, 16% of mothers were dissatisfied with the amount of help they were receiving from their partner with child care, and that this proportion increased to 24% at 6 months, and 26% at a year. Although 23% of fathers felt they were not doing enough child care at 9 weeks, only 18% did so at 1 year, so their perceptions of 'enough' did not correspond with those of their partners. Other aspects of relationship strain are discussed below.

Relationship changes in the postnatal period

Scott-Heyes (1983, 1984) has found that it was not uncommon for both partners to have unsatisfied emotional needs for a full 6 months after the birth. Indeed almost a third of the 70 couples studied were unable to satisfy one another's needs at this time. Her Northern Ireland study, which was discussed in Chapter 1, highlighted relationship changes during pregnancy. Scott-Heyes found that the nurturance/dependence balance between husband and wife was altered at this time. The woman's need for nurturance (being looked after and emotionally cared for) by her husband increased and the man's need for continued nurturance by his wife was sometimes unfulfilled (Scott-Heyes, 1983). This imbalance continues into the early postnatal period, as the mother, though less dependent than in pregnancy, is in need of her husband's support, reassurance and 'ego-boosting'. Husbands were found to continue to be more nurturant than they had been before the pregnancy but still failed to satisfy their wives' needs in approximately 40% of cases. Fathers were found to be at their most needy during the postnatal period when, despite no decrease in dependence, they received substantially less nurturance from their wives; the baby was the primary recipient of her nurturance. Fathers in families with more than one child were shown to suffer from this lack of nurturance most severely. This finding demonstrates the impossibility of a mother 'mothering' her new baby, her existing children and their father, all at the same time. Multiparous mothers were however less dependent on their husbands than first-time mothers, reflecting the increased confidence which normally accompanies the rearing of the second and subsequent child. Primiparous couples were more affectionate to one another during pregnancy than multiparous couples but their rates of affection, especially from the wife to the husband, declined postnatally where the multiparous couples did not. In the sexual domain too, the imbalance between the couple's desires, apparent in pregnancy, continues. Scott-Heyes found that most husbands' ratings of sexual interest were unchanged throughout the period covered by the study whereas their wives were substantially less interested postnatally (than they had been antenatally), especially if they had been married for some time. The recently married women resumed their interest in sex more rapidly.

Thus the father may continue to feel deprived of love and affection for a considerable time after the birth and it is easy to see that a man who feels somewhat deprived of his partner's attention, in and out of bed, may react in ways which will exacerbate his partner's adjustment problems rather than minimize them. He could for instance become more demanding, both in and out of bed; become jealous of the baby (perhaps especially of the breast-fed baby); or shut himself off, becoming absorbed in work or hobbies and reducing his involvement in the home and family – Lewis (1986) found just such an effect in some of his subjects. The father may on the other hand react in a more mature manner, becoming more helpful, more understanding and more supportive. Scott-Heyes (1984) found that such men, who gave a lot of support to their wives but received less affection and nurturance in return, were only stressed by this in the early postnatal period if the couple were dissatisfied with their marriage overall. However 6 months later the picture had changed. At this point, men whose needs for affection and nurturance were not met were significantly more depressed. Scott-Heyes comments that 6 months 'seemed to indicate the end of a period when the men had expected less from their wives, accepting that they had other additional demands to cope with' (Scott-Heyes, 1984, p. 148).

And what of the poor harassed wives? Women whose own emotional needs were unmet early in the postnatal period seemed in many cases to give up on their husbands by 6 months after the birth. So at that stage, the wives who had unmet needs were not meeting the needs of their husbands either, and the stage appeared to be set for a significant downturn in the marital relationship. However the couples' ratings of their overall satisfaction with their relationship remained unchanged, so despite the problems which the study made apparent, the participants evidently did not feel at that time that they had seriously damaged their marriage. Lewis (1986), however, in asking his male subjects about the course of their relationship over the first postnatal year, found that 70 out of 100 husbands reported that the couple had drifted apart in certain ways during this period. So the effect of parenthood on marriage may not be catastrophic but may still be significantly detrimental.

The low rates of sexual interest noted by Scott-Heyes in her study are reflected in low rates of sexual intercourse in the first postnatal year (see Adler, 1989). The infrequency of intercourse may be due to a number of factors. Fear of future pregnancy was not found to be a significant factor in the majority of women studied by Adler and colleagues in Edinburgh (Adler, 1989). Vaginal and perineal pain and consequent dyspareunia were much more significant. These may be related to delivery and episiotomy. For instance, Reading (1982) found that 60 out of 68 subjects still experienced dyspareunia 3 months postpartum associated with midline episiotomy, and Hillan (1989) found that three out of six vaginally delivered mothers who reported 'serious sexual problems' 6 months postpartum attributed this to dyspareunia.

In a prospective study of breast-feeding persistence, sexuality and mood in postpartum women, Adler and Bancroft (1988) found that all women, both breast-feeders and non-breast-feeders, were significantly less sexually motivated 6 months postnatally than in the early months of pregnancy. This affected their arousal, orgasm and emotional responsivity. However breast-feeders experienced more pain during intercourse than bottle-feeders, with 36% reporting pain at 6 months compared with 16% of bottle-feeders. This dyspareunia is likely to be a result of a poorly lubricated hypo-oestrogenized vagina which would make penetration painful and inhibit its pleasurable anticipation. It is likely to have led to a marked reduction in sexual motivation for these women who demonstrated lower preferred frequency of intercourse with their partner than non-breast-feeders.

The breast-feeding mothers delayed resuming intercourse for longer than the bottle-feeding mothers, which may reflect their lack of interest in sex or their fatigue. Breast-fed babies are likely to be night-waking for longer (16 versus 10 weeks) than bottle-fed babies (Wright and MacLeod, 1983) and as a result their feeders will be more tired. Breast-fed babies tend to remain in their parents' room for longer and their presence may have an inhibitory effect on their parents' sexual activity. For instance, not one out of a sample of 25 women who kept diaries of sexual activity and feeding (breast and bottle) for 24 weeks following delivery said they would be comfortable having sexual intercourse in the presence of the baby (see Adler, 1989).

The results of research into sexual relationships during the postnatal period therefore suggest that the majority of women are less sexually motivated in the first few months following the birth than they were before they got pregnant. This is normal, and couples should be informed so. This may make their expectations more realistic and prevent the couple blaming themselves, or one another, for their lack of success in bed. Women who are breast-feeding are likely to delay a return to intercourse for longer than women who are bottle-feeding. In part this is due to dyspareunia associated with a poorly lubricated vagina. This is probably simply remedied (baby oil may be more acceptable and accessible than KY jelly *but not if condoms are used*). A night-waking baby, an exclusively feeding, exhausted mother and a sleeping or jealous father (see Relationship changes in the postnatal period, above) all may conspire together to put breast-feeding mothers off sex for longer. There may be hormonal factors involved as well (Adler, 1989).

There is little the midwife or health visitor can do to relieve these problems, except recommend that the mother should sleep when she can (a generally helpful recommendation) and that the baby be moved to where his or her presence is less of a 'turn-off'. It is one of the aspects of breast-feeding which make it not necessarily 'best for mother', nor for father. However, a couple who are prepared for these inconveniences are less likely to be upset by them, so again realistic preparation and explanation are likely to be helpful.

The results of an early North American study by Masters and Johnson (1966) have been taken to indicate that breast-feeding women will have greater sexual interest than bottle-feeders and that breast-feeding is sexually arousing (in 3 out of 24 cases to orgasm). Despite a number of factors which make these findings difficult to apply to women today in the UK, they have found their way into many texts on breast-feeding and have been widely promulgated. Thus couples who find that breast-feeding is rarely sexually arousing (15%; Adler, 1989) and that it is associated with dyspareunia and a delayed return to sexual intercourse (Adler and Bancroft, 1988) will be even more disappointed. These more recent findings need to be equally widely disseminated.

Many midwives and health visitors may feel uncomfortable about discussing sexual adjustment with the mothers and fathers they care for and the recipients of their care may similarly feel that it is their own private business. Their feelings need to be respected. However, clinicians have noted that sexual problems often appear in the first year following the birth of a first child (Adler, 1989) so health professionals need to be aware that sexual problems may be developing in the postpartum period which could be ameliorated by the provision of simple advice and treatment. An association between breast-feeding and postnatal depression has also been found (Adler and Bancroft, 1988) which may reflect the marital disharmony caused by sexual problems. This finding would again suggest that sexual problems in the postnatal period should be taken seriously. The advice of a specialist psychiatrist or psychologist can be invaluable for staff who are inexperienced in sexual counselling, and midwives and health visitors should endeavour to make contact with such professionals if practicable.

In the postnatal clinics studied by Porter and McIntyre (1989), several of the 50 married primigravidae mentioned sexual problems. These were noted by the doctors without comment. This would suggest that sexual problems are not taken as seriously as they should be by medical staff even when they are spontaneously raised by mothers. The midwifery and/or nursing staff working in such clinics may find it useful to include some general questions about potential sexual problems in their assessment of mothers at 6 weeks postpartum.

Adjustment in siblings

When mothers are asked why they had a second baby, one of their most typical replies is 'so the first child will not be an only child', which is clearly seen as not being in the first-born's best interest. However the first-born rarely has any say in the matter and might disagree with the mother's opinion. The necessity of sharing the mother's time, energy and attention with a newborn usually provokes some degree of sibling rivalry. Dunn and Kendrick (1982), in a study carried out in a largely working-class population living in and around Cambridge, showed clearly that a majority of first-borns (93%) were seen to become more naughty and more demanding following the birth of a sibling than they had been during the last month of their mother's pregnancy. Some of the children, more especially the first-born boys, became withdrawn, and feeding, sleeping and toilet training problems also increased. The first-borns were aged 19–43 months, so they were all still quite dependent on their carers. The younger children were more likely to be clingy as compared to the older ones, and the boys were more likely to be withdrawn. Most of these behaviours can be understood as an attempt to gain more of the mother's attention. They were more marked in children who had a very close relationship with their mother before the birth of their younger sibling.

First-borns who had a close relationship with their father showed fewer of these changes in behaviour, presumably because their father's time, energy and attention were less taken up by the new baby and their relationship with their first-born could therefore continue relatively unchanged. However overt jealousy of the baby was most apparent when the father or grandparents showed pleasure and interest in the baby. Deliberate naughtiness (doing things they had specifically been told not to do, or physically attacking the mother) and confrontation with the mother were observed by the researchers most frequently when the mother was caring for the baby. This was less notable when the mother breast- rather than bottle-fed the baby. This finding runs contrary to common opinion expressed by 'experts' such as Dr Spock (1969) that sibs will be most upset by the sight of the baby being breast-fed. Dunn and Kendrick observed that breast-feeding mothers played more with their first-borns when they were not engaged in baby care than bottle-feeding mothers, and provided more distractors at the beginning of a feeding session – drinks, potty, books, crayons, puzzles were all made available before feeding started. The breast-feeding mothers were also more likely to interrupt feeding in order to help or attend to the older child. The approach of these mothers to the feeding situation seemed therefore to be effective in reducing jealousy or distress in the first-born, and in preventing confrontation between mother and child. It might usefully be copied by other mothers.

Aggression towards the baby was found to be relatively infrequent, the majority of children demonstrating interest and some affectionate behaviour. For instance, 22 out of the sample of 40 tried to entertain the baby with books, toys or play and 30 wanted to cuddle and caress him or her. Ninety-five per cent were keen to help in caring for him/her. Although many of the children became more babyish in some ways, reverting to wanting the occasional bottle or to being fed, in other ways they became more independent, perhaps dressing themselves 'like a big girl' or going to the toilet alone. Therefore overall, sibling rivalry was shown to be less of a problem than is often feared. However, its manifestations do make life more difficult for the mother who has to cope with a child who is being more naughty and difficult than usual as well as being more demanding and clingy, and at the same time cope with the needs of the new baby.

No wonder Daddy gets neglected. Yet Daddy's role is vital here. It seems that he holds the key to relieving much of the first-born's distress if he has established a close relationship with him or her before the birth of the new baby, and if he can maintain it after the birth. In doing so, he will not only help the child, but also his partner and therefore the baby. Since close relationships between adults and children are usually mutually reinforcing, he is also likely to benefit himself. Research by both Lewis (1986) and Scott-Heyes (1984), detailed earlier in this chapter, has found that this is one of the tasks in which fathers often become involved, following the birth of a new baby. While the mother concentrates on the baby, the father looks after the older children.

Dunn and Kendrick (1982) found that mothers who felt very depressed or exhausted in the first 3 postpartum weeks were more likely to report that their older child had been tearful at that time. These reports were substantiated by the researchers' observations that these children were more withdrawn, so it seems the mother's state had affected the child's behaviour rather than merely affected the mother's perceptions of her child's behaviour. These mothers were also more likely to be getting little sleep and to be having difficulties with the new baby, showing clearly how the dynamics of this kind of situation can affect the entire family, not just its individual members.

Difficulties in adjustment

These are, as shown above, normal and should be anticipated. Most families will experience them and most families will cope with them. Preparation for parenthood which is realistic rather than euphemistic is likely to help dispel the rosy glow conjured up by much of the media. It would also allow mothers to understand that feeling lonely and a bit miserable after having a baby isn't a sign of postnatal depression; fathers to recognize that a lack of sex doesn't equal a lack of love; and parents to realize that, for a child, having a little sister or brother has good points and bad ones. Such preparation could be incorporated into antenatal training or form a part of informal postnatal education. Chapter 6 details some examples of how this kind of preparation has been incorporated into programmes designed to prevent postnatal depression.

Severe problems of adjustment are dealt with in Chapter 6. One group not mentioned there are teenage mothers. This is because recent research has suggested that young mothers between the ages of 16 and

19 do not necessarily have unusually severe problems in adjusting to motherhood and coping with a baby. The study (Phoenix, 1991) was carried out in London and used women from a variety of ethnic backgrounds. It found that the majority of the subjects had wanted to have a baby at some time, though not necessarily at the time they had become pregnant. They were familiar with child care and were well supported, especially by their mothers, many of whom had also had children at a young age. The subjects therefore did not regard themselves as 'too young' and were generally satisfied with motherhood. Sixty-two per cent thought they were coping 'OK' with the baby and 30% thought they were coping very well. This study, while not focusing on the very young or totally unsupported mother, provided a different and more optimistic picture than is generally available about the consequences of teenage pregnancy. Its findings are supported by those of another recently presented study which showed that the infant care practices of unmarried teenage mothers are quite similar to those of a random sample of mothers living in the same area, though the teenage mothers were less likely to breast-feed (Lilley, 1990).

Adult–infant interaction

In most textbooks this section would be referred to as 'mother–infant' interaction, and indeed much of the research I will be discussing focuses on just that. However, although the baby's primary caretaker is usually the biological mother, she need not necessarily be a mother, a female or even an adult. Fathers can care for babies, as can siblings, and some people who never act as physical caretakers, for example Grandad, or the woman next door, still spend a lot of time interacting with the baby through play.

In the early postnatal period the kind of interactions which dominate are very basic. They mainly concern feeding and the stabilization of sleep/wake cycles and are described in detail in Chapter 3. These aspects of baby care might be regarded as one-way actions rather than two-way interactions. However, the baby contributes to them as well as the mother, and the mutual effect the action of each has upon the other makes the label of 'interaction' an accurate one.

When the baby is approximately 2 months old, the nature of adult–infant interaction changes. The baby's basic states – sleeping, waking, feeding – are usually relatively stable by this time, i.e. they don't fluctuate wildly from day to day. Although the baby's activity and feeding cycles may not be ideal from the mother's point of view, they are at least fairly predictable and so they don't attract the same amount of attention as they did in the first weeks. At 2 months, the baby is more alert when awake. S/he is able to make volitional eye contact with the mother and can produce real smiles – smiles which respond to external stimuli such as the sight of the caretaker's face. This makes talking to and playing with the baby enormously rewarding for the adult, and adult–infant interaction becomes more person-centred, rather than task-centred.

Mothers, and other primary caretakers, of course play with babies in the early postnatal weeks. They talk to them, sing to them, poke and tickle them, dandle them and snuggle them. But at that stage there is usually little response from the baby. The slightly older baby responds. S/he smiles, laughs, makes noises, wriggles about. The mother in turn responds to the baby's response, and so develops an interactive routine or game (Schaffer, 1984). These games are apparently very simple, but when studied in depth, often using slow-motion simultaneous video recording of the mother's and the baby's actions and reactions, they turn out to be quite complex.

Firstly studies of the kind of human behaviour which is directed towards young babies show it to be quite bizarre. Close and continuous eye contact is made, with the adult keeping her/his face aligned with the baby's. This *en face* position is seen from the first days, even though the baby at that time can't focus on the adult's face and almost appears to look through the adult. After 2 months the baby's ability to focus improves and s/he appears really to look at the caretaker, which is immensely rewarding for the adult who now feels as if the baby is a real person who recognizes the caretaker's identity (Wolff, 1963). This prolonged gazing into another's eyes is not normally seen in human interactions where eye contact is usually on/off in nature, except when mothers (or others) are looking at babies, or when lovers are looking into one another's eyes.

Once mutual eye contact has been established with the baby, adults engage in strange behaviours. They speak to babies in a funny way, often waggling their heads like dog mascots in the back of cars, using a highly pitched tone, speaking slowly, emphasizing the vowels and repeating the same simple sound, word or phrase time and time again. Accompanying this strange speech are equally odd expressions. Again they are exaggerated; the expression of mock surprise for instance involves wide open eyes, wide open mouth, raised eyebrows and a highly exaggerated 'aaah' or 'oooh'.

This so called infant-elicited behaviour – the continuous eye contact; the exaggeration and repetition of a limited range of sounds and expressions (Stern, 1977) – seems to be produced automatically by most adults in response to young babies. Children do it too. Watch a 5-year-old playing with her baby doll and you'll likely see a good demonstration of it. You sometimes see it when humans talk to baby animals or to pets who retain the features of baby animals – round faces with protruding cheeks, big eyes set low in a wide forehead, large head relative to the size of the body – animals like Pekinese dogs or other lap dogs. It is suggested (see Stern, 1977) that infant-elicited behaviour is an inbuilt human response, which may become refined through contact with babies, but can be produced in a rudimentary form by most of us. It appears to serve the function of grabbing and keeping the baby's attention and of presenting him or her with a simple, exaggerated model of human interactive behaviour with which they can gradually become familiar and from which, over the months of repetition, they can learn (Schaffer, 1984).

Secondly, adult–infant interactive behaviour is complex in that it is organized into little segments or runs which are repeated with slight variations, time and time again. Stern gives the example of a mother interacting with her $3\frac{1}{2}$-month-old son.

The cycles [runs] in the game went something like this. The mother moved closer, leaning in, frowning but with a twinkle in her eyes and her mouth pursed into a circle always on the edge of breaking into a smile. She said 'This time I'm gonna get ya', simultaneously poising her hand over the baby's belly ready to begin a finger-tickle march up the baby's belly and into the hilarious recesses of his neck and armpits. As she hovered and spoke, he smiled and squirmed but always stayed in eye contact with her (Stern, 1977, p. 12).

The intensity of each run is determined by the reaction of the baby to the previous run. If the baby signals pleasure, maintaining eye contact, smiling, laughing, wriggling about, the subsequent run will be at an equal or slightly increased intensity. If the baby signals displeasure, alarm or distress, breaking eye contact or turning away, crying or fussing, the mother will either discontinue the game altogether or continue at a lower pitch. Stern again:

Finally the mother rushed forward again, perhaps a bit earlier and with more acceleration than the times before. His readiness was not fully settled yet, he was caught a split second off guard. His face showed more surprise than pleasure. He slightly averted his face but still held his end of the mutual gaze. When she returned at the end of that cycle she saw that it had missed somehow – not quite backfired but missed enough. The pleasure had disappeared. She sat back in her chair for several seconds without doing anything, just evaluating. Then she resumed the game. This time however, she left out the tickle-march and established a more regular and marked cadence in her actions. The baby's attention was again rivetted to her, and he began to show an easy smile with his mouth slightly open, the face tilted up and the eyes slightly closed . . . (She escalates the intensity of each run again until) . . . this one proved too much for him. He broke gaze immediately, face averted and frowned. The mother picked it up immediately. She stopped dead in her tracks (Stern, 1977, pp. 13, 14).

Stern's description is thus of a mother whose behaviour in playing the simplest of interactive games is subtly but powerfully determined by the baby's response to each of its runs or segments. This is one reason why the mother maintains such close eye contact with the baby during interaction – she is constantly engaged in monitoring the baby's response.

It has been suggested that babies learn through these interactive games that what they do has an effect. Watson (1973) labelled adult–infant interaction games as 'contingency games'. Every time the baby does something, the adult responds in a regular manner, e.g. every time the baby waves his arms, the adult will poke him in the tummy (a favourite game with children of all ages!). Therefore after a few rounds of this game and a few repeats of the same sequence, the baby learns the contingency between his behaviour – waving his arms – and the adult's response – poking him in the tummy. It's not the specific behaviours of the players which are important, Watson suggests, but the contingency between what the baby does and the reliable response. Because adults respond in this way to the baby's behaviour in their interactive games, the baby learns that adults are normally responsive: an important and perhaps fundamental thing to learn.

More recent research, for instance that on interaction during feeding, outlined in Chapter 3, would suggest that adults typically follow the lead of the baby during any interactive episode, not just when playing games. Therefore it seems that most adult–infant interaction shares the characteristic of being infant-led/adult-responsive.

As the baby matures, s/he becomes a more equal partner in the game, initiating it perhaps by catching the mother's eye rather than passively waiting for the mother to seize the most opportune moment to commence their favourite game, or terminating it by focusing attention on another stimulus such as a toy or another player who has just come along. Kaye and Fogel (1980), for example, followed up a number of mother–infant pairs from 6 to 26 weeks old and found that the baby's attention was initially attracted and totally held by the mother's infant-elicited behaviour. However by 26 weeks, the babies could stop attending and look away from their mothers' antics, thus clearly signalling when they had had enough, and that the interactions were as likely to be initiated by the baby greeting the mother as by the mother greeting the baby. So over time, the baby becomes a more powerful player and her or his behaviour provokes more contingency – it makes more things happen, for instance it can make a game begin or end.

As the baby ages, s/he probably becomes more able to tolerate stimulation which was experienced as too arousing in the early weeks. Stern describes in detail a mother–infant pair where initially the mother seemed to overstimulate the baby and seemed insensitive to the baby's signals that the game was 'too much'. The mother for instance ignored any breaking of eye contact, so that the baby was forced to avoid the stimulation by turning her head away from the mother completely.

> The mother never interpreted this as a cue to lower her level of behaviour. Instead she would swing her head around following Jenny's [the 3-month-old baby] to re-establish the full face position. Once the mother achieved this she would re-initiate the same level of [over] stimulation. Jenny again turned away, pushing her face further into the pillow, to try to break all visual contact. Again the mother instead of holding back, continued to chase Jenny. . . . She escalated the level of her stimulation even more by adding touching and tickling to the unabated flow of vocal and verbal behaviour. With Jenny's head now pinned in the corner, the baby's next recourse was to perform a 'pass-through'. She rapidly swung her face from one side to the other right past her mother's face. When her face passed her mother's face, Jenny closed her eyes to avoid any mutual visual contact and only opened them again after the head aversion was established on the other side. All of these behaviours on Jenny's part were completed with a sober face and sometimes a grimace' (Stern, 1977, p. 123).

These unfortunate interactions left the baby upset and the mother frustrated, angry and confused. However, over time, Jenny seemed to have learned how to deal with her mother's insensitivity. At 4 months old:

Somehow Jenny and her mother were achieving more mutual gaze. The chase and dodge game, while still ominous looking, had lightened enough so that it had some joyful teasing moments and a few smiles were seen. The mother had lowered her level of stimulation only slightly and become only a bit less controlling and intrusive. [But] Jenny seemed better able to handle the level of stimulation from her mother and in doing so began to give her mother more of the positive feedback that allowed the mother to alter her behaviour. A vicious cycle was broken. (Stern, 1977, p. 126).

The case of Jenny is probably quite unusual. But the way that she dealt with a difficult interactive situation is very illuminating. It demonstrates clearly that the baby, as well as the mother, is a central player within the interactive games. At first s/he is a relatively passive partner, but rapidly becomes more active, more powerful, more of an equal partner.

At one level, anyone can play these games with babies. Peek-boo, round-and-round-the-garden, raspberry-blowing, smiling at one another, copying the baby's noises and getting them recopied by the baby – any of us could play these interactive games with any baby. (The next time you do, note how truly interactive they are – how your behaviour is influenced by the baby's and in turn influences the baby's, which again influences yours.) However, individual mother–infant pairs develop and refine their own versions of these routines, one pair for instance specializing in dialogue (the mother using very simple speech and overemphasizing tone and verbal and facial expression; the baby using sound and body movement) while another will predominantly utilize touch and body contact. These interactive routines are sometimes compared to conversations – two people taking it in turn to interact with one another with one 'speaking' (verbally or using body language) while the other 'listens' (is silent or still), and then it becoming the speaker's turn to fall silent and listen while the other partner 'talks'. As such these early interactive 'conversations' may have some function in relation to the later development of verbal communication in the child (Trevarthen, 1977).

The timing of the to-and-fro of these routines becomes distinctive so that different adult–infant pairs, e.g. a mother with each of her twins, or a father with his baby versus the mother with the same baby, utilize different timing (see Schaffer, 1984; Stern, 1977). Researchers have 'scanned' them, just as you have scanned poetry in school, and can identify one mother–infant pair by its iambic pattern of dialogue (remember iambic pentameter?) and another by its trochaic pattern.

Perhaps for those of us not engaged in such painstaking research, it's easier to think of a pair's characteristic routine as akin to a dance. One pair will go in for waltzes where another pair will be into tangos. Whatever dance it is, both partners become increasingly skilled at performing it – 'Come Dancing' standards are the norm, with each partner following the other's steps smoothly and effortlessly. As the interactions between a baby and her/his regular partner become more refined, more skilled and more practised, so the baby finds it harder and harder to interact in a similar way with 'just anyone'. The regular partner is needed for a satisfactory game. So increasingly, babies can't just play with anyone. They need people they are familiar with.

One familiar playmate is the primary caretaker, since care-taking necessarily involves interaction and is nearly always accompanied by some sort of game, no matter how simple (see above, and Chapter 3). However, people who don't look after the baby but do interact with him or her on a regular basis can also become familiar playmates: for instance, a father or sibling who never feeds the baby or changes her nappies but instead plays with her endlessly. When they are older (around 8 months of age) many babies will demonstrate great attachment to these playmates (Bower, 1979). Schaffer and Emerson (1964), in a longitudinal study of attachment, found that 87% of their 18-month-old subjects protested as loudly and as long when they were separated from their regular playmates as when separated from their primary caretaker. This protest was interpreted as a sign that these babies were as attached to their fathers, grandparents and brothers as they were to their mothers, despite the fact that many of these attachment figures had never looked after the baby in a practical sense but had merely played with her or him.

These findings therefore suggested strongly that playing with babies is very important in cementing the relationship between the baby and those who wish to be close to her or him. More modern research seems to show that attachment to the mother is primary so that, especially when distressed, the baby will prefer to go to his mother or primary caretaker rather than to anyone else (Lamb, 1981; Russell, 1983). However, these studies make it clear that babies become attached to non-care-taking fathers as well as to fathers who are highly involved in child care, and that the father is as likely as the mother to be chosen as the preferred playmate or companion except in moments of distress (Lamb, 1981; Russell, 1983; Lewis, 1986; Hwang, 1987). Thus they reinforce the idea that playing with babies is almost as important as looking after them. Of course feeding and bathing and changing and putting to bed are more vital for physical health, but having a simple game with the baby while doing so seems equally vital for psychological well-being.

A word of caution here! Because of the importance currently attributed to mother–infant interaction, many studies are focusing on 'abnormal' interactions. For instance, in the following chapter we will discuss studies which suggest that mother–infant interaction is affected by maternal postnatal depression. You might therefore be on the look-out for such abnormal interactions, and take any deviation from the interactions described in this chapter as symptomatic of such abnormality. You should not do so.

The descriptions given here are not detailed enough. They were included only to give you an idea of the richness and complexity of the adult–infant relationship in the early months of the postnatal period. They refer to the early postnatal months only (up to around 5 months). I haven't described how these interactions change as the baby becomes more dextrous and more involved in interacting with objects around 5 months of age, or how they change again around 8 months (Schaffer, 1984, details these). The interactions described in the literature tend to involve mothers who have the time and the inclination to participate in research, or who are involved because of some already existing problem such as postnatal depression. Either way these mothers may not be typical of the mothers you are caring for.

Cross-cultural research has shown that mother–infant interaction which is regarded as normal here is atypical elsewhere, e.g. in the Mayan Indians in Mexico where the level of mother–infant interaction is much reduced. Other research suggests that there are differences in mother–infant interaction within ethnic groups living in a shared society, e.g. in the USA, and within different social class groups (see Schaffer, 1984). These findings would suggest that there is a much wider range of normality than that which is reflected by current research findings, and that practitioners should be wary of pronouncing any interaction as 'abnormal'. Furthermore, as Stern's research has shown, apparent abnormality in interaction can become normality because interaction involves a dynamic, changing relationship between two partners. So any shortcomings in the action of one of the partners can be compensated for by the actions of the other. (More examples of how difficulties in interaction can be overcome are detailed in Chapter 6.)

Overview and summary

In the first few months of the postnatal period, the mother, father and sibs continue to adjust to the realities of having a new baby. Typically the mother will shoulder most of the burden of babycare and house-work while the father returns to work. Caring for a young baby is a lonely and tiring task which typically involves some anxiety, especially about feeding. Breast-feeding mothers may be more prone to such concerns. They may not fully understand some aspects of the breast-feeding process, particularly those which change over time. They may also lack support for their chosen method of feeding, for instance from their partner, or from friends and family who have bottle-fed. These factors can cause the mother to doubt her ability to feed her baby adequately and can lead her to abandon breast-feeding after a few weeks. Education and encouragement provided by midwives, health visitors and fellow breast-feeders could alleviate some of these con-cerns. Enlisting the father's support could be extremely useful, so pre- and postnatal education should be directed towards him as well as towards his partner.

Some fathers may wish to be closely involved in babycare and, given the requisite amount of experience, are usually as efficient feeders, bathers and nappy changers as mothers. Occasionally their expertise is resented by the mother, but a significant proportion of other mothers instead resent the lack of help that they get from their partners. Such resentments can put strain on the marital (or cohabiting) relationship. Maternal preoccupation with the baby and the needs of older children, who normally exhibit some unhelpful manifestations of sibling rivalry, can lead to a degree of neglect of the father. Paternal preoccupation with work and an inability to meet his partner's practical and emotional needs can leave the mother feeling unsupported. The mother's (particularly the breast-feeding mother's) level of sexual desire is also likely to be reduced compared with pre-pregnancy and with that of her partner. So during the postnatal period both the father and mother may have needs which are unsatisfied. This may set the scene for long-term relationship problems. It is therefore important that postnatal staff strive to support the family in its entirety. Focusing solely on the needs of the mother and baby will not help a mother whose husband feels neglected and consequently is jealous of the baby, unhelpful in practical matters and distances himself emotionally. Nor will it help deal with the consequences of sibling rivalry – an increas-ingly naughty or withdrawn child.

The mother's interaction with her baby is initially dominated by the need to stabilize the baby's feeding and sleeping states. After approximately 8 weeks, however, the baby's increased social abilities focus her attention onto the fundamentals of social interaction itself. So mothers and other members of the baby's 'family' – fathers, grannies, sibs, the woman next door – spend much of their time playing simple interactive games with the baby. These are *inter*active from the beginning, with the baby participating to the best of his or her ability. For instance, early on s/he responds to the mother's overtures with smiles and gurgles and body movements, and the mother in turn observes and responds to these reponses. Later, as the baby develops, these interactive games can be initiated or terminated by the baby so they become more balanced and equitable.

Research suggests that babies become closely attached to their regular playmates as their joint interactive sequences become increasingly refined and specialized. This may be one reason why fathers, who spend relatively little time with their offspring, concentrate the time they do have with them on play.

Further reading

Lewis C. (1989). Fathers and postnatal mood disturbance. *Marce Soc. Bull.*, Spring issue.
Schaffer H. R. (1984). *The Child's Entry into a Social World*. London: Academic Press.
Stern D. (1977). *The First Relationship*. London: Open Books/Fontana.
Thomson A. M. (1989). Why don't women breast feed? In *Midwives, Research and Childbirth. Volume 1* (Robinson S., Thomson A. M., eds). London: Chapman and Hall.
Wright P., Woolet A. (1987). *J. Reprod. Infant Psychol.*, **5**, special issue on breast-feeding.

References

Adler E. (1989). Sexual behaviour in pregnancy, after childbirth and during breast-feeding. In *Baillière's Clinical Obstetrics and Gynaecology, Volume 3* (Oates M., ed.). London: Baillière Tindall.
Adler E., Bancroft J. (1988). The relationship between breast feeding persistence, sexuality and mood in postpartum women. *Psychol. Med.*, **18**, 389–96.

Ball J. (1989). Postnatal care and adjustment to motherhood. In *Midwives, Research and Childbirth. Volume I* (Robinson S., Thomson A. M., eds). London: Chapman and Hall.

Beail N. (1985). Fathers and infant caretaking. *J. Reprod. Infant Psychol.*, **3**, 54–64.

Bower T. G. (1979). *Human Development*. San Francisco: W. H. Freeman.

Butler N. R., Goldring J. (1986). *From Birth to Five: a Study of the Health and Behaviour of Britain's Five Year Olds*. London: Pergamon.

Crow R. A., Wright P. (1976). The development of feeding behaviour in early infancy. *Nursing Mirror*, **142**, 57–9.

Department of Health and Social Security (1989). *Present Day Practice in Infant Feeding: Third Report*. No. 32. London: DHSS.

Dunn J., Kendrick C. (1982). *Siblings*. London: Grant McIntyre.

Graham H., McKee L. (1979). *The First Months of Motherhood*. London: Health Education Council.

Hellin K. (1990). The association between maternal mood, obstetric complications and infant feeding difficulties. *J. Reprod. Infant Psychol.*, **8**, 276–7.

Hillan E. M. (1989). Caesarian section: indications and outcomes. Unpublished PhD thesis, University of Glasgow.

Hwang C. P. (1987). The changing role of Swedish fathers. In *The Father's Role. Cross-cultural Perspectives* (Lamb M. E., ed.). New York: LEA.

Kaye K., Fogel A. (1980). The temporal structure of face-to-face communication between mothers and infants. *Dev. Psychol.*, **16**, 454–64.

Lamb M. E. (1981). *The Father's Role in Child Development*. New York: Wiley.

Lamb M. E. (1987). *The Father's Role. Cross-cultural Perspectives*. New York: LEA.

Lewis C. (1986). *Becoming a Father*. Milton Keynes: Open University Press.

Lewis C. (1989). Fathers and postnatal mood disturbance. *Marce Soc. Bull.*, Spring issue.

Lilley J. (1990). The infant care practices of young unmarried mothers. *J. Reprod. Infant Psychol.*, **8**, 277–8.

McIntosh J. (1985). Barriers to breast feeding: choice of method in a sample of working class primiparae. *Midwifery*, **1**, 213–24.

Martin J., Monk J. (1982). *Infant Feeding 1980*. Office of Population Censuses and Surveys, Social Survey Division. London: HMSO.

Masters W. H., Johnson V. E. (1966). *Human Sexual Response*. Boston: Brown.

Moss P., Bolland G., Foxman R., Owen C. (1987). The division of household work during the transition to parenthood. *J. Reprod. Infant Psychol.*, **5**, 71–87.

Oakley A. (1980). *Women Confined.* London: Martin Robinson.

Oates M. (1989). Normal emotional changes in pregnancy and the puerperium. In *Psychological Aspects of Obstetrics and Gynaecology. Volume 3. Clinical Obstetrics and Gynaecology.* (Oates M., ed.). London: Baillière Tindall.

Phoenix A. (1991). *Young Mothers.* Cambridge: Polity Press.

Porter M., McIntyre S. (1989). Psychosocial effectiveness of antenatal and postnatal care. In *Midwives, Research and Childbirth. Volume 1* (Robinson S., Thomson A., eds). London: Chapman and Hall.

Reading A. E. (1982). How women view post episiotomy pain. *Br. Med. J.*, **284**, 28.

Russell G. (1983). *The Changing Role of Fathers.* Milton Keynes: Open University Press.

Sanjack M. (1988). Commentary articles on special issue on breast feeding. *J. Reprod. Infant Psychol.*, **6**, 251–9.

Schaffer H. R. (1984). *The Child's Entry into a Social World.* London: Academic Press.

Schaffer H. R., Emerson P. (1964). The development of social attachments in infancy. *Monogr. Soc. Res. Child Dev.*, **29**, series 94.

Scott-Heyes G. (1983). Marital adaptation during pregnancy and after childbirth. *J. Reprod. Infant Psychol.*, **1**, 18–29.

Scott-Heyes G. (1984). Childbearing as a mutual experience. Unpublished D. Phil thesis. New University of Ulster.

Spock B. (1969). *Baby and Child Care.* New York: Pocket Books.

Stern D. (1977). *The First Relationship.* London: Open Books/Fontana.

Thomson A. M. (1989). Why don't women breast feed? In *Midwives, Research and Childbirth. Volume 1* (Robinson S., Thomson A. M. eds). London: Chapman and Hall.

Trevarthen C. (1977). Descriptive analyses of infant communicative behaviour. In *Studies in Mother–Infant Interaction* (Schaffer H. R., ed.). London: Academic Press.

Watson J. S. (1973). Smiling, cooing and 'the game'. *Merril-Palmer Q.*, **18**, 323–39.

Wolff P. H. (1963). Observations on the early development of smiling. In *Determinants of Infant Behaviour. Volume 2.* (Foss B. M., ed.). London: Methuen.

Wright P. (1990). Psychological insights into early feeding experience.

In *Excellence in Nursing: The Research Route. Midwifery* (Faulkner A., Murphy-Black T., eds). London: Scutari Press.

Wright P., MacLeod H. (1983). Waking at night; the effect of early feeding experience. *Child Care Health Dev.*, **9**, 272–82.

6 Problems

This chapter will focus on serious problems which the mother, father, siblings and baby may experience through their mutual interactions and in their adjustment to one another. Although some of these problems may be manifest in the first weeks of the baby's life, many will not become obvious till later in the postnatal year. Consequently, this chapter does not restrict itself to the early months, as does Chapter 5. The material in this chapter is however closely linked to that of Chapter 5 where normal adjustment and normal interaction are described.

The mother

As we discussed in Chapter 5, feelings of mild anxiety, inadequacy and transient unhappiness are quite normal for mothers in the postnatal period. However, in a proportion of mothers these feelings will be much more marked, will be long-lasting and will not be easily overturned. Such feelings are nowadays often characterized as post-natal depression.

Much current debate centres on the exact definition of postnatal depression (see, for example, Cox, 1986; Elliot et al., 1988; Sharp, 1989). Should postnatal depression be characterized by symptoms of classic depression (i.e. depression occurring outside childbirth) exper-ienced by women who have recently given birth, severe enough to be rated by psychiatrists as constituting a form of mental illness? Or should it instead refer to any relatively long-lasting distress occurring in the postnatal period which is sufficient to cause upset to the mother and her family? Should it only refer to disturbances of affect (depres-sion, sadness, guilt, low self-esteem, anxiety) which develop after a baby's birth, or include perinatal disturbances and long-term mental health problems which are affecting women who have recently given birth? This debate, while fascinating for researchers and academics, may not overly concern those who care for the postnatal woman and her family. If a new mother is very distressed, crying all the time for no apparent reason, incredibly anxious about her baby who seems to be healthy and well enough cared for, exhausted but not sleeping well when she gets the chance, miserable and not cheered up by the things which usually brighten up her life, excessively irritable with her husband and uninterested in her baby, then something is wrong. And what you call that something – postnatal depression, perinatal distur-bance, affective disorder – matters less than making it better.

For convenience I will call the something postnatal depression, since this is the term which has been most commonly used in the literature to date. However it should be noted that this term typically describes a syndrome which is characterized by feelings of anxiety as well as feelings of depression (Cox, 1986) and which may not be exclusive to the postnatal period (Cooper et al., 1988; Dinnerstein et al., 1988; Sharp, 1989). The label 'postnatal depression' is intended to distin-guish it from the blues, a transient disturbance of mood typically occurring towards the end of the first postnatal week, described in Chapter 3, and from puerperal psychosis which also develops early on in the puerperium. Puerperal psychosis is a rare (0.5–1 per 1000 deliveries) but serious form of psychotic illness, most common in first-time mothers and typically involving delusions and often halluci-nations in a mother who is obviously disturbed and out of touch with reality (Kendall et al., 1987). It normally requires hospital admission or treatment by a specialist community psychiatric team and so does not fall within the remit of the midwife or health visitor. However, the onset of the illness often occurs around the time when the mother is being discharged from hospital or when her care is being transferred from the midwife to the health visitor. It is important that there is no breakdown in communication between the various professionals involved at this time, since skilled care is needed urgently; suicide and infanticide are not common sequelae, but do occur. The provision of this care usually results in complete recovery though women who have had a puerperal psychosis have a 20–30% increased chance of suffering another episode following a subsequent birth. Though a midwife or health visitor may only see one case of puerperal psychosis in her/his professional career, the seriousness of the illness is such that s/he should be prepared to take rapid action if it is suspected. Knowledge of the local provision for affected mothers and their babies is essential, and contacts should be established between specialist units and hospital and community staff. These contacts will facilitate follow-up care for a mother and should also serve as useful sources of help for staff dealing with less serious forms of mental illness (Cox, 1986).

Since an agreed definition of postnatal depression remains elusive, it is not surprising that its diagnosis can be problematic. Differences in the criteria for the existence of postnatal depression have led to difficulty in establishing reliable incidence rates. Hence you will see rates between 3% and 25% quoted in different studies (see Elliot et al., 1988). A number of British studies which have used standard psychiatric interviews to diagnose postnatal depression according to psychiatric criteria have estimated the incidence at around 10–15% (Cox et al., 1982; Kumar and Robson, 1984; Watson et al., 1984). A recent study carried out in two south London general practitioner practices used criteria of a psychiatric disorder of sufficient severity to require care from a general practitioner, as opposed to a psychiatrist (Sharp, 1989). It found an incidence of 24% at 3 months after birth. Ball (1989), in her study of postnatal care and adjustment to motherhood described in Chapters 3 and 5, found 20% of mothers to be emotionally distressed at 6 weeks postpartum according to their responses to an emotional well-being rating scale. And an international collaborative study carried out on primigravid women in Australia, the Netherlands and Italy which used standardized self-rating scales found rates of 20% at 4 months postpartum (Dinnerstein et al., 1988). A small intensive study carried out in South Asian women in Bristol (Fenton and Sadiq, in press), found that 'a considerable number of South Asian women experience that syndrome of thoughts and feelings which are very much akin to what English speakers describe as depression. They experience this as illness and as an illness of the mind'. The authors suggest therefore that the claim that 'ethnic minority women from third world countries do not experience depression in anything like the same sense as native born English women do, or that they do suffer depression but do not perceive it as an illness' is incorrect (Fenton and Sadiq, 1990, pp. 1, 2).

Whichever study you read, it will be perfectly clear that postnatal depression is a fairly common and deeply distressing problem. Kumar (1989) has calculated that at least 75 000 cases will occur in the UK annually. Each of these cases will involve a profoundly miserable mother, whose distress is likely to last for at least a few months or may go on for as long as a year (Watson et al., 1984). This prolonged depression makes the mother feel she has missed out on a vital phase of her life – the first year of her child's life; and, when it is unremitting, leads to a sense of 'depression about being depressed' which further adds to her misery. Depression following the birth of one child may sometimes merge into a depression following the birth of a subsequent child and eventually become part and parcel of normal life (Cox, 1986).

Depression in the mother will inevitably affect the rest of the family. The marital relationship which, as we have discussed in Chapter 5, is under some strain in the postpartum period anyway will be subject to further difficulties due to the unhappiness, irritability, lassitude, and even lower than normal postnatal libido of the female partner. If this is matched by a lack of understanding and support from the male partner and the depression is long-lasting, then some degree of marital disharmony seems inevitable. Holden et al. (1989) in a study of postnatal depression found that 4 out of the 55 couples who formed their sample split up during the course of the research (which covered approximately the first 6 months postpartum). A further three couples intimated that their marriage had been at considerable risk.

Many mothers who have been depressed in the postnatal period report problems with their children. Some of these problems seem to predate the depression and may have been instrumental in its development. (This possibility is discussed in more detail below.) But other problems seem more likely to have resulted from the effects of maternal depression. We know from experimental studies that infants react with protest, distress and withdrawal when interacting with mothers who simulate depression by being blank-faced and non-responsive (Cohn and Tronik, 1983). A number of studies, including ongoing research in Cambridge by Murray and Marwick (see Murray and Stein, 1989), have found that the interactions of many though not all depressed mothers produce similar disruption in the baby. The Cambridge study has found that where mother–infant speech patterns were distorted at 3 months (not showing the typical features of infant-elicited behaviour described in Chapter 5), tests of cognitive development in these infants showed a decrement at 9 months of age. So disruption of normal mother–infant interaction may have long-lasting effects on the infant's development.

Some primigravid mothers also seem to have more problems in infant-rearing if they are depressed. Research in Australia found that a proportion of babies of first-time mothers developed sleeping, feeding and crying difficulties after the onset of maternal depression (Williams and Carmichael, 1985). In families where there was an older child, the pattern of disruption was different. These mothers had problems with the older preschool siblings but not with the baby. Research concerned with older children reared by depressed mothers has found that behavioural problems are more common during a maternal depressive episode and that the presence of such problems is additionally related to marital conflict, as well as to paternal psychiatric difficulties (Caplan et al., 1989).

So overall the picture that emerges is of potential disruption of the entire family when the mother is depressed. The father, the baby and the older children can all be affected by it. This is because the mother is so central to the well-being of every family member. In recognizing that postnatal depression can affect the wider family, however, I don't think we should be distracted from the central problem of the mother. It is she who is distraught. It is she who feels inadequate, guilty and consumed by anxiety and a sense of failure. The problem of postnatal depression is firstly the mother's problem. The difficulties it causes the rest of the family are secondary, though also of importance not least because they will exacerbate the mother's difficulties.

Postnatal depression used to be a hidden problem, but it has received a lot of publicity in the past few years with articles in magazines and features in soap operas helping the public to understand the condition and removing some of the stigma associated with any form of mental illness. This has made it easier for depressed mothers to admit to themselves and their families that they have a problem and to seek help. However, there are still mothers who haven't heard of postnatal depression, or who don't understand what it is, or who are horrified by the thought that their atypical behaviour means they are going mad.

These women may well try to hide their misery, denying that they have any problems and insisting that 'everything's fine'. That of course is their prerogative. Doctors, psychiatric nurses, midwives and health visitors have no God-given right to force people to consult them about their problems. However many women might be reassured and helped if they discussed their depression and anxiety with a sympathetic professional (see Resolution, below).

Professionals who wish to be alert to the possible presence of postnatal depression can rely on informal or formal means of assessing the mother's psychological state. Informal assessment, at its most basic, involves asking the mother how she is and listening carefully to the answer. This seems insultingly simple. However it is remarkable how often the mother is ignored and attention is focused on the baby when routine postnatal visits are carried out. True, a polite 'how are you?' may be included but often the answer is taken for granted, so that a hesitation is missed or a brave smile that should deceive nobody is not noticed. Hennessy (1985) found that health visitors only recognized depression in 27% of mothers whom she identified with the condition. The mother should be a focus of concern for the postnatal visitor as well as the baby. If her needs, her worries, her feelings are dealt with sympathetically, this will encourage the mother to share any problems she has and seek help if she so wishes. Indeed, the development of a close supportive relationship between a new mother and a professional such as the health visitor who has regular contact with postnatal women not only helps in identifying postnatal depression but may also help to alleviate it (see Resolution).

Murray (1990) has noted that the depressed Cambridge mothers she is studying seemed to often project their depressed feelings on to their babies. So they may refer to the baby as 'poor baby', commenting that s/he looks miserable or that the world is a rotten place for the baby to live in. These comments are at odds with the baby's state – the baby doesn't look unhappy, isn't crying or suffering; it's the mother who is. This pattern of behaviour obviously couldn't be used to diagnose postnatal depression but if it is observed it might indicate that the health visitor should concentrate more attention on the mother.

The possible existence of postnatal depression can be detected by non-medical personnel through the use of structured questionnaires (diagnosis is, as always, a medical matter). Many of the questionnaires which have been used in research into postnatal depression were developed to detect depression unassociated with childbirth. They may include inappropriate items concerning, for instance, sleep disturbance or somatic symptoms which are normal (though inconvenient) for new mothers and which are therefore not indicative of postnatal depression.

A series of studies carried out by Cox et al. (1987) in Edinburgh aimed to develop a structured questionnaire which was specifically designed to detect postnatal depression. The Edinburgh Postnatal Depression Scale (EPDS) was validated on a substantial group of postnatally depressed mothers who had been independently diagnosed as such by psychiatrists. The EPDS provides a short, simple question- naire which can be used by non-medical personnel to detect the likelihood that a mother is suffering from postnatal depression. Both the health visitors who administered it and the mothers who completed the questionnaire found it acceptable and easy to understand. Health visitors who participated in a further study of postnatal depression initiated by the Edinburgh group (see Holden et al., 1989 and Resolution) incorporated it into their clinic routines without too much disruption. It was well received by their clients, many of whom indicated that it gave them the impression that the health visitors were interested in them as individuals, and in their feelings (Holden et al., 1989).

Health visitors and other professionals working with postnatal women could use the EPDS as a screening instrument by administering it to all postnatal women. (If they wish to do so, they should consult Cox et al., 1987. This describes how the EPDS should be administered and determines what scores on the EPDS are indicative of postnatal depression.) Alternatively, they could utilize the questions contained in the EPDS as part of their informal enquiry about the mother's psychological state. Professor Cox has kindly agreed that the EPDS can be reproduced here (Figure 6.1).

Much current research is directed towards finding out which women are most likely to suffer from postnatal depression. Unfortunately the findings are as yet unclear. As John Cox says in the introduction to his book *Postnatal Depression*, 'We are much clearer about what happens than why' (Cox, 1986, p. v). A host of theories have been advanced about its aetiology and many factors have been related to its occur- rence.

A major focus of research has concerned the role of hormones. Although individual research studies have produced some promising findings, no clear-cut hormonal aetiology has yet been established, perhaps because the immense complexity of neuroendocrine interac- tions makes simple analysis of causation impracticable. Hormonal

Name: Date:
Address: Age:
               Date of delivery:

As you have recently had a baby, we would like to know how you are feeling now.
Please UNDERLINE the answer which comes closest to how you have felt IN THE PAST WEEK.

Here is an example, already completed.
I have felt happy:

  Yes, all the time
  Yes, most of the time
  No, not very often
  No, not at all

This would mean: 'I have felt happy most of the time' during the past week.
Please complete the other questions in the same way.

IN THE PAST 7 DAYS

1. I have been able to laugh and see the funny side of things

  As much as I always could
  Not quite so much now
  Definitely not so much now
  Not at all

2. People upset me so that I felt like slamming doors and banging about

  Yes, often
  Yes, sometimes
  Only occasionally
  Not at all

3. I have looked forward with enjoyment to things

  As much as I ever did
  Rather less than I used to
  Definitely less than I used to
  Hardly at all

4. I have blamed myself unnecessarily when things went wrong

  Yes, most of the time
  Yes, some of the time
  Not very often
  No, never

5. I have been anxious or worried for no good reason

  No, not at all
  Hardly ever
  Yes, sometimes
  Yes, very often

6. I have enjoyed being a mother

  Yes, very much so
  Yes, on the whole
  Rather less than usual
  No, not very much

7. I have felt scared or panicky for no very good reason

  Yes, quite a lot
  Yes, sometimes
  No, not much
  No, not at all

8. Thing have been getting on top of me

  Yes, most of the time I haven't been able to cope at all
  Yes, sometimes I haven't been coping as well as usual
  No, most of the time I have coped quite well
  No, I have been coping as well as ever

9. I have been so unhappy that I have had difficulty sleeping

  Yes, most of the time
  Yes, sometimes
  Not very often
  No, not at all

10. I have felt sad or miserable

  Yes, most of the time
  Yes, quite often
  Not very often
  Not at all

11. I have felt I might lose control and hit someone

  Yes, frequently
  Yes, sometimes
  Only occasionally
  Never

12. I have been so unhappy that I have been crying

  Yes, most of the time
  Yes, quite often
  Only occasionally
  No, never

13. The thought of harming myself has occurred to me

  Yes, quite often
  Sometimes
  Hardly ever
  Never

Figure 6.1 Detection of postnatal depression: development of the 10-item Edinburgh Postnatal Depression Scale. From Cox et al. (1987), with permission

factors are anyway much more likely to be centrally involved in the development of the blues or puerperal psychosis, as these disorders occur at the time when hormone levels are changing dramatically. Postnatal depression typically develops around 6–14 weeks postpartum when a woman's hormonal status is much more stable. Recently it has become apparent that some cases of postnatal depression are in fact the continuation of a prenatal depression (Dinnerstein et al., 1988; Sharp, 1989). As pre- and postnatal hormonal profiles are vastly different, these findings again suggest that the role of hormones in causing postnatal depression is not a simple and obvious one. However, the idea that 'it's your hormones' has been widely promulgated and is comforting to many women, who thus feel that postnatal depression is not due to some personal inadequacy. Continuing research may uncover an as yet hidden hormonal story, so this consoling notion should not be dismissed out of hand. It is likely to be a complicated story, however, with hormonal factors interacting with other biological, social and psychological variables (Cox, 1986).

Research results indicate that women who have a history of mental illness or psychological disturbance (ranging from severe illness necessitating admission to hospital, through previous episodes of postnatal depression, to consulting the general practitioner for 'nerves') are more likely to suffer postnatal depression (Kumar and Robson, 1984; Watson et al., 1984; Dinnerstein et al., 1988). High levels of anxiety in pregnancy (Watson et al., 1984) and marked depression in pregnancy have also been linked to postnatal depression (Watson et al., 1984; Sharp, 1989; Fox et al., 1990), as have marked and prolonged blues (Cox, 1986, Hannah et al., 1990). These findings suggest that women who are generally prone to psychiatric illness, or who react to stress by becoming depressed and/or anxious, are more likely to react to the stresses of the postnatal period by developing postnatal depression. It is also possible that the links between pre- and early postnatal disturbance and subsequent depression may reflect the lingering effects of a stressful pregnancy and a difficult first few postnatal days. When these are added to the problems of the postnatal period, they provide the 'straw that breaks the camel's back'. For example, the EPDS has now been used in both the antenatal period and in the first postnatal week to detect the likelihood of depression occurring at that time. Fox et al. (1990) found that high antenatal EPDS scores were significantly related to subsequent postnatal depression. And Sandler et al. (1990) found that the most significant risk factor for postnatal depression in primiparous subjects at 6 weeks postpartum was high EPDS scores at 5 days postpartum. If this link between pre- and postnatal disturbance does reflect the enduring effects of perinatal stress, then everything that has been discussed in this book so far about the problems of pregnancy and the immediate postnatal period is of relevance to our consideration of the causes of postnatal depression, and about how to prevent it.

Many studies have suggested that the quality of the marital relationship is also important. For example, Sharp (1988), in her community-based study of postnatal depression, found that a poor marital relationship and little support were significantly related to depression at 3 months postpartum. Ball (1989), in her study of adjustment to motherhood, similarly found that marital tension was strongly related to reports of emotional distress 6 weeks after the birth. And Scott-Heyes (1984), in her study of marital adaptation after childbirth, found that women whose husbands provided less affection and nurturance in the postnatal period were the most prone to depression at that time.

The association between breast-feeding and prolonged avoidance of sexual intercourse described by Adler and Bancroft (1988; see Chapter 5) may be related to the higher rates of postnatal depression found by them in their breast-feeding subjects. Dinnerstein et al. (1988), using the statistical techniques of factor analysis, found that mood change (depression), breast-feeding and sexual functioning all clustered together in their analysis of their postnatal data. This suggests that these factors were interrelated. A poor sexual relationship may contribute to a poor marital relationship, so breast-feeding mothers may become depressed because their marital relationship is suffering from the consequences of a lack of sex. An alternative explanation might be that sexual activity relieves depression to some extent (a kiss and a cuddle make most of us feel better after all) and that breast-feeding mothers are less likely to have, or seek, access to this form of therapy.

The lack of emotional support and of a confiding relationship (most often but not invariably provided by the husband) have also been associated with postnatal depression (see Elliot et al., 1988). Taken together, all the above findings strongly suggest that everything that can be done to maintain and support the marital relationship during the postnatal period should be done. Gordon et al. (1965) showed that women who were encouraged during pregnancy to confide in their husband and enlist his practical help were less likely to become depressed postnatally, so comparatively simple measures may affect the way that mothers and fathers relate during the perinatal period. It has also been suggested that the quality of the relationship between the mother and her own mother may be important (Kumar and Robson,

1984; Cox, 1989), so that encouraging grandmothers to support their daughters emotionally as well as practically can be useful.

The Australian study of Williams and Carmichael (1985), discussed above, found that some postnatally depressed mothers reported that they had experienced difficulties with their baby on the postnatal ward, and that when they returned home the baby cried persistently, was difficult to feed or soothe, and slept for short periods only. The difficulties preceded their depression and may have contributed to it. Cutrona and Troutman (1986) carried out an assessment of infant temperament at 3 months and found that depression in the mother was much more likely to persist when the infant cried excessively and was difficult to soothe. Thus a 'difficult baby' may contribute to the development or persistence of depression. Midwives and health visitors are well placed to advise mothers on how best to cope with infant problems and this aspect of their work can be of great benefit to the mother who is under stress.

A host of other factors have been related to postnatal depression, some of which have not been reliably established as aetiological through replication as yet. New research is uncovering more and more psychological, sociological and physiological aspects of the disorder and is becoming more concerned with the interactions between these aspects. Many researchers consider that the way forward is to combine psychosocial research with physiological research.

> Further progress towards understanding the causes of postnatal depression will occur when neurobiological research is carried out in close collaboration with social scientists (Cox, 1989, p. 848).

Theories about the aetiological mechanisms involved in postnatal depression similarly abound (see Cox, 1986 for a résumé of some of these). Some researchers have questioned the whole foundation of the concept, suggesting that its existence is merely a 'pseudo scientific tag for the description of maternal discontent' (Oakley, 1980, p. 27). This view relates to the ongoing debate about the nature of mental illness and the way in which societies conceptualize unusual or undesirable behaviour. Other researchers agree that the mothers concerned are suffering from a syndrome they would classify as depression. They argue however that this syndrome is not specific to the postnatal period, but instead reflects the high rates of depression which women of childbearing age suffer from anyway. Two British studies have addressed the issue. One (Cooper et al., 1988) found similar prevalence rates of depression in postpartum and non-postpartum women, but with a bunching of new cases in the postpartum group around 3 months after the birth. Another (Cox, Murray and Chapman; see Cox, 1989) is currently under way. The debate continues, but in my view whatever its outcome it cannot lessen our concern for the misery of the depressed postpartum woman and her family. The high rates of depression found in non-postpartum women should lead us to extend our concern to those women outside the postnatal period who are also suffering intense, severe and long-lasting depression. Brown and Harris's (1978) classic text on this topic is included in the list of further reading.

Leverton (see Elliot et al., 1988) constructed a vulnerability scale for postnatal depression based on many of the findings discussed above. This consisted of five items – a previous psychiatric history; a previous episode of postnatal depression; high anxiety in pregnancy; a poor marital relationship; and the lack of a confiding relationship. Forty per cent of women who had these identified vulnerability factors were judged to have definite, or borderline, depression at some time during the first 3 postnatal months. This compared with only 16% who did not have these vulnerability factors. The research group of Elliot et al. then went on to test a programme of preventive treatment using a proportion of the vulnerable group as subjects, and comparing their progress postnatally with a control group of vulnerable women who had not been offered the preventive treatment. The rationale for the treatment programme, a detailed description of its content and a discussion of the practicalities of its implementation, are all contained in Elliot et al. (1988) and interested readers are directed to this publication. I want to outline some salient facets of the study here, because they relate to the general provision of psychological care and support during pregnancy and in the postnatal period.

The programme consisted of a monthly series of group meetings which started as early as possible in pregnancy and continued until 6 months after the birth. These meetings were designed firstly to provide social support for the mothers attending them. They were therefore structured to encourage a warm, comfortable atmosphere with plenty of time available for chatting over coffee as well as for informal discussion between the participants. First-time mothers were grouped together, as were multiparous mothers, and the group numbers were kept low. In these ways it was hoped to foster friendships between the group members which could be maintained outside the group. Such friendships can be formed between mothers-to-be when they attend antenatal classes, but sometimes the format of these classes makes it difficult; for example, there may be no provision for the all-important chat, or the classes may serve a widely distributed geographical area so the participants can't keep in touch. The importance of having access to continuing social support both before and after the birth was discussed in the groups – for example, through making friends with other mothers – and the continuation of the groups from pregnancy into the postnatal period provided a regular (albeit only monthly) source of social support which could be depended upon. A degree of continuity of care was also provided by the woman's health visitor who visited at least once during pregnancy before commencing her/his regular postnatal visits. Thus this programme differed from conventional NHS antenatal education in its continuation into the postnatal period.

The groups were marketed as educational groups, similar to antenatal groups. Thus off-putting terms such as 'counselling' or 'psychotherapy' or 'vulnerability' were avoided. The topics discussed included postnatal depression; the realities of the postnatal period and early child development; ways of preparing for parenting; and where and how to get help when you are a parent. The aim was to 'convey an understanding of parenting as a tough but survivable experience' (Elliot et al., 1988, p. 104) and to make it easy for the participants to obtain help and support throughout pregnancy and the postnatal period from the group members, the group leaders, their health visitor and from other sources.

The groups were run by either the psychologist or the health visitor member of the research team but it is anticipated that similar programmes will be run by midwives or health visitors. The group leaders adopted a non-directive style; they didn't tell the participants how 'parenting would or should be, but how it might be' (Elliot et al., 1988, p. 96). They encouraged a lot of open discussion with participants, rather than the leader doing much of the talking. The last pregnancy meeting and all of the postnatal meetings had no set agenda and thus their content was determined by the participants. This kind of empowering, educative style may be difficult for staff who have been trained in a more formal lecture-based system and who tend to utilize a similar teaching style. Murphy-Black and Faulkner (1990), who observed 37 midwives and health visitors conducting antenatal classes, found that on average the teachers talked for about four-fifths of the class, the mothers contributed less than one-fifth and 'the remainder of the time was spent in silence or confusion' (Murphy-Black and

Faulkner, 1990, p. 89). However, after attending a teaching and group skills training course, the midwives and health visitors who had chosen to attend the course made substantial improvements. The mothers in their classes talked more and initiated more content, and the teachers talked less, responded more to the mothers' ideas and feelings and didn't dominate the class. The midwives and health visitors who had been sent on the course by management, rather than choosing to do so themselves, showed little if any improvement overall – a real demonstration of the principle that you can lead a horse to water but you can't make it drink. It is also a lesson for any educator who thinks that all you have to do to improve or change people is to tell them what to do and how to do it! An informal teaching style is easier to adopt in a one-to-one setting, so individual antenatal and postnatal education may be more effective than group education unless the educator has been specially trained in the use of group methods and/or has a natural inclination for this approach. As nursing and midwifery education becomes more student-centred and less didactic, it should become easier for those who have been its students to become less authoritarian teachers.

Out of 22 first-time mothers who were offered participation in the preventive programme, 3 were diagnosed as depressed at 2 months postpartum, and none at 3 months. This compares with 9 out of 25 control primigravidae at 2 months, and 2 out of 25 at 3 months after birth. Three out of the 26 second-time mothers who had been offered participation became depressed at 2 months, compared with 9 out of 25 control mothers. However at 3 months postpartum, there was no statistically significant difference between the participating multiparous subjects and their controls. Thus the prevention programme seemed to be effective in reducing rates of depression in first-time mothers. Results were more mixed when the data from second-time mothers was considered. These mothers attended fewer group meetings and were less enthusiastic than first-time mothers about those they did attend. This may account for the differences found between these two groups of subjects. Alternatively the strain of caring for two children may make second-time mothers more susceptible to depression later in the postnatal period. The very reasons which made attendance at the group meetings more difficult for second-timers – greater physical discomfort in pregnancy and exhaustion in the postnatal period; problems of child care particularly in the evenings when their partners could attend the meetings with them; problems of travelling with a small child while pregnant, or with a baby as well as a small child –

may contribute to depression in vulnerable individuals such as those selected to participate in this preventive programme.

Leverton's 'vulnerability' study which preceded the preventive study described above indicates that the vulnerability factors of previous psychiatric history, previous postnatal depression, high anxiety in pregnancy, poor marital relationship, and the lack of a confiding relationship, have some sort of predictive value in identifying women likely to suffer postnatal depression. But it also shows that many (60%) women who are thus defined as vulnerable do not go on to have depression and that some (16%) who might be termed 'invulnerable' do subsequently develop it. Thus it is obvious that we are still a long way from understanding what causes postnatal depression. As the results of more studies become available and the condition itself is better understood, the nature of predictive factors is likely to change. It is therefore unwise to restrict screening or support to women with a previous psychiatric history or with a poor marital relationship. Such restriction would miss a substantial number of women who go on to develop the condition. As we have discussed in Chapter 5, the non-postnatally depressed mother still has a pretty hard time of it, so it would be no waste of resources to support her too. If the principles of realistic preparation for parenthood, some continuity of care from pregnancy to postpartum and the provision of psychological and social support for mothers are to be generally implemented, then they should be made available to all parturients.

The father

The postnatal period can be a difficult time for fathers as well as for mothers. A number of research studies have found that fathers suffer from mood disorders, anxiety and depression in the early postnatal months (Scott-Heyes, 1984; Lewis, 1989). Estimations of the proportion of fathers thus affected vary (as in comparable mother research), with Lewis reporting that 43% of his subjects experienced feelings of depression during early fatherhood, but Elliot et al. (1985) finding that less than 3% of fathers were rated as experiencing severe difficulties in adjusting during the first postnatal year. Given the milder adjustment problems that most men experience at this time (see Chapter 5) it is not surprising that a small proportion of fathers will be unable to adapt satisfactorily and will encounter serious psychological problems in the postnatal period. These adjustment problems may be exacerbated by a sense of neglect – 'my wife only cares for the baby now' – of exclusion – from the charmed circle of mother and baby – and of impotence – not only sexual: 'I can't turn her on any more', but within the family: 'nobody needs me', particularly if the man's expectations of fatherhood are unrealistic. Scott-Heyes (1984) found that dissatisfaction with the marital relationship was significantly associated with anxiety and depression in fathers at 1 month after birth, and that men who received less affection from their wives at 6 months after the birth were more likely to be depressed.

Siblings

The older children within a family can, like the father, feel unloved and unwanted, particularly if their relationship with their mother before the birth of the baby was very close and exclusive (Dunn and Kendrick, 1982). These feelings can affect children of any age, but young children are especially susceptible since their relationship with the mother is, relatively speaking, more central to their minute-to-minute well-being. If the child is very young, s/he is very dependent on the kind of intimate symbiotic mother–infant interaction described in Chapter 5. The nature of this interaction changes as the child grows older, but remains fairly exclusive until the child is of an age (around 3–4 years) to communicate easily with large numbers of people outside the family. Until then, the young child can interact satisfactorily with only a small number of people with whom s/he has established a close relationship, whereas the older child can interact satisfactorily with many people. If the young child's only, or principal, interactive partner is the mother, then the birth of a younger sibling will deprive him or her of that partner, since much of the mother's interactive capacity will be taken up by the new baby. This is not to say that the mother will not continue to talk to, care for and play with the child. Dunn and Kendrick's study shows quite clearly that she does. But the needs of a newborn baby are such that inevitably the older child will receive less focused attention.

Children who suffer in this way may display their distress by becoming withdrawn, but more commonly it is evidenced by intense sibling rivalry, aggression and/or regression. These behaviours certainly gain the child attention but usually in the form of anger, punishment and disapproval. This exacerbates the child's distress and a vicious circle can easily be established. This difficult situation can be, and usually is, avoided if the child has a close relationship with someone other than the mother. This ideally needs to be established before the baby is born, as adult–infant interactions take time to become established.

Consequences of serious psychological distress in mothers, fathers and siblings during the postnatal period

Postnatal depression should concern all those who are involved in the care of the postnatal woman and her family. It obviously causes deep unhappiness to the mother who, apart from suffering depression and anxiety, often fears she is 'going mad' and therefore suffers the additional burden of trying to come to terms with mental illness. Her unhappiness and atypical behaviour will obviously disturb her husband or partner who, as we have noted before (Chapter 5), has his own adjustments to make to the new baby.

There is little evidence of associations between postnatal depression and physical neglect or abuse of the baby. Although these sometimes do co-occur (Cox, 1986), non-postnatally depressed mothers are as likely to abuse their babies (see Chapter 4). However, some research indicates that normal mother–infant interaction can be attenuated (see above). Our discussion of mother–infant interaction in Chapter 5 shows that the mother's close attention to the baby's signals is crucial to the development of smooth, well co-ordinated interaction. The exhausted, miserable, postnatally depressed mother may be unable to focus her attention on the baby in this way, and her anxiety may cause her to misinterpret the baby's signals. Other research suggests that postnatal depression in the mother is associated with feeding and sleeping problems in her baby.

A postnatally depressed mother will also have less energy and motivation to direct to her other children who, like the father, are consequently likely to feel neglected or excluded. These feelings may influence their reactions to the new baby, exacerbating their feelings of rivalry, which in turn will make the mother's life more difficult since, as Dunn and Kendrick have shown, the principal focus of a sibling's aggression is the mother.

Within a family, distress in one member typically affects all the remaining members. So postnatal depression in the mother is likely to affect the father and the children. Similarly a distressed or depressed father, or an intensely rivalrous sibling, will affect the mother. Depressed, distressed fathers require emotional support (remember how wives are the main source of emotional support for husbands) and are likely to be less able or willing to contribute to baby care and to maintain a close relationship with the other children. Intensely rivalrous siblings often require more 'baby care' since regression in feeding, dressing and toileting can be a common response to the birth of a baby brother or sister. They usually demand more attention and they may require more close supervision to prevent serious naughtiness and occasional aggression towards the baby (see Chapter 5).

Resolution

The above section paints a picture of a family caught in a vicious circle. Many families react differently to the distress of the mother, father or child. They mobilize their resources to reduce that distress. The father is perhaps the crucial person here. The mother may wish to increase her care of the father or the sibling but her resources are already overstretched in caring for the new baby. The siblings are usually too young to understand how to help a distressed parent and can instead only react with their own empathic unhappiness.

The father can ease the mother's burden of child care; can reassure her that her intense anxiety about the baby is groundless (or, if it is justified, can help her to resolve its causes); and is best placed to be a sympathetic listener, a knowledgeable 'cheerer-upper', and an effective comforter. His role in ameliorating his partner's distress may account for the association demonstrated in a number of research studies between postnatal depression and the quality of the marital relationship; that is, postnatal depression may not develop or may be more quickly resolved in women who have a supportive and caring partner (Watson et al., 1984), whereas postnatal depression will be exacerbated where the partner is unsupportive and uncaring and where the marital relationship is breaking down. A recent study has suggested that the quality of the marital relationship may also be important in preventing postnatal relapse in women who have had major psychotic illness. Marks et al. (1990) found a significantly lower rate of relapse in women whose husbands communicated positively with them and were generally uncritical.

The father can also do much to alleviate sibling rivalry. Research shows that where a strong father–child relationship exists before the birth of the new baby, sibling rivalry is less intense (Dunn and Kendrick, 1982). It is therefore likely that the formation of a close father–child relationship *after* the birth of the baby will ameliorate an already existing, intense rivalry. Even if it doesn't, the amount of time the father spends with the older child, and the quality of attention he shows to his son or daughter, will be effective in removing some of the burden of sibling care from the mother.

If fathers are to play this key role they must be educated and supported. Education is needed to help them to understand the needs of their family and the ways in which they can contribute to their care. Fathers as well as mothers should be prepared for parenthood in a realistic manner. Such preparation might do much to prevent the development of serious problems of postnatal adjustment. If their partner has postnatal depression, if their child is intensely rivalrous, then these conditions should be carefully explained to the father and ways in which he can help should be suggested, always remembering that the professionals' ideas about support may not equate with those of their clients. Support, encouragement and reinforcement should be given to the father as well as to the rest of the family. It's scary living with a seriously depressed person. Supporting a family emotionally and practically is stressful (as women know to their cost) and keeping a job going at the same time is doubly stressful (as every working woman will recognize). So involved, caring, supportive fathers need support. They need someone to tell them they're doing a good job. They need someone to talk to. They perhaps need a phone number so they can contact a professional they know and trust when they get worried or when things get too much.

Of course mothers need all this too. And many mothers who are depressed, or who are struggling to cope with distressed families, don't have supportive, caring partners to turn to. They may have relatives or friends who act as practical or emotional supporters and in which case they, individually or collectively, make take the place of the father, or complement and supplement his involvement. They may have no one – except you, the professional. You can't replace a caring family network, but you should aim to provide as many substitutes as possible. Our discussion so far would suggest that there are two important aspects to such provision. Firstly, practical help is crucial. Someone to help with the baby; help with the sibling; help with the housework, the shopping, the cooking. Someone to give the mother a break, a night's sleep, an afternoon off. Secondly, emotional support is equally important and within that context I echo everything I have said throughout this book concerning the provision of psychological care.

A study carried out by Jenifer Holden, who is a psychologist and a health visitor, and her colleagues Cox and Sagovsky (Holden et al., 1989) used health visitors to provide counselling for postnatally depressed mothers. These mothers were identified using the EPDS (see above) and their depression was confirmed by psychiatric interview. They were randomly assigned to either a counselling group or to a control group who continued to receive only the normal, routine visits from their health visitors. The general practitioner was informed of his/her patient's depression in each case.

The counselled group received up to eight sessions of non-directive counselling from their regular health visitor, who made extra weekly visits for the duration of the study. All participants were then reassessed. Thirteen per cent of the control group reported that participating in the study had been helpful i.e. that assessing their mood using their EPDS, being interviewed by the research psychiatrist and receiving any treatment offered to them by the general practitioner had been helpful. One hundred per cent of the counselled group rated their participation as being helpful. Ninety-two per cent reported that it was talking to their health visitor which had been most helpful. In the control group, 15 mothers remained depressed throughout the 13 weeks of the study, and 9 recovered. Amongst the counselled group, 8 remained depressed and 18 recovered. This difference in recovery rates was statistically significant and was not accounted for by differences in demographic or obstetric variables, degree of depression on entering the trial, antidepressant or medical contact between assessments. This is a remarkable result. Eight hours of counselling by health visitors produced a very significant improvement in recovery from postnatal depression.

What did this magic counselling consist of, and how did the health visitors learn how to use it? All the health visitors who wished to participate in the study were given notes on the Rogerian method of non-directive, client-centred counselling prepared by Ms Holden (see Cox, 1986) and three sessions of role play, video and discussion. They were also visited regularly by one of the researchers while the study was in progress. The preparation the health visitors were given could only provide an introduction to this form of counselling, but served to emphasize its basic tenets – allowing the clients (the mothers in this case) to 'share their feelings with an empathic and non-judgemental person who helps the client to analyse her problems and find her own solutions' (Holden, 1990, p. 49) or more simply 'to encourage the mothers to talk about how they were feeling and to listen constructively rather than making suggestions' (Holden, 1990, p. 49). This approach is fundamentally empowering because it places the client in the position of expert. She knows more about her problems and about how they may be ameliorated than any professional. Within the client therefore, not the professional, resides the power to do something about these problems, or not to do anything about them if she so chooses. The professional merely acts as a sounding board for the client. S/he does not give advice, no matter how well intentioned, nor tell the person what to do. Instead, the counsellor acknowledges the client's own wisdom and strength and treats her thoughts, feelings and decisions with respect.

Most of the health visitors involved in the study felt more confident about acting as counsellors following their brief introduction to counselling principles and techniques, and their experiences with their clients, the depressed mothers. However they were nearly unanimous in their demand that more counselling should be included in health-visiting courses.

The health-visiting counsellors arranged to call on each mother weekly for at least half an hour, in order to discuss how the mother was feeling. Babycare was discussed at another time. It was stressed that privacy was important and that, if possible, the baby and any other preschool children should be looked after by someone else at that time. Thus the mother set aside a time for talking about and thinking about herself, not her baby, and someone was there to listen to her thoughts. Someone who neither condemned them nor denied them, but sought to understand them. Someone who offered no good advice or suggestions, or recommendations, but was concerned to find out about the mother's ideas; about what *she* thought might help. Someone who treated everything said in total confidence and didn't blab it all around the neighbourhood, or the surgery, or the clinic. Thus the type of counselling undertaken by the health visitors was relatively simple. Perhaps the most cogent piece of advice about such counselling offered by Ms Holden (bold typing included) was **'If in doubt, keep quiet'** (Cox, 1986, p. 55) – something which is difficult, but surely not impossible, for health care professionals who have generally been trained to give advice and information and who are inclined to give their opinions as well. Most midwives, health visitors and nurses who are interested in incorporating non-directive counselling in their work should be able to achieve this aim given the correct preparation. However as Holden points out, professionals working in this way need to be supported themselves, a point which I have constantly reiterated in this book.

Twenty-two out of the 26 mothers who were counselled reported that their perception of the role of the health visitor had changed because of this experience.

> When my health visitor first came to the house, I thought she was a bit officious. She seemed so competent, so good at dealing with the baby. She kept telling me things to do with the baby, and I thought she meant I was doing it wrongly. . . . Then when I was depressed, she came every week. I found her very easy to talk to and she didn't seem to be shocked by anything I said. It was such a relief to talk it out. Now I could talk to her about anything (Holden, 1990, p. 51).

Before their participation in the study, the health visitor was seen by the counselled mothers as being concerned with the baby. As with the control group, despite often having a good relationship with their health visitor, the mothers felt that they couldn't talk to her about how they were feeling. It took a specific commitment from the health visitors to persuade the mothers that they could talk about themselves. It seems therefore that health visitors could usefully provide a sympathetic listening ear for the mothers in their care, but that they need to make it clear that they are willing to do so. And that they have the time and the opportunity to do so; listening of this sort can't be done with half an ear open for the phone, or with half an eye on the clock. Simple non-directive counselling could be provided for all mothers if the health visitor included some mother-centred time in her/his routine visits. Alternatively a commitment to a more formal counselling session, like the ones described above, could be made for mothers who were discovered, through screening, to be suffering from postnatal depression. Holden comments that the partners of some of her subjects felt left out because no one asked how they were coping. As I comment above, supporting the partners of postnatally depressed women is likely to be important, and consideration should be given to the husband's/partner's needs when supportive interventions are planned.

A study is currently under way in London, Edinburgh and Nottingham which combines the preventive aspects of Elliot et al.'s research, described earlier in this chapter, with the counselling approach of Holden and colleagues. The study will involve health visitors in both preventive support and education, and in screening and counselling. Its results are eagerly awaited.

The research studies detailed above show that a useful degree of postpartum emotional support can come from health professionals. Practical and emotional support can also come from neighbourhood, community or religious groups, from voluntary societies, charities, self-help groups, local authority, and government sources. The task of the professional working with families who are experiencing serious problems during the postnatal period is to access that help wherever it is available, and offer it to the mother to use if she chooses. The professional should also be aware of the provision for referral so that when and if a problem becomes so severe that it is beyond her/his own resources, it can be referred to more intensive regimens. For instance, you should note that 8 out of the 26 counselled mothers who participated in Holden et al.'s study remained depressed, despite finding participation generally helpful. These women needed to be offered further treatment. This treatment often involved antidepressant medication, the use of which in the postnatal period is apparently poorly understood by many practitioners (Cox, 1986). Psychotherapy, electro-convulsive therapy and intensive hospital- or community-based treatment can also be considered (Cox, 1986).

The baby

Babies, like their mothers, fathers and siblings, can have serious difficulty in adjusting to their life within the family. Babies who have been hospitalized for some time following birth because of prematurity, low birthweight, medical or surgical conditions, will have become accustomed to an institutional environment – that of the hospital. Even the most sensitive, well staffed neonatal units cannot care for their babies in the way that a family does. The baby will have become adapted to the routines of the unit where, for instance, day and night are relatively indistinguishable; people who pick you up are as likely to stick needles into you as to cuddle you, and where your family is just a small proportion of the adult population with whom you are required to interact.

When a baby who has been hospitalized comes home, s/he has to adjust to a new environment which is usually quieter, duller (in light intensity terms) and less smelly than that of the hospital. Night and day have different routines associated with them, with diurnal rhythms affecting the caretaker's behaviour. Feeding methods and frequency may change. The baby also has to adjust to new caretakers. The mother and father may have looked after her/him for some of the time in hospital, but so too did the midwifery and nursing staff (especially the night staff). And as well as Mummy and Daddy, Granny and

Grandad, big sister or brother, and the woman next door, may all feature more markedly in the social environment of the baby at home compared with that of the baby in hospital.

The baby coming home from hospital has therefore to make a large number of adjustments. These would be demanding enough for a healthy baby. For an immature or sick baby they can be overwhelming. Research into the effects of changing the caretaker of healthy 10-day-old infants (awaiting adoption, see Chapter 5) found that the babies cried a lot and that their feeding patterns were markedly disrupted (Sander et al., 1979). This kind of behavioural upset is likely to be shown by babies coming home from hospital, where caretakers, routines, sounds, sights and smells are all being changed simultaneously (Sander's subjects stayed within the same environment). Parmelee et al. (1984) have shown that premature babies have disorganized sleeping patterns, so that parents are faced with a baby who is sleeping and feeding irregularly, and is crying more than usual. This would worry and upset most parents. When the baby is frail, sick, immature or underweight anyway, or there are two or more babies, it is likely to make the mother frantic.

Many neonatal units have tried to ease the transition between hospital and home by encouraging the primary caretakers to assume control of their baby's care 24 hours a day within the hospital. For a few days prior to the baby's discharge, the mother will room-in with the baby, allowing each to become more familiar with one another's behaviours and routines whilst still having the safety net of skilled professional care available if necessary. (A very few units have facilities which enable mothers to room-in for the entirety of the baby's stay.) Another way of linking home and hospital is for the neonatal unit staff to visit the family on a regular basis for a period of time once the baby has gone home. Alternatively the health visitor may spend time with the baby and her/his carers in hospital, so that s/he can advise better on how to ease the baby's adaptation to the changes that will be experienced. A number of such transitional arrangements are discussed in Davis et al. 1983 (see Further reading).

Handicapped babies may have specific incapacities which affect feeding, sleeping and interaction (see below). However many of these babies will seem very normal in the early postnatal months and indeed throughout much of the first postnatal year, so their parents will experience a euphoric phase (Cunningham and Sloper, 1977) when their baby seems just like everybody else's. Developmental delay is often not apparent until the baby fails to walk or talk at the expected time, and all babies need to be fed and changed and carried, so the handicapped baby is no different. Babies who have very slight neurological impairment may demonstrate subtle deficiencies in feeding behaviours which are not apparent to the mother but which make ingestion of semisolids difficult and may lead to failure to thrive (Mathisen et al., 1989). These babies also seem to be unable to signal hunger, satiation or dislike as clearly as 'normal' babies (Mathisen et al., 1989).

Research studies have shown that the fathers of premature or low birthweight babies tend to be more involved in their routine care than the fathers of full-term babies (Richards, 1983; Levy-Shiff and Mogilner, 1989). This demonstrates one of the ways that families react when faced with even higher than normal needs for child care. The father in these cases is compensating for the increased child care demands placed on the family, and seems to do this by both supplementing and complementing the care provided by the mother. A recent Israeli study (Levy-Schiff and Mogilner, 1989) has noted how such fathers become more involved in the traditional care-giving aspects of 'maternal care' – holding, feeding and changing – than a comparable group of full-term babies' fathers. Both the mothers and the fathers were more involved in stimulating and playing with their preterm babies than their full-term counterparts, so both parents appeared to adapt their traditional parenting patterns to meet the needs of their baby for increased care and stimulation.

However, if the prematurity was associated with continued medical complications, the fathers were typically less involved, leaving the care of the sick child to the mother. The authors suggested that involvement with a sick as well as premature child is too overwhelming for fathers, causing them to withdraw from interaction and care-giving and leave these to the 'expertise' of the mother. This is a much less adaptive pattern of family reaction to increased child care demands, where the mother is left to cope (or not cope) very much on her own, without receiving even the normal amount of support.

The families of premature or low birthweight babies also often get support from grandparents, but the advice and information that grandparents can provide for families with normal healthy full-term babies is often felt to be completely inappropriate when the baby has been the recipient of long-term intensive 'high-tech' hospital care. This has sometimes been found to create difficulties for both the grandparents and the parents, which can accentuate the intergenerational family friction which is common when a new generation enters the scene (McHaffie, 1991). This conflict can deprive the parents of a much needed source of support, and can leave the grandparents feeling helpless, stupid and unappreciated. A tactful health visitor, who occasionally includes the grandparents in discussion and suggests the kind of help which will be of most use to the parents, can alleviate much of this friction. The health visitor can also, of course, provide direct support for the families. However, McHaffie found that only 46% of her 88 subjects who were parents of very low birthweight babies rated the health visitor as supportive, whereas 90% had so rated hospital midwifery and nursing staff.

McConachie (1982) reported that fathers of mentally handicapped babies were like ordinary fathers, in that their participation in child care was on average low compared to the mothers, and in that there were tremendous differences between fathers, with some being highly involved and others minimally. Byrne et al. (1988) found that most mothers of Down's syndrome children got little extra support to help them to cope with the extra demands of looking after their handicapped child, but that what help they did receive came from their family, especially from their partner and from their own female relatives, rather than from outside sources. It seems, therefore, that while some families mobilize all their resources to meet the increased child care demands caused by handicap or illness, others react in the opposite fashion with the increased burdens falling heavily on the mother. Health visitors, midwives, nurses and other professionals who are involved with such families need to encourage the mobilization of the family's own resources as much as possible. They also need to be alert to the 'abandoned' mother who, though she has a husband and other family members who could help, is in reality as alone as a lone mother.

Problems in mother–infant interaction

Many of the problems the baby coming home from hospital experiences are related to interaction. These interactive problems can also be experienced by 'difficult' normal babies and by healthy handicapped babies. The establishment of smooth feeding routines and sleep–activity cycles are, as we have discussed in Chapters 3 and 5, a matter of interaction between baby and mother, or other primary caretaker. These depend on the mother being sensitive to the baby's signals – signals of hunger, for instance, or of satiation, and to the baby's display of his or her regularities of behaviour, such as the length of the sleep cycle or the duration of pauses in the suck/pause routine. By coming to understand what her baby's signals mean and to predict what, when and how s/he is likely to feed, sleep and play, the mother can adapt to the baby's needs, at the same time as gradually shaping her/his behaviour. The baby in turn has to learn about the mother's routines and predictable behaviour – how she lifts him and holds him; how she settles him or stimulates him; when she will be maximally responsive and when minimally (at 3 a.m. for instance), and has to adapt to these. (See Chapter 5 for a more detailed description of this process.)

Mothers and babies who have been separated, and whose behaviour has been governed by institutional routines and the necessities of survival, have not had the opportunity for lengthy mutual adaptation. They need time to adapt when they get home, and families should be prepared for this process to take some considerable while. As many premature, 'difficult' or ill babies will not display consistent regularities in behaviour, nor signal their needs clearly, the interactive partner's task is particularly difficult (Brown and Bakeman, 1979; Field, 1980; Goldberg et al., 1980). Research into mothers' interactions with their Down's syndrome infants (whose social signals are of unusually low intensity, see below) has shown that they respond to low-intensity signals which would normally be missed, recalibrating their criteria of the strength of signal which requires a response, and thus establishing mutually satisfying interaction. Mothers of sick or premature babies could, and probably do, adjust their interactive behaviour in a similar manner, allowing them to respond to any slight regularity that the baby demonstrates, and to discern and act on the baby's signals, however faint and confusing they might appear to a less involved observer. Again, this adaptation takes time. It also requires strong and continued motivation (at first, nothing the mother does will seem to work) and acute observational skills.

As time at home passes, the baby will mature and recover from the experience of hospitalization. This will allow her/him to display behaviour patterns and needs and wants more clearly, and to increase her/his capacity to respond to the mother's behaviour. Just as it helps the mother when the baby's signals become clearer – so that she can tell when he's hungry, or tired, or feeling sociable – so it helps the baby if his mother's signals are clear – if, for instance, her 'now it's time to go to sleep' signals can be easily distinguished from her 'now it's time for play' signals. This clarity allows the baby to learn and thus gradually to alter her/his behaviour. (Playing with a recently hospitalized baby at 3 a.m. as if it were 3 p.m. is not going to help her/him to learn the difference between night and day.) Of course this is not an easy task for a young, sick baby, whose hospital experience has taught her/him about other routines and time schedules. So it's important that the primary caretaker learns to cope with the temporary reality of caring for a baby who sleeps for short periods of time, whose feeding requirements are frequent and whose behaviour is generally unpredictable. This coping probably involves the utilization of strategies such as sleeping when the baby sleeps, letting the housework go to pot, and not planning anything which requires the baby to sleep, feed, or charm visitors to order. And of course the mother requires all the intrafamilial and extrafamilial support described in the earlier sections of this chapter, as do the other members of her support network.

Full-term babies described as 'difficult' by their parents are typically recognized as such by independent, trained observers (Hewson et al., 1987). Many of these babies will be immature though not premature, and thus their difficultness will abate with time. Others may suffer more long-lasting problems of sleeping (see Richman, 1986), feeding (for instance, involving minimal neurological impairment and poor oral–motor behaviour associated with failure to thrive (see Mathisen et al., 1989) or crying, or will develop them later on in the postnatal period, for instance associated with 3-month colic (Hewson et al., 1987).

Since interaction involves two partners, difficulties in interaction can emanate from either. Factors in the mother which can interfere with normal interaction can be physical or psychological. Physical handicap, particularly that which involves blindness, can make it difficult for the mother to perceive her baby's signals. She can obviously hear when the baby cries, but cannot distinguish the quiet sleeping baby from the quiet ill baby or read the baby's expression or respond to her/his visual communications, for example those involving eye contact. Adamson et al. (1977) made a study of a sighted infant reared by blind parents. Feeding was disrupted by the mother running her fingers over the baby's face in order to obtain information about her state. This touching, which of course is widely used by blind people to learn about the emotional state of people they are close to, unfortunately caused the baby to root to the mother's fingers, and so interfered both with the baby's feeding and with the mother's attempt to 'see' how she was. The same baby later developed the tendency to avoid looking at the mother's face during playful interactions, since her face conveyed little information, being uniformly bland and conveying no visual messages.

Deaf mothers tend to have less severe problems of interaction since early interactions are dominated by vision and touch (see Chapter 5). Obviously the deaf mother needs to find some way of detecting her baby's cries when she is not beside her/him, but as soon as she is in visual contact with her baby she can perceive his/her needs and interactive overtures quite easily. Language-based interaction comes when the child is out of infancy, and is thus beyond the scope of this book. However by the time the child uses language, s/he will have had considerable experience in communicating with the mother, using signs and visual expressions so that non-verbal interaction between them can continue satisfactorily.

Early mother–infant interactions are dependent on the mother observing the baby's behaviour closely, responding to the baby in a relatively consistent manner, monitoring the effects of her responses and adjusting them appropriately (see Chapter 5). A mother who is under stress or is depressed may not be motivated to observe and monitor her interaction with her baby closely. The mother who is physically ill or exhausted may also lack the required energy to respond to the baby in any but the most basic fashion. A mother who is very anxious may, on the other hand, observe her baby very closely, being ever-ready and over-ready to feed or wind, lift or lay, stimulate or rock. In all these cases the mother's behaviour (or lack of it) may interfere with her interaction with her baby.

Factors in the baby can affect interaction as well, although it is generally easier for the mother to compensate for difficulties emanating from the baby than for the baby to compensate for problems emanating from the mother. Blind babies will be unable to perceive their mother's visual communications and to respond with their own. Thus the cues of eye contact, facial expression and aversion of gaze which are so important in establishing and maintaining mother–infant interaction will be unavailable to both partners (Fraiberg et al., 1980). Mentally handicapped babies may display relatively little emotional expression, as shown in a study of Down's syndrome infants by Sorce and Emde (1982), making it difficult for their mothers to interpret their affective state, or they may display very unpredictable behaviour which disrupts the consistency of dyadic interaction. Malnourished babies, like sick babies and some multi-handicapped babies are lethargic and so produce few signals on which the mother can base her responses.

Consequences of disrupted mother–infant interaction

Most of the factors described above can lead to understimulation of the baby or to overstimulation. Understimulation, resulting for instance from a depressed mother or a mentally handicapped baby, could reduce the total amount of interaction between mother and baby, with feeding being solely concerned with the ingestion of milk and not with the social interchanges which normally accompany it (a pattern which is seen in older failure-to-thrive children; Mathisen et al., 1989), and playful interactions being almost totally absent. This could have serious consequences for the social and intellectual development of the child if the lack of stimulation persisted for long enough, as studies of institutionalized children reared in non-stimulating environments have shown (see Rutter, 1972). Alternatively, understimulation or inappropriate stimulation resulting from a sensory handicap in either the mother or the baby could lead to a reduced quality of interaction. A simple experiment shows the kinds of effects this can have. Cohn and Tronik (1983) asked mothers to remain blank-faced as they sat opposite their infants. Initially the infants tried to engage their mothers in their normal interactions, producing repeated greeting behaviours, with eye contact, smiles and body movement. As the mothers failed to respond, the infants became unhappy. Some withdrew, and some became very upset. This upset lasted for some time, even once the mothers resumed their normal interactive behaviour.

Overstimulation may occur when the mother is overanxious, or when the mother is compensating for a baby's lack of responsiveness which might be due to handicap or illness. A study of preterm babies, for instance, showed that mothers stimulated these babies excessively and at inappropriate times during feeding, because preterm babies are more restless and distractible than normal babies during feeds and do not signal hunger and satiation as clearly (Field, 1980). Overstimulation has been graphically described by Stern (see Chapter 5) and can result in the baby avoiding stimulation and hence interaction with the mother. Thus the end-result of overstimulation can be much the same as that of understimulation, in that the baby receives relatively little appropriate stimulation. The overstimulating mother is likely to end up frustrated and upset, perhaps feeling that her baby is rejecting her. The understimulating mother (who may have started out as an overstimulating mother but altered her approach because of her baby's 'rejection') will miss out on the positive reinforcement that comes from playful and mutually satisfying interactions with babies. However, she may not be aware of what she's missing and may feel relieved that she's got 'such a good, quiet baby'.

Resolution

Interaction is a dynamic process involving two partners. In mother–infant interaction, one partner, the mother or other primary carer, has more skills and experience in interaction per se though not necessarily with babies. The other partner, the baby, though totally inexperienced and unskilled at the outset of the relationship, is changing, maturing, developing and learning at a rapid rate. In a dynamic process, compensatory mechanisms operate. In mother–infant interaction this happens too. For instance, Stern tells how the overstimulated baby that he described gradually became able to handle the intensity of interaction as she matured (see Chapter 5). Blind mothers compensate for their inability to read their baby's expression by eye through hearing it and feeling it (but not during feeding). They can tell if the baby is attending to them by checking his/her bodily and facial orientation. They, and their babies, develop playful routines which are based on body games, sound and touch, so that social interaction, looked at over time, develops normally despite its initial disruption (Adamson et al., 1977; Collis and Bryant, 1981). The mothers of blind babies can learn to utilize these kinds of interactive routes as well (Fraiberg et al., 1980) and the mothers of premature babies or babies with Down's syndrome to respond to faint and subtle signals which initially they would have hardly noticed (Goldberg et al., 1980; Sorce and Emde, 1982).

In many cases mothers and babies learn together, and from one another, how to moderate their interactions so they become more satisfying. In some cases, however, professional help is required. In the case of the baby with a mental or sensory handicap, this help may be provided by a clinical or educational psychologist or other professional who, together with the mother, will examine and chart the baby's behaviour in order to detail its hidden regularities, e.g. in sleep/activity or feeding cycles. This charting makes the baby's behaviour more predictable, and allows the mother to understand how to fit in her own interventions. Similar attention will be paid to the minutiae of interaction: the modalities utilized by mother and baby, the cues that the baby gives when s/he wants to interact and when it all becomes too much, the responses of the mother and how she modulates them. This mapping out of interaction is not done in order to tell the mother where she is going wrong, but in order to allow her to see for herself how she might utilize different modalities for interaction or respond more sensitively to the baby's interactive signals.

This general principle of careful and detailed observation of the baby's behaviour could be utilized by midwives, paediatric nurses or health visitors working with mothers who are experiencing difficulty in interaction. By getting the mother to note when, and for how long, the baby sleeps or feeds, the professional can enable the mother to see for herself that, for instance, the baby is sleeping enough, it's just that the timing is inconvenient; or that waking the baby up for a feed at 10 p.m. is counterproductive because the baby cries a lot and feeds poorly. Mapping the baby's interactive behaviour can allow the mother to notice how the baby greets her, what s/he likes and dislikes, and this in itself may improve their interaction. Advising on how to interact is a skilled and difficult business, so unless the professional has received extensive training in the appropriate areas, mothers are perhaps best directed by the health visitor, midwife or nurse towards careful observation and left to draw their own conscious or unconscious conclusions. They should never be made to feel that they are failing at interacting since this would merely add to their difficulties and be counterproductive.

In families where there are actual or potential difficulties in parent–infant interaction, interventions based on the Brazelton Neonatal Behavioural Assessment Scale (BNBAS) have been used to enhance the parent's perception of the newborn as an interesting social being. The BNBAS is an interactive assessment which reveals the 'complexities and competencies of the newborn' (Worobey, 1985, p. 65). By demonstrating that the baby has some impressive abilities (see Chapter 3) and that s/he can interact with adults (Chapter 5), this assessment makes it obvious to the parents that they have a baby who is an individual human being capable of responding to their overtures, rather than a passive, helpless, boring creature who just needs to be fed and changed and does nothing but sleep (not enough) and cry (too much). A review of the effectiveness of these interventions concludes that they are especially successful in improving interaction patterns, as well as having an effect on play and feeding behaviours (Worobey, 1985).

Administering the BNBAS requires specialist training, but the principles of its use as an aid to improving parents' appreciation of the capabilities of their baby are fairly simple and could be utilized by midwives, paediatric nurses or health visitors. Firstly they stress the baby's abilities – all the fascinating little tricks a neonate can perform such as 'walking', 'swimming' and grasping fingers. These make up the content of most neurological assessments, but in this context they are directed towards showing off what the baby can do. With an older baby, the developmental markers noted by the health visitor could also be incorporated into this 'look, isn't s/he amazing' routine, always stressing the things the baby can do, rather than focusing on what s/he can't. Secondly, they demonstrate how adults and babies interact; the very material that we have discussed in some detail in Chapters 3, 5 and 6. The parent's lack of interaction, or faulty interaction, is not analysed or criticized. Instead the professional interacts with the baby, pointing out how the baby responds, how this affects the adult's behaviour, and how that in turn produces a new response from the baby. This is not put over as a scientific lecture on parent–infant interaction but as fun; as something which the baby and the adult both obviously enjoy.

When dealing with a premature or handicapped baby whose abilities may be limited, it is doubly important to focus on what the baby can do, rather than on what s/he can't. Mothers who are struggling with a difficult baby or with some depression or disability of their own similarly need to have their successes recognized – what they *can do* with this baby, what they have managed to achieve, must receive lots of attention and praise. This doesn't mean that their difficulties should be ignored, but that they are set in the context of something positive. Otherwise the professional's visit becomes something to be dreaded – 'what have I done wrong this time?' – and will be counterproductive. Sometimes you will have to look very hard for something positive to recognize and praise, and you will only find it if you look at the mother's behaviour and the infant's in great detail. This detailed observation may require the involvement of specialist professionals who are experienced in dealing with the consequences of prematurity, developmental delay, mental, physical and sensory handicap.

Mothers who are over- or understimulating their babies because of stress, depression, anxiety or exhaustion should be given the appropriate practical and psychological support. Their need for support ties the second half of this chapter in with the first half, where we discussed postnatal depression and how to alleviate it. The two sections are in fact intertwined, since having a difficult, premature, sick or handicapped baby increases the stress on the mother, and this stress may make it more likely that she will become depressed.

Disability is often associated with exceptional ability, where the individual has developed the faculties which are intact to a greater degree than is normal in 'ordinary' human beings. For instance, blind people often have enhanced auditory, olfactory and tactile abilities. Mary Cronk (personal communication) tells of a blind primiparous mother whom she delivered. The mother was holding the baby who was a few minutes old, whilst the midwife was examining the placenta. The mother sensed that something was wrong with the baby because he sounded 'wrong' and felt floppy. The baby had stopped breathing and required aspiration. As Mary comments 'then he was given back to his mother who was the best monitor of his condition'. This incident indicates how sensitive this mother was to her baby despite her sensory handicap. Midwives and other staff who work with handicapped parents should not assume that disabled mothers will be less skilled than 'normal' mothers. The opposite may be the case, because the disabled mother utilizes the abilities she has to the full – something that those of us who are fortunate enough to have all our abilities operational may sometimes fail to do.

Overview and summary

The arrival of a new baby puts strain on all families. Most mothers, fathers and siblings adapt successfully to the changes involved, but all will experience some degree of strain. In a minority of cases this strain will be extreme. The person who is central to the well-being of the entire family is the mother. She is also the person who is normally most involved with the care of the new baby and consequently is the most exhausted, physically and psychologically. When she experiences severe postnatal psychological distress, usually labelled postnatal depression, her entire family suffer. Recent research has shown that postnatal depression can be ameliorated in many cases through counselling provided by health visitors, the health professionals who currently have the greatest contact with women in the postnatal period. The facets of this intervention which seemed to be most important were non-judgemental listening and a focus on the needs and feelings of the mother. The provision of structured support and educational preparation commencing in pregnancy and continuing for some time after the birth has also been shown to be effective in preventing the development of postnatal depression in vulnerable women. Such provision emphasized realistic preparation for parenthood and access to social support.

All health care professionals working with families before and after birth could utilize aspects of these preventive and ameliorative programmes.

Postnatal families can face a wide variety of difficult problems: maternal or paternal depression, intense sibling rivalry, illness or handicap in the baby. In order to accommodate to these problems and move towards solving them, the family needs to maximize its resources. The mother's coping abilities are usually fully stretched (if not overstretched), so additional help has to come from other family members, or be acquired from elsewhere – from friends and neighbours and/or from midwives, health visitors, nurses, doctors, psychologists, social workers, voluntary agencies. Many families accommodate to their increased needs by utilizing the energies and abilities of the father, the grandparents, and of female relatives. They may become involved in the care of the baby, or more often help the mother by caring for older children, and by providing her with practical and emotional support. These people need support, encouragement and reassurance from the health care professionals. More help might be forthcoming from fathers if they were educated appropriately, so that they understood the nature of the problem and realized how they could be involved in alleviating it. Thus midwives, paediatric nurses and health visitors should seek to inform the father as well as the mother about the nature of any problem facing the family, and about how it may be resolved.

Despite their best efforts, however, many mothers experiencing postnatal depression or struggling to cope with a premature, sick or handicapped baby will be unsupported, either because there is no father, grandparent or close friend or relative available, or because they are available but refuse to give the necessary support. Others may attempt to provide support, but be incapable of providing the right sort, adding to the mother's problems rather than alleviating them. In these cases, the midwife, health visitor or nurse needs to provide maximal practical and emotional support directly, and should seek to find other sources of support for the mother from neighbours, self-help groups and local organizations. S/he also needs to acknowledge her/his own limitations (see Epilogue), so direct provision of support from the health care professional should always be bolstered by indirect support obtained from other sources.

Further reading

Brown G. W., Harris T. (1978). *The Social Origins of Depression*. London: Tavistock.
Campion M. J. (1990). *The Baby Challenge*. London: Tavistock/ Routledge.
Cox J. L. (1986). *Postnatal Depression: A Guide for Health Professionals*. Edinburgh: Churchill Livingstone.
Davis J. A., Richards M. P. M., Robertson N. C. R. (1983). *Parent–Baby Attachment in Premature Infants*. Kent: Croom Helm.

References

Adamson L., Als H., Tronic E., Brazelton T. B. (1977). The development of social reciprocity between a sighted infant and her blind parents. *J. Am. Acad. Child Psychiatry*, **16**,194–207.
Adler E., Bancroft J. (1988). The relationship between breast feeding persistence, sexuality and mood in postpartum women. *Psychol. Med.*, **18**, 389–96.
Ball J. (1989). Postnatal care and adjustment to motherhood. In *Midwives, Research and Childbirth. Volume I* (Robinson S., Thomson A. M., eds). London: Chapman and Hall.
Brown J. V., Bakeman R. (1979). Relationships of human mothers with their infants during the first years of life. In *Maternal Influences and Early Behaviour* (Bell R. W., Smotherman W. P., eds). New York: Spectrum.
Byrne E. A., Cunningham C. C., Sloper P. (1988). *Families and their Children with Down's Syndrome: One Feature in Common*. London: Croom Helm.
Caplan H., Cogill S. R., Alexandra H. et al. (1989). Maternal depression and the emotional development of the child. *Br. J. Psychiatry*, **154**, 818–23.
Cohn J. F., Tronik E. Z. (1983). Three month old infant's reaction to simulated maternal depression. *Child Dev.*, **54**, 185–93.
Collis G. M., Bryant C. A. (1981). Interactions between blind parents and their young children. *Child Care, Health Dev.*, **7**, 41–50.
Cooper P. J., Campbell E. A., Day A. (1988). Non-psychotic psychiatric disorder after childbirth: a prospective study of prevalence, incidence, course and nature. *Br. J. Psychiatry*, **152**, 799–806.

Cox J. L. (1986). *Postnatal Depression: A Guide for Health Professionals.* Edinburgh: Churchill Livingstone.

Cox J. L. (1989). Postnatal depression. In *Clinical Obstetrics and Gynaecology. Volume 3, part 4. Psychological Aspects of Obstetrics and Gynaecology* (Oates M., ed.). London: Baillière Tindall.

Cox J. L., Connor Y. M., Kendall R. E. (1982). Prospective study of the psychiatric disorders of childbirth. *Br. J. Psychiatry*, **140**, 111–17.

Cox J. L., Holden J. M., Sagovsky R. (1987). Detection of postnatal depression: development of the 10 item Edinburgh Postnatal Depression Scale. *Br. J. Psychiatry*, **150**, 782–6.

Cunningham C. C., Sloper P. (1977). A positive approach to parent and professional collaboration. *Health Visitor*, **50**, 32–7.

Cutrona C. E., Troutman B. R. (1986). Social support, infant temperament and parenting self efficacy: a mediational model of postpartum depression. *Child Dev.*, **57**, 1507–18.

Dinnerstein L., Lehert P., Riphagen F. (1988). Factors affecting psychological adjustment in pregnancy and postpartum. Paper presented at The Family and Mental Illness. The 4th International Conference of the Marcé Society, University of Keele, England.

Dunn J., Kendrick C. (1982). *Siblings.* London: Grant McIntyre.

Elliot S. A., Sanjack M., Leverton T. J. (1988). Parents' groups in pregnancy. In *Marshalling Social Support* (Gottlieb B. H., ed.). London: Sage Publications.

Elliot S. A., Watson J.P., Brough D. I. (1985). Transition to parenthood by British couples. *J. Reprod. Infant Psychol.*, **3**, 28–39.

Fenton S., Sadiq A. *Voices of Depression.* London: Commission for Racial Equality. In press.

Field T. M. (1980). *High Risk Infants and Children.* New York: Academic Press.

Fox H., Hipwell A., Cooper D., Kumar R. (1990). The King's College Hospital Antenatal Questionnaire (KCHAQ): development of an antenatal screening instrument to predict postnatal depression. Paper presented at the 5th International Conference of the Marce Society, University of York, England.

Fraiberg S. H. (1977). *Insights from the Blind.* New York: Basic Books.

Goldberg S., Brachfield S., Di Vitto B. (1980). Feeding, fussing and play: Parent–infant interaction in the first year as a function of prematurity and perinatal medical problems. In *High Risk Infants and Children: Adult and Peer Interactions* (Field T., Goldberg S., Brackfield S., Di Vitto B., eds). New York: Academic Press.

Gordon R. E., Kapostins E. E., Gordon K. K. (1965). Factors in postpartum emotional adjustment. *Obstet. Gynaecol.*, **25**, 158–66.

Hennessy D. A. (1985). Should health visitors also care for mothers? In *Proceedings of the RCN Research Society Annual Conference, University of Nottingham* (Hawthorne P. J., ed.). London: RCN.

Hewson P., Oberklaid F., Menahem S. (1987). Infant colic, distress and crying. *Clin. Pediatr.*, **26**, 69–76.

Holden J. (1990). Postnatal depression: the health visitor as counsellor. In *Excellence in Nursing: The Research Route. Midwifery* (Faulkner A., Murphy-Black T., eds). London: Scutari Press.

Holden J. A., Sagovsky R. S., Cox J. L. (1989). Counselling in a general practice setting: a controlled trial of health visitor intervention in postnatal depression. *Br. Med. J.*, **298**, 233–6.

Kendall R. E., Chalmers J. C., Platz C. (1987). Epidemiology of puerperal psychosis. *Br. J. Psychiatry*, **150**, 662–73.

Kumar R. (1989). Postpartum psychosis. In *Clinical Obstetrics and Gynaecology. Volume 3, part 4. Psychological Aspects of Obstetrics and Gynaecology* (Oates M., ed.). London: Baillière Tindall.

Kumar R., Robson K. (1984). A prospective study of emotional disorders in childbearing women. *Br. J. Psychiatry*, **144**, 35–47.

Levy-Schiff R., Mogilner M. B. (1989). Mother's and father's interactions with their preterm infants during the initial period at home. *J. Reprod. Infant Psychol.*, **7**, 25–39.

Lewis C. (1989). Fathers and postnatal mood disturbance. *Marce Soc. Bull.*, Spring issue.

McConachie H. (1982). Fathers of mentally handicapped children. In *Fathers: Psychological Perspectives* (Beail N., McGuire J., eds). London: Junction Books.

McHaffie H. (1991). A study of support for families with very low birth rate babies. Nursing Research Unit Report, Department of Nursing Studies, University of Edinburgh.

Marks M., Wiek A., Kumar R. (1990). The association of husband factors with variations in the risk of postnatal relapse in women with a history of affective psychosis. Paper presented at the 5th International Conference of the Marcé Society, University of York, England.

Mathisen B., Skuse D., Wolke D., Reilly S. (1989). Oral–motor dysfunction and failure to thrive among inner-city infants. *Dev. Med. Child Neurol.*, **31**, 293–302.

Murphy-Black T., Faulkner A. (1990). Antenatal education. In *Excellence in Nursing: The Research Route. Midwifery* (Faulkner A., Murphy-Black T., eds). London: Scutari Press.

Murray L. (1990). Interaction and infant development. Paper presented at European Society of Developmental Psychology. University of Stirling, Scotland.

Murray L., Stein A. (1989). The effects of postnatal depression on mother–infant relations and infant development. In *Clinical Obstetrics and Gynaecology. Volume 3, part 4. Psychological Aspects of Obstetrics and Gynaecology* (Oates M., ed.). London: Baillière Tindall.

Oakley A. (1980). *Women Confined.* Oxford: Martin Robertson.

Parmelee A. H., Weiner N. H., Schulz H. R. (1984). Infant sleep patterns from birth to 16 weeks of age. *J. Pediatr.*, **65**, 576–82.

Richards M. P. M. (1983). Parent–child relationships: some general considerations. In *Parent–baby Attachment in Premature Infants.* (Davis J. A., Richards M. P. M., Roberton N. C. R., eds). Kent: Croom Helm.

Richman N. (1986). Recent progress in understanding sleep disorder. *Adv. Dev. Behav. Pediatr.*, **7**, 45–63.

Rutter M. (1972). *Maternal Deprivation Reassessed.* Harmondsworth: Penguin.

Sander L., Stechler G., Burns P., Lee A. (1979). Changes in infant and caregiver variables over the first two months of life. In *Origins of the Infant's Social Responsiveness* (Thoman E. B., ed.). Hillsdale, New Jersey: Lawrence Erlbaum.

Sandler M., Glover V., Hannah P. (1990). Postnatal depression predisposition and prediction. *Journal of Obstetrics and Gynaecology*, **10**, 229–41.

Scott-Heyes G. (1984). Childbearing as a mutual experience. Unpublished D. Phil thesis. New University of Ulster.

Sharp D. J. (1989). Emotional disorders during pregnancy and the puerperium – a longitudinal prospective study in primary care. *Marce Soc. Bull.*, Spring issue.

Sorce J. E., Emde R. N. (1982). The meaning of infant emotional expressions: regularities in caregiving responses in normal and Down's syndrome infants. *J. Child Psychol., Psychiatry*, **23**, 145–58.

Watson J. P., Elliot S. A., Rugg A. J., Brough D. I. (1984). Psychiatric disorder in pregnancy and in the first postnatal year. *Br. J. Psychiatry*, **144**, 453–62.

Williams H., Carmichael A. (1985). Depression in mothers in a multi-ethnic urban industrial municipality in Melbourne. Aetiological factors and effects on infants and pre-school children. *J. Child Psychol. Psychiatry Allied Disc.*, **26**, 277–88.

Worobey J. (1985). A review of Brazelton based interventions to enhance parent–infant interaction. *J. Reprod. Infant Psychol.*, **3**, 64–74.

Epilogue: Caring for and caring about

Midwives, health visitors and nurses care *for* the families they are responsible for. They look after them, do things for them, help them, and support them. It's hard work and they get tired. They also get fed up sometimes and want a break. A break can be coffee with colleagues, a look round the shops, going home at night, going on holiday. If these breaks involve looking after colleagues, shopping for the tea, going home to care for the kids, the man or woman in their life, an elderly relative or any combination of these, then it may provide a bit of a change but it won't provide a rest. So the professional is likely to end up putting less energy into caring for either her/his professional families, or for her/his own family.

Mothers care *for* their babies. In pregnancy they nourish and protect them; they carry them about; and they deal with their waste products. The mother's body does all this 'caring for' by itself, automatically, and it can leave the mother feeling pretty tired and drained as a result. During birth the mother's body continues to do these things, and in addition, delivers the baby into the outside world – hard labour indeed! After birth most mothers continue to care for their baby, nourishing and protecting it, feeding it, maintaining its warmth and safety; dealing with vomit, urine and faeces; and carrying the baby about. At this stage all this caring becomes conscious. It doesn't happen automatically and it involves a huge amount of physical energy, so just like the over-worked professional, they feel exhausted. They need a rest and they want a break. But they don't get much rest – breast-feeding mothers can go for months without a single complete night's sleep, and breaks can be few and far between.

If the mother has more than one person to care for – other children, older relatives, a 'helpless husband' – then her resources, just like those of the overworked professional, are going to be overstretched, and something's got to give. Typically, her energy will go first and foremost to the baby, whose very survival is dependent upon her care, so the last thing to 'give' is the mother's care of the baby. The order in which she prioritizes the other demands on her time and energy will vary. Some mothers will put their husband next on the list, others their older children; still others will put the house high on the list, but few, in my experience, put themselves there.

Mothers care *about* their families as well as caring *for* them. They are constantly concerned about their well-being. When the family is happy, she is relieved. When they are miserable, she feels upset (and often guilty). When they are there she shares their joys and sorrows, and when they are somewhere else she worries about them. During pregnancy, she worries about the baby's well-being. She worries about whether her husband is happy about having the baby, and about how her other kids will feel about having a little brother or sister. Fathers-to-be usually care more *about* their partners than about the baby during pregnancy, and usually do more caring *for* them than usual. So their ratio of caring increases during pregnancy, but nowhere near as much as the mother's.

During birth, the well-being of the baby often preoccupies the mother and she sometimes manages to worry about the father and her other children as well. The father is typically anxious about his partner's well-being, especially if she is in pain. During birth, as in pregnancy, he can care *for* his partner to a limited extent but cannot care for the baby directly at all. After the birth, fathers can care *for* their offspring directly, but often their care is expressed indirectly through helping or substituting for their partner, rather than sharing child care with her.

The ability to care *for* other people seems to be finite. There is a limit to it. When the mother is looking after a new baby, she is physically incapable of looking after a toddler, a husband and an aged mother as well. (Though some mothers do try to do this.) The ability to care *about* family and loved ones, while not perhaps truly infinite, seems to be pretty elastic. So the mother who cannot manage totally physically to care *for* everyone in her family, still cares *about* them. She still worries about the older children, her husband, her mother, particularly if she thinks they are not being cared for properly, as she would have done. She also cares *about* a baby she has lost – there is nothing to care *for*, nothing physical to be done, no nourishing, protecting, cleaning or carrying, and maybe that is part of her loss. The father who cares *about* his partner and their baby during pregnancy and birth may also fret because there is little that he can do to care *for* their well-being directly, so an imbalance between caring *for* and caring *about* may always be troublesome.

Professionals who get overinvolved, who care *about* their patients/ clients/families as well as caring *for* them, and whose jobs are demanding and stressful and exhausting, are at risk of being 'burnt-out'. As we have seen in this book, motherhood is demanding, stressful and exhausting, and most mothers are overinvolved up to the hilt. So why don't they get burnt out? Well, of course, some of them do – perhaps being 'burnt-out' would be a better term than being 'postnatally depressed'. But I would suggest that most of them don't become burnt out because someone cares *for* them and *about* them too.

Fathers often care *for* their partners during pregnancy and birth and in the early postnatal period. And they often care *about* them. Children may not be big enough to care *for* their parents at these times but they do care *about* them. The baby even occasionally seems to care about his/her mother, in that s/he appears to welcome her presence and appreciate her ministrations. Friends and relatives, and the community at large, can also care *for* and *about* mothers and so can the midwife, the health visitor, the nurse and the doctor.

I might suggest a simple and simplistic equation here. The more caring a mother or father gives out – to one another, to the baby, to their other children, relatives and friends – the more they need to be given in return – from one another, from family and friends and from professional carers. A sick baby, a premature baby, a difficult baby, more than one baby, very young siblings, a disabled, disturbed, distressed or sick family member – all these things increase the burden of caring that a family carries. These families will need to be given extra care which emanates from professional sources. A mother who does not receive a certain amount of physical and psychological support from her partner or from her family or friends is similarly in great need of care from the professionals. And that care cannot just be caring for. Someone needs to care about her as well.

Professional staff also need to be cared *for* and cared *about*. If they are giving out a lot of care, particularly a lot of psychological care – caring *about* their 'patients' as well as *for* them – then they need to balance their own caring equation. Turning the equation the other way round means that if they aren't receiving good psychological care, then they can't provide good psychological care.

So if you, the reader, are physically and psychologically unsupported then you won't be able to give a lot to the families in your professional care. If you have an increased burden of caring at home – a new baby, a sick, disabled, disturbed, distressed or sick family member – then you can't expect to provide the standards of psychological care at work that you might wish. It is important for you to recognize these facts, and not to blame yourself if you can't always listen properly; if you can't take a family's troubles, because you've got too many of your own; if you can't be understanding and sympathetic, because someone has just been nasty to you, and no one has listened to your problems.

Midwives, health visitors, nurses and other health care professionals need to look after themselves, if there is no one else willing or able to do that for them. So they need to learn when to say 'no'. Sometimes that means saying 'no' to the provision of psychological care – temporarily ignoring some of what I've said in this book. In such circumstances, midwifery, health-visiting and nursing personnel can still provide plenty of practical care for mothers and babies, and the benefits of that care should never be underestimated. They can also give advice about how families can maximize their own resources, and they can provide access to the many other sources of practical and emotional support, some of which are listed in the Appendix.

Hopefully, in most circumstances, professional staff will receive adequate personal support in the workplace, as well as within their own homes. This should allow them to care properly, i.e. psychologically as well as physically and practically, for mothers, and fathers, and babies, and siblings, etcetera, etcetera – for all the members of the family, during pregnancy, birth and the postnatal period.

Appendix: Sources of support and advice

Association for Improvement of Midwifery Services
21 Iver Lane
Iver
Buckinghamshire

Association for Spina Bifida and Hydrocephalus
23 Upper Woburn Place
London WC1

CHAT (counselling service for nurses)
Royal College of Nursing
20 Cavendish Square
London W1M 0BA
071–629–3870

Down's Children's Association
4 Oxford Street
London SW1 9SB

National Council for One Parent Families
255 Kentish Town Road
London NW5 2LX

Marcé Society (for study of postnatal mental illness)
Dr Beth Alder
Queen Margaret College
Clerkwood Terrace
Edinburgh EH12 8TS

Maternity Alliance
15 Britannia Street
London WC1

Multiple Births Foundation Bereavement Clinic
Queen Charlotte's and Chelsea Hospital
Goldhawk Road
London W6 0XG

National Childbirth Trust
Alexander House
Oldham Terrace
London W3 6NH

Relate (marriage guidance)
Herbert Gray College
Little Church Street
Rugby CV21 3AP

Society for Reproductive and Infant Psychology
(multidisciplinary, welcomes midwives, health visitors and nurses as
members)
Membership Secretary Dr Ann Walker
Dept of Business Studies
Dundee Institute of Technology
Bell Street
Dundee DD1 1HG

Spastics Society
12 Park Crescent
London W1N 4EQ

Stillbirth and Neonatal Death Society
Argyle House
21–31 Euston Road
London NW1 2SD

Twin and Multiple Birth Association (TAMBRA; bereavement
support group)
56 Chase Court Gardens
Enfield
Middlesex

Working Mothers Association, also Working for Childcare
77 Holloway Road
London N7 8JZ

Index